ROBERT HARRIS

What to
Listen
for in
MOZART

SIMON & SCHUSTER

NEW YORK LONDON TORONTO
SYDNEY TOKYO SINGAPORE

SIMON & SCHUSTER
Simon & Schuster Building
Rockefeller Center
1230 Avenue of the Americas
New York, New York 10020

Manufactured in the United States of America

10   9   8   7   6   5   4   3   2   1

Library of Congress Cataloging in Publication Data

Harris, Robert
    What to listen for in Mozart / Robert Harris.
        p.   cm.
    "Originally published in Canada by Macfarlane, Walter & Ross"—
    T.p.   verso.
    Includes index.
    1. Mozart, Wolfgang Amadeus. 1756–1791.   2. Mozart, Wolfgang
Amadeus, 1756–1791—Criticism and interpretation.
3. Composers—Austria—Biography.   1. Title.
ML410.M9H17   1992
780'.92—dc20
[B]   92-13248
                                                                    CIP
                                                                     MN

ISBN: 0-671-75092-5

*Lyrics from "I Got Rhythm" (George Gershwin, Ira Gershwin)
© 1930 WB MUSIC CORP (Renewed) All rights reserved. Used by
permission.*

To Cassie, with love

LIST OF WORKS DISCUSSED

CONTENTS

CONTENTS

INTRODUCTION

T HIS BOOK is based on a simple premise: that the music of generations of classical composers is one of the great cultural treasures of the world, but one which is appreciated by too few people, through no fault of their own. It would take a sociologist to sift through the layers of elitism and snobbery that have accumulated on the clear, brilliant surface of classical music. The composers who labored long and hard to communicate as simply and directly as they could to their audiences would be astonished, if not furious, at the treatment their art receives today. The very people they wanted to reach consider their art inaccessible, if not incomprehensible. An apparently unbridgable gulf separates classical music from many contemporary listeners.

It needn't exist. Yes, classical music is different from other forms of music that are more familiar to us, and yes, the language and terms used to describe classical music may seem foreign. But there is no reason why normal audiences cannot learn to appreciate this music. With a little curiosity, and the willingness to do a little work, classical music can come alive to anyone.

The music of Mozart is a good place to start. Deceptively simple, Mozart's musical legacy is one of the great achievements in all Western art. And Mozart himself, clouded and mysterious, remains one of the most intriguing figures in the history of classical music.

Two hundred years after his death, his personality and his art remain as compellingly fascinating as they were in the 1780s. Consequently the means by which we can make the music of Mozart come alive will stand us in good stead for any other composer or style of composition.

A brief note on how to use this book. It is really two books in one. The biography and interpretation of Mozart the man can be read as any normal book. This is not necessarily so for the chapters describing Mozart's music. Although I have attempted everywhere to describe his music in the clearest language, these chapters should be read with the music itself close at hand. They really work best when you can listen and read at the same time. And don't worry if the music chapters need more than a single perusal. If you find yourself assimilating too much information on the first go, skip the rest of that chapter, and return to it later. After a while, all these chapters will begin to fit together and a new world will open up to you — a world of extreme beauty and great excitement.

My thanks go to five wonderful women for encouraging and supporting me in this endeavor. First, to Jan Walter — the Walter of Macfarlane, Walter and Ross — who brought me the idea for this book, and whose combination of persistence and dedication to quality was a constant inspiration to this first-time author. Kathryn Dean edited the messy manuscript with sympathy for the material and an uncompromising eye to detail and exactitude. Suzan Wookey provided support and encouragement throughout the process, even when she was in the Greek Isles. My wife, Candace, always my best critic, asked me the right questions when they needed to be asked, stayed my hand hovering over the wastepaper basket when it needed to be stayed and provided the kind of supportive environment that made it possible to keep working. Finally, there is my five-year-old daughter, Dory, who was fascinated by the process of writing a book and whose interest reminded me of why this endeavor was worthwhile.

Robert Harris

CHAPTER ONE

A Titan Charming the Gods

H E CAME hurtling into our world in January of 1756. His father's people were bookbinders; his mother's family, court officials. His full name was Johannes Chrysostomus Wolfgangus Theophilus Mozart. Wolfgang was his grandfather's name on his mother's side. Theophilus (the Greek form of Amadeus) had been his brother's name, his brother who had lived a mere four months in the winter of 1752.

He was the last of seven children born to Maria Anna Pertl and Leopold Mozart of Salzburg, but only the second to survive. A brother, Leopold, lived six months in 1748; a sister, Maria Anna, six days in 1749; a second sister, also named Maria Anna, three months in 1750. Carolus Amadeus lived and died in four months in 1752, Maria Francesca the same in 1754. Of the first six children, only the fourth survived, the third Maria Anna, born in 1751. She became Nannerl, Mozart's first partner in the fun and practical jokes that filled his entire life. His mother, thirty-six when he was born, had been pregnant seven times since her twenty-eighth birthday. She almost died giving birth to Wolfgang.

He was a short man, perhaps five-foot-four. His family and his contemporaries were forever remarking on his height. "Who would believe that such great things could be hidden in so small a head," exclaimed the Elector of Bavaria, upon hearing a rehearsal of Mozart's opera *Idomeneo* in 1781, when the composer was twenty-five. From Rome, where he had been traveling with his father, the fourteen-year-old Wolfgang wrote his sister and mother:

> Praise and thanks be to God, I and my wretched pen are well and I kiss Mama and Nannerl a thousand or 1000 times. I have had the honour of kissing St. Peter's foot in St. Peter's church and as I have the misfortune to be so small, I that same old dunce, Wolfgang Mozart
> had to be lifted up.

He was fastidious about his appearance and spent much time and a fair amount of the little money he had on his clothes and wigs. His skin was sallow, his face pockmarked, the residue of an attack of smallpox he had suffered as a child. By the end of his life he had developed a nasty double chin. He was restless and excitable, always shuffling his feet or moving his hands about unconsciously.

His was a mysterious personality, full of contradictions, as though the musical power he had been granted allowed him to speak clearly and fully only in the artistic realm, but prevented him from expressing himself honestly and simply in personal relations, even to himself. He was the greatest musician of his time — perhaps of all time — yet he died in depressing poverty, unable to secure a single decent position in his life, despite twenty years of trying. His compositions are among the most refined and sublime the world has ever heard, yet he was obsessed with defecation and defecating, and wrote many hilarious letters on the subject. He approached the world with an odd combination of vanity and innocence, of scorn and naïveté, and was totally defeated all his life by mundane forces that lesser men handled with ease. Not until the very end of his life did he attempt to understand himself — what he was, what he had become — but by then the self-knowledge was of no use.

He loved to laugh, to joke, to play. After his piano, the most expensive article of furniture he owned was his billiard table. He was a constant player. Often he would compose while playing, carrying on a conversation at the same time. His practical jokes seemed to leap out of him involuntarily; it was almost as though his exalted musical thoughts were too much for him to bear without some release. His friends and associates were often astonished by his behavior; even those who knew him well were caught off guard by his unpredictability. Caroline Pichler was a Viennese author in the late eighteenth century, the center of a literary circle in the Austrian capital. She remembered one scene from the mid-1780s, when Mozart was in his thirties:

> One day when I was sitting at the pianoforte playing the "Non più andrai" from *Figaro*, Mozart, who was paying a visit to us, came up behind me; I must have been playing it to his satisfaction, for he hummed the melody as I played and beat the time on my shoulders; but then he suddenly moved a chair up, sat down, told me to carry on playing the bass and began to improvise such wonderfully beautiful variations that everyone listened to the tones of the German Orpheus with bated breath. But then he suddenly tired of it, jumped up, and, in the mad mood which so often came over him, he began to leap over tables and chairs, miaow like a cat, and turn somersaults like an unruly boy.

Mozart was an enigma to most of his contemporaries, and he has remained a deep mystery to us: a sublime artist who reveled in the simplest and crudest of practical jokes; a precarious freelance musician who could run through money at astonishing speeds; a friend who could be loyal to those closest to him, but cold and cutting to them as well. Eventually, Mozart's erratic behavior alienated him from his family and his society. Both his father and his sister lost contact with him in his later years (his mother died when he was in his twenties); friends and associates became fewer as he withdrew from Viennese society near the end of his life. Even after his death, Mozart proved something of an embarrassment to those who longed to celebrate his extraordinary musical achievements. For a hundred years, a variety of attempts was made to censor his biography, to create an image of the man that corresponded more closely to the divine and magnificent music he had created. To this day, two hundred years after they were written, Mozart's letters have seldom been published without judicious removal of the more obscene and scatological references with which they are liberally scattered.

He wrote his first piece of music, K. 1,* when he was six years old — a minuet and trio for piano in G. His last composition, the **Requiem**, K. 626, lay uncompleted on the covers of his bed when he died just weeks short of his thirty-sixth birthday. In between, he wrote an astonishing amount of music. From his twelfth year on, he wrote almost constantly, producing forty-one symphonies, twenty-seven piano concertos, twenty-five string quartets, seventeen operas, hundreds of marches, dances, serenades, a good deal of church music, canons, fugues, piano sonatas; there is no form of music in which he was not active. Simply put, Mozart possessed the most powerful musical mind in history. His natural talent was awesome in its completeness, almost otherworldly. There was no musical feat that he could not accomplish with ease. The exploits of his youth have been the yardstick against which child prodigies have been measured for two centuries. His mature pieces remain some of the most revered works in the history of Western art.

His work, unlike his life, presents an almost unbroken string of development and improvement. You can count on the fingers of

---

* All of Mozart's works are identified by "K" numbers, which refer to the catalog of his compositions compiled in the nineteenth century by Ludwig von Köchel. Using letters, manuscripts and Mozart's own catalogs, Köchel attempted to list all of Mozart's compositions in chronological order. The notion of appending opus numbers to compositions — basically the way composers today keep track of their works — never crossed Mozart's mind, since so little of his output was published when he was alive.

one hand his artistic failures: some early string quartets, perhaps his late opera, *La Clemenza di Tito*. Virtually everything else is assured, polished, successful — even the early symphonies and sonatas, written in his teens. If we listen less to the early Mozart today, it is not because the works are unpolished, but because musical styles have developed since then. Virtually every major piece he wrote during the last ten years of his life is still in the active repertoire; nearly every major piece he wrote during the last five years of his life is a towering masterpiece. No other classical musician — indeed, few other artists in any field — can boast such incredible consistency. For most musicians, fallow periods of several years are common. Even a composer of such intensity as Beethoven ran into periods of limited inspiration or no inspiration. Not so Mozart. His development is a straight, unbroken, ascending line.

What is even more remarkable about the Mozart output — and this has confounded Mozart scholars for two centuries — is that the work seems to bear no relationship of any kind to the external circumstances of his life. Pieces of elfin lightness and grace were composed during periods of intense emotional distress; they were also composed during times of happiness and contentment. Pieces of intense foreboding and tragic presentiment pop out of his imagination during the sunniest moments of his life. His most innocent and joyful work, *The Magic Flute*, and one of his most serious and tragic, the *Requiem*, were composed at exactly the same time, near the end of his life. It is as though the path of his musical development was prompted by forces deep within him, that spun themselves out in an inevitable pattern that connected only vaguely with the events of his life.

Yet we know of perhaps only three or four pieces in his entire output that were not written on commission or for a very specific purpose. He was a composer who wrote to order, to earn a living. Rarely did he compose a work out of inner necessity alone, unprompted by some external circumstance. When he was touring as a virtuoso, he wrote piano sonatas to have something to perform; when he received a commission, he would write an outdoor serenade, or a mass for the next Sunday's service. When he could snare an order for an opera, he would write it, sometimes in as little as six weeks. If the next commission was three years in coming, so was the next opera. Mozart's most famous piano concertos, pieces that have been performed tens of thousands of times since their composition, were written in groups of three for the fall and spring concert seasons in the mid-1780s in Vienna. They were performed once by Mozart, and then abandoned. Often, he would not bother to write out the solo piano part, since he assumed that no one else would ever play the piece.

At twenty-five, Mozart left the safety of his employment with the Archbishop of Salzburg and became a freelance musician in Vienna, the first in history. He was a failure, a decade or so ahead of his time. If the output of the later years falls off a little, compared to the prodigious output of the early Vienna years, it is simply because the call for his services dried up.

Mozart lived in a revolutionary age. He was a contemporary of Voltaire, Goethe, Benjamin Franklin and Thomas Jefferson. Feudal Europe had mere decades to live when he was born. The philosophies of the Enlightenment, of Diderot, Voltaire and Rousseau, reached their full development in his lifetime, first in America, then in France. The Declaration of Independence was written when he was twenty; the Bastille was stormed when he was thirty-three. The forces liberated by the French Revolution, which began in his lifetime, would eventually change both the external circumstances and the spiritual climate of Europe. Mozart caught the early breezes of the coming storm. His father, Leopold, was a servant, a musical servant, of the absolute ruler of Salzburg, the Archbishop, and until he was twenty-five, Mozart was also a servant of this same prince. According to the custom of the court, musicians were attached to the prince's kitchen staff, providing, as they did, pleasant entertainment by which to dine. Mozart chafed at the restrictions this service placed on him. While he was in the Archbishop's hire, he had little opportunity to fulfil his desire to travel and make a name for himself as a composer and virtuoso. His eventual break with his ecclesiastical employer, although it took place just before the revolutionary age descended on Europe, was more an act of personal rebellion than a political statement.

In fact, Mozart's relationship to the politics of his time was as ambiguous as his relationship to so many of the other external factors of his existence. Nevertheless, Mozart was sensitive to the tenor of his times, to its spirit, and so his life and work do reflect the tension between the old hierarchical order of European society and the emerging sense that the individual could control his own destiny, outside the bounds of aristocratic rule.

The forces liberating society in the late eighteenth century included music and art. Mozart lived through a musical revolution in his teens and early twenties. The old Baroque order had disappeared, with its emphasis on somber, complex musical statement. A new style, the "Classical" style, took its place, a music full of direct, tuneful simplicity, which appealed to a wider audience.

The revolution in music was seized upon by those intent on extending it to the heart of government. Jean-Jacques Rousseau, the intellectual and spiritual father of the French Revolution, began life as a composer and critic. The new musical styles of the mid to late 1770s were the first palpable evidence for him that society might be able to change, that this artistic revolution could be followed by a political revolution. Although completely foreign to the way in which we conceive of art and politics today, such thinking was common in the time in which Mozart and Rousseau lived.

In many ways we have a much more difficult time imagining the ways of life of Europe in this time period — the late eighteenth century — than in just about any other era. The occasional movie or historical romance attempts to make it come alive for us today, but our twentieth-century imaginations cannot come to grips with the essential realities of the Enlightenment, as the European pre-revolutionary age is called. This time, Mozart's time, was rough — conditions of comfort were rudimentary by our standards, houses were small, heating poor, sanitation primitive. At least those were the conditions for the vast majority of the inhabitants of Europe.

In contrast to the harsh life of the many was the incredible luxury enjoyed by the few — Europe's nobility and aristocracy. Perhaps never before in the history of Europe had the distinctions between the rich and the poor been so dramatic. Eventually, of course, the tension between these two worlds helped create a revolution, and the opulent lifestyles of the privileged classes began to fade from history. However, these developments properly belonged to the very end of the eighteenth century and the early nineteenth century. For Mozart, and for the rest of Europe in the second half of the eighteenth century, the two co-existing worlds of rich and poor were an inevitable and incontestable fact of life.

Mozart moved back and forth between these two worlds all his life, as did his father. Indeed, some of Leopold's most telling insights came at the expense of the aristocracy, which he observed at close quarters, though he never for a moment considered himself to be part of that class. Wolfgang also spent a great deal of his time in the world of the aristocracy, but he had a more difficult time maintaining the appropriate distance between himself and the aristocrats for whom he provided entertainment most of his life. He often mistook the cheerful informality of certain aristocrats for an implicit invitation to equality. His anger, consequently, at the often boorish treatment he received at the hands of the nobility roused him to a passion, where it would have been borne with sad resignation by his father.

Nonetheless, Mozart has passed down to us, through his polished, elegant phrases and textures, perhaps the most vivid and palpable portrait of late-eighteenth-century aristocratic life that has ever been drawn. It has been said that Mozart, unlike his two most famous contemporaries, Haydn and Beethoven, was an indoors composer. Mozart's colleagues loved nothing better than a traipse through the woods and an elemental connection with nature, and they brought these values to their music. The rustic charm found in the music of Haydn and the longing for a connection with a greater spirit that you can hear in Beethoven have little to do with the elegant perfection that was Mozart's stock-in-trade. Everything is indoors for Mozart; his music is full of the salon, the ballroom, the dining room and the artificial world that these rooms represent.

At the same time, Mozart's music reflects the ambiguity and contradiction that was part of late-eighteenth-century society. As much as his music provided a perfect reflection of the elegance and decorum to which the era aspired, there is a fiercely independent voice in his art. Though never able to escape his financial link to the aristocracy, Mozart managed somehow to write music that satisfied his employers and his own artistic conscience at one and the same time. Long after Mozart's world has passed into history's antechamber, his music still speaks to us as clearly and freshly as it did when it was first composed.

He left us with music of sublime grace, in works like the slow movement of his Clarinet Quintet and the Andante movement of the *Elvira Madigan* Piano Concerto, but he also wrote with exuberance and joy — especially in his serenades and symphonies. The characters in his operas live for us today as brightly as they did two hundred years ago — the Countess in *Figaro*, Papageno in *The Magic Flute*, Fiordiligi in *Così fan tutte* and Don Giovanni in the opera of the same name. The times in which he lived and his own musical genius worked together to create the most finely polished, perfectly balanced, formally exquisite art in the repertoire. Yet there is more to Mozart than just polish. At the same time charming and profound, funny and moving, Mozart's music seems to be totally under his control at every moment. Indeed, Mozart's complete control over his music, the sense that nothing was beyond him musically, has seemed almost otherworldly to many observers. Where another composer — a Beethoven, for instance — struggled to wrest meaning from stubborn musical forces, Mozart seems to have toyed with them effortlessly. He tamed the wild beasts of musical technique by the sheer force of his artistic genius.

The ambiguity in Mozart's music, like the ambiguities in the man himself, have meant that succeeding generations have interpreted his art quite differently, depending on that generation's understanding of itself. For the Romantic era, the era of the nineteenth century, music and art had to be dramatic, personal and emotional. This was understandable for a century that discovered the individual and the centrality of the individual in the political storms of the French Revolution and the upheavals that followed. Beethoven is the quintessential Romantic composer — a proud, personal hero, "a Titan wrestling with the Gods," as

Richard Wagner described him, an individual struggling against the forces of man and nature.

No one would call Mozart "a Titan wrestling with the Gods"; perhaps a Titan sharing a laugh with the gods or a Titan charming the gods. In no other composer is the sense of struggle less evident; Mozart's genius seems effortless. For this reason, his music was praised in the nineteenth century for its charm and easy grace, but beneath the praise was an undercurrent of scorn. The music was too graceful, too charming; it lacked true spiritual depth. Mozart was passed over as a society composer — a wonderful society composer, to be sure — but a society composer nonetheless, for a social class that had been swept away by the tides of revolution.

Oddly enough, and tellingly, the reaction to Mozart's music in his own day was exactly the opposite. Accustomed to listening to the musical efforts of true society composers and their vapid charms, Mozart's contemporaries heard in him only the complex, the confusing and the difficult. Especially in his later years, his music was criticized for being too "highly spiced," too difficult to perform, too hard to understand.

Only in our time has Mozart begun to be appreciated for his true worth, with all his ambiguities. For one thing, we are less afraid to look at the real man clearly and without prejudice. Perhaps the passing of time has made us more tolerant of the contradictions between the inner and the outer man that drove Mozart's contemporaries to distraction and his idolators to despair a hundred years ago. We seem more prepared to accept Mozart for what he was. Our century also believes less in the artistic principles that the nineteenth century took for granted. We are more willing to listen, indeed even delight in listening to music that expresses its beauties indirectly, rather than forcefully and emotionally, as Romantic music does. Our artistic reach is broadening.

In the end, perhaps we of all generations are most able to appreciate Mozart's art for what it is: a great composer's struggle to communicate eternal truths to his listeners, truths expressed in purely musical form, across the centuries. Of course, if we are to understand Mozart's message more fully, we need to know a little more about the language he spoke, the language of classical music.

It is not difficult to understand, but it is different from our own, it takes a little translation. When we can appreciate the wonders of Mozart in his own tongue, the mystery of his genius at once comes nearer to us and becomes more deeply mysterious than ever before.

CHAPTER TWO

Mozart's
Musical
Atoms

APPROACHING a piece of classical music can sometimes be a daunting experience for uninitiated listeners. On the one hand, they are confronted with the ecstatic claims of the cognoscenti that such and such a piece is marvelous, or sublime, or whatever. Yet when they themselves listen to the piece in question, or any classical piece for that matter, they don't hear any of those things. Because they don't always know what is happening in the music, the experience often leaves them uninvolved and frustrated. They feel angry or guilty that the "sublime" music seems not to touch them. They end up rejecting the music and thus cut themselves off from potentially rewarding experiences. Even those listeners familiar with classical music are not always tuned in to the fullest appreciation of the sounds they are hearing. They know the music, but could learn to love it more completely. What they need is a guide.

It should be no surprise that classical music is not immediately understood by all who listen to it for the first time. For one thing, classical music (by which we mean the art-music of Europe from the sixteenth to the twentieth centuries) is old. Its techniques, its sounds, its underlying structures represent the values and mores, ideas and attitudes of worlds now largely disappeared. However, the wonderful thing about the music is that, mysteriously, it can conjure up these lost worlds when it is performed. We can re-live the religious fervor of Baroque Germany when we listen to Bach, re-fight the battles of the French Revolution when we encounter Beethoven, share in the edgy charm of the late eighteenth century when we hear the works of Mozart. Of course, many of the values of those bygone eras are still the values of the Western world today, so the music also speaks to us of our times and our lives, not just of times and lives gone by.

However, we need a means to unravel the complexities of the music of the past, a guide to understanding the works as the people who wrote them and first heard them might have understood them. Their musical language is a bit foreign to our late-twentieth-century ears, bombarded, as they are, by a constant stream of popular music. We need some translation.

Our familiarity with popular music — indeed, our inability to escape it — acts as a barrier to our appreciation of classical music for a couple of reasons. The point of pop music, whether it is by Irving Berlin or the Beatles, is to make an immediate impression. It does so by focusing on one or two of the most visceral elements of music and ignoring the rest. Generally, this means either a catchy tune or a catchy beat. Pop music is music that we can understand without hesitation, untroubled by any complex musical sophistication.

Classical music is different. Its point is not necessarily to make the strongest immediate impression, but to create a sophisticated texture of sound that reveals its connections only gradually and to the careful ear. Indeed, one of the joys of listening to classical music is hearing the interrelationships between various parts of a piece that might have escaped your attention on the first, or even the fiftieth, hearing. Classical music is more complicated than popular music; it is meant to be listened to again and again. Each time you hear the piece, you will hear something in it you might never have noticed before. Your response to a work, rather than being quick and immediate, develops and changes over time.

So the first step in listening to classical music is to let your ear wander through all the various parts of a piece. Each instrument, each line in a classical work is important, not just the melody or the rhythm. In a piece of pop music, the music has been constructed to focus almost completely on the melody or the beat. The parts in between are there for background only, to provide a cushion for the melody or the rhythm. Not so for classical music. Classical composers delight in creating musical structures that involve all the instruments in the work. Sometimes they present a melody using the highest instrument, perhaps a violin, and then have that melody repeated a bar later by the lowest instrument, perhaps the string bass. Sometimes rhythms show up in the middle parts, played by the woodwinds, that had first been heard several bars earlier in the top part. Sometimes a theme played frontwards in one part will be played backwards in another. Often one group of instruments will echo another. There is almost no end to the kinds of techniques classical composers use to create a complete musical experience. Over the centuries, they developed the means to express a wider and wider range of emotions in their music. The history of Western art-music, at least until our century, was the history of composers deepening and broadening the potential emotional response to their art.

So if you want to appreciate the richness and expressiveness of classical music, listen to all the instruments that are playing, and see if you can hear how they interrelate. And listen to the piece over and over again. Maybe the first time through, you will just listen for the melody, usually played by the highest instrument. Maybe the next time through, you will consciously focus on the bass part and the main rhythm of the piece. Perhaps on a third listening, you will be able to hear the inner voices (they're the hardest to pick out) and you might have the pleasure of discovering that the music for these voices has been carefully composed as well. Only by listening to all parts of the work will you hear the full range of a composer's musical language.

We're going to use one of Mozart's most famous compositions, *Eine Kleine Nachtmusik*, to help us become familiar with classical music in general, as well as with Mozart's specific musical language. Written in the late summer of 1787, originally for five stringed instruments, *Eine Kleine Nachtmusik* is a perfect beginner's piece. It is one of Mozart's clearest, sunniest works, a simple evening's entertainment that has delighted audiences for two hundred years. All his life, Mozart took pleasure in writing happy, joyful music: *Eine Kleine Nachtmusik* represents the pinnacle of his achievement in this aspect of his art.

However, as breathtakingly simple as the piece appears, it is actually the work of a consummate and mature master. In miniature form, Mozart poured into *Eine Kleine Nachtmusik* all he had learned about writing music. Simple it may be, simple-minded it is not. What we will find within its pages will help us understand the unique combination of sophistication and simplicity that is a chief hallmark of Mozart's style. *Eine Kleine Nachtmusik* can also provide us with a wonderful introduction to the language of classical music.

Before we start, however, a reminder. Don't feel you have to plow through every paragraph of the analysis portions of this book the first time through. Read as much as you can digest, then take a break. Maybe skip ahead a bit, or re-read a part. This is probably the best way to use all the chapters in this book where Mozart's actual music is discussed in detail. Because so much goes on in a piece of classical music, it may take a little while for it all to sink in. Don't worry if it seems a little complicated: it isn't. You simply have to acclimatize yourself to a different world and a different way of speaking about that world.

On top of it all, we're trying to write about something that you eventually have to hear — music. The chapters that deal with the music directly — like this one — will make a lot more sense if you have the music nearby. Either try to listen to the work as you read (the ideal) or have a record player, cassette machine or CD player not too far away so you can try out the listening hints right after you've read about the piece. Eventually, I am sure, you'll be able to hear things in the music of Mozart that you didn't know were there before, and you'll start to build your own appreciation of his musical artistry.

Although classical music is more sophisticated and complex than virtually any other kind of music, the basic elements that help create a classical piece are relatively simple, and not that different from those contained in any kind of music. We'll start our investigation by looking at these elements individually. There are four altogether: *rhythm* (and meter), *melody*, *harmony* and *texture*.

Out of these four basic musical atoms, classical composers were able to concoct the most fabulous compounds and musical polymers. Over the centuries, experiments with each component of the musical mix taught composers techniques that were passed on from generation to generation and which helped establish the Western musical language. While differing musical generations applied these techniques differently, a common style emerged that became the basis for classical composition.

Of the four elements, the most indefinable and yet the one we first notice, is texture. Texture is the word we use to refer to the actual sound of the music: the instruments with which it is played, its "tone colors," its dynamic range, loud to soft, its sparseness or complexity — anything to do with the actual sound experience. Like so many other terms describing music, texture is borrowed from another sensual realm. Texture refers to the way things feel, whether it is the softness of cotton batting or the smoothness of silk or the roughness of burlap. In music, texture is the word we use to explain the overall impression that a piece of music creates in our emotional imagination.

Because it is concerned with virtually every aspect of a piece of music, texture is not immediately identifiable as a separate musical element. Yet our first and most lasting impressions of a piece of music, classical or not, are often made on the basis of that work's texture, even if we're not aware of it. Think of the sound of a forties big band, with its sweetly blended saxophone section, or the harsh whine of an electric guitar in a sixties rock group, and you'll get a sense of how powerful the texture of music can be, apart from the actual piece that might be being played. We receive strong musical impressions from the physical sound of any music that determine our emotional reaction to the work.

For classical music, as for any music, the texture of any given piece is often an embodiment of the culture and society in which it was written. Music does not exist in a vacuum. It is part and parcel of a social, political and cultural world, a world that can be brought to life by the music. Certain classical pieces are so evocative that they almost give off an odor of a specific time and place. Mozart's music is very much like that. All you have to do is listen to a few seconds of *Eine Kleine Nachtmusik* to get a powerfully immediate sense of the times in which it was written. You can hardly stop imagining yourself in a sumptuous ballroom, lit by thousands of candles, with servants running to and fro, a Barry Lyndon-esque scene, as you listen to the music.

Mozart's music may be the most perfect reflection we now have of the society in which he lived. It was written for the salon and the drawing room; the concert hall did not exist in Mozart's day, because a concert-going, middle-class public did not exist. Mozart saw the end of the feudal era in Europe, but he was still living and composing in it. Since his music was written for the nobility, to charm and entertain them, it was often quiet, restrained, modest and pleasant. The orchestral forces at his disposal were often small; Mozart's orchestra was perhaps only half as large as modern ones. The dynamic range — that is, the range of louds and softs — was also limited in the late eighteenth century for reasons of taste. It was considered unseemly to display emotion too violently in art, just as it was inappropriate to do so in polite company. Large variations in volume, dramatic pauses, plaintive arias — none of these would have been countenanced by a nobility intent on amusing itself at all costs. Balance was a great virtue in life and in art; symmetry and order were valued more highly than expression and passion.

Mozart, genius that he was, provided the most perfect expression of the virtues of order and balance, grace and elegance, to which his era aspired. In his hands, they transcend the mundane and take on heavenly proportions. Those who love Mozart's music love it first for this texture of order, elegance and proportion. At the heart of the music is a sense of perfection and completeness that exists in its own, otherworldly realm of art.

Here is the first of many mysteries we will encounter in the music of Mozart. Working strictly within the limitations imposed upon him by his time, he managed to create a musical universe that nonetheless overcomes those very limitations and sounds as fresh for us today as it was for the nobility of the *ancien régime* two hundred years ago. Within his music is a perfection which transcends time and place.

As you listen to Mozart's music or any other classical work, remember to focus your listening on its texture from time to time. Of course, you can never escape the impact the texture of the music is making, but it is valuable to listen to it consciously every so often. What you are hearing is an entire world coming to life once again in music.

As you do this, you will be listening to every aspect of the work in combination. To listen for the other basic elements of classical music, we reverse this kind of listening, and focus on one single feature at a time.

The most visceral and fundamental of these musical elements is rhythm. Whether it is the tribal drumming of Africa, the sophisticated interplay of instruments in Indian music or the beat of a rock tune, rhythm is the time element in music. Music takes place in time, and composers have discovered that rhythms and the relationships between rhythms can express many moods and musical thoughts.

For most forms of music, rhythm is used to provide a primal, instinctive kind of foundation for the other musical thoughts to build upon. In extremely basic music, there is only rhythm. Western music, however, developed a special kind of organization of time over the centuries that is now one of its most significant features: the concept of meter. We are so used to meter in our music that we sometimes forget it was an invention of generations of composers, not a spontaneous method of music making. We are the only musical civilization to use meter as an organizing principle in our music, and our whole concept of rhythm is tied to this fundamental idea.

Here's one way of understanding meter. Imagine someone sauntering along a downtown street at lunchtime. They're in no particular hurry; they're just watching the world go by. Maybe they stop to do a little window shopping or hurry to catch a light at an intersection or slow down to catch sight of a friend. Their progress is spontaneous and unplanned.

Now imagine that that person has joined the armed forces, and is marching down the same street — left, right, left right — 1-2, 1-2. Time, rather than flowing freely and unpredictably, as it did in the lunch-hour walk, is now measured out in equal parcels of unvarying length. The amount of time between each of the marching steps, or beats, is identical: it is the meter of the march. If the person marches more quickly, the meter speeds up, if they slow down, the meter slows down. For any meter, any marching speed, a symmetry has been created, imposing order on the seeming chaos of "real time."

This is where every piece of Western music written after about 1600 starts, with an invisible organization of time into equal measures. The music may sound as free-flowing as Bach's "Jesu, Joy of Man's Desiring" or as languid as the slow movement of Beethoven's Ninth Symphony, but the meter is always there, counting away in the background, in either 2 beats, 3 beats or 4, providing the basic metric scaffolding for the piece, a grid upon which any number of musical events can be constructed.

Try an experiment for yourself. Take any piece of music — popular or classical — and start counting to yourself as you listen. You'll find, within a few moments, that you can hear a pattern in the music of equal beats, generally in groups of 2, 3 or 4. Once you establish this pattern, you will be able to anticipate when notes will begin and end, and when sections of the piece are likely to occur. Meter provides us with an invisible security blanket, allowing us a sense of continuity that is emotionally satisfying.

This equal measuring out of time as a primary organizing tool for the creation of music corresponds to the rational organizing principles of Western thought that equally affect our scientific, political and social thinking. Eastern music is also based on measurements of time, but in a much more subtle and changeable way. An Indian raga may start with a section of 2 beats, followed by one of 11 beats, followed by another of 18 beats, followed by yet another of 3 beats, a pattern which is then repeated. The Indian musician finds our 1-2, 1-2 metric organization simple-minded and laughable. However, these meters, whether they consist of two beats (1-2, 1-2), three beats (1-2-3, 1-2-3, the waltz tempo) or four (hup-2-3-4) lie at the heart of our music, and very much at the heart of Mozart's music. Mozart needed the regularity and symmetry of that metric scaffolding to allow him to create music of infinite variety and charm.

If we go back to that imaginary march down the imaginary street, we will see that in a march, one step, or beat, within a given pattern is always stronger than the others. When the march is in two, the steps are patterned this way: LEFT-right; LEFT-right; STRONG-weak; STRONG-weak. If the march were in four, the pattern would be: HUP-two-three-four; STRONG-weak-weak-weak. If the march turned into a waltz, the pattern would be ONE-two-three; ONE-two-three; STRONG-weak-weak. Not only does the meter create equal divisions of time, called beats, in a piece, it establishes patterns of beats as well — patterns of strong and weak accents. It is these patterns that are the true background for virtually all pieces of classical music, patterns that all by themselves carry a certain emotional weight.

Count to yourself once more the three patterns mentioned above. Can you feel how different the waltz pattern is from the other two? Merely by choosing to write a piece with this meter, the composer determines the character of the piece. And there are differences, as well, although they are more subtle, between a meter of 2 beats and a meter of 4. Left-right, left-right as a marching pattern is more insistent and brutal than Hup-two-three-four, Hup-two-three-four.

Meter is the foundation on which all rhythm rests in classical music. The rhythms of the piece, the actual pattern of long and short lengths of time that the notes of the piece express, are always consistent with the basic metrical pulse counting away in the background. Even though composers discovered dozens of different kinds of rhythms and rhythmic patterns, the rhythm and the meter are always in harmony with each other.

It's time now to listen to a real piece of music to see how rhythm and meter actually work. Let's take a look at the opening page or so of *Eine Kleine Nachtmusik*. But before we start, a brief word about reading scores. Perhaps you've never seen a score before or maybe you haven't read a note of music since you struggled through a piece propped up on your music teacher's stand when you were ten. In either case, you might not be that anxious to dive into reading scores now. But it's not as hard as you think. There's a lot of information you can glean from a score just by looking at it — even if you can't hear the sounds the notes represent. If the score is a piece you already know, you can actually use the score to remind yourself of the way the piece sounds. For musicians across the centuries, scores have proved an invaluable tool for documenting visually the ephemeral world of sound. Scores have allowed musicians to transmit their ideas to one another in written form for study and performance. That's why they are also valuable to us.

Here's the way the opening to *Eine Kleine Nachtmusik* looks in the score:

Serenade
Eine Kleine Nachtmusik

W.A. Mozart
1756-1791
Köchel No. 525

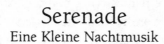

Let's start with a few preliminaries about how the score is set up. Each instrument in the piece has its own line of music; generally the higher the instrument, the higher the line. There are four lines of music in *Eine Kleine*, although there are five instruments; the cellos and the basses play the same music all the way through the piece. Sometimes instruments that play different music most of the time play the same music every so often. That is what is happening at the beginning of *Eine Kleine*. If you look at the excerpt, you'll see that the first violin part and the second violin part are identical, note for note. In fact, all four parts are nearly identical. You can see, looking down the page, that the notes for each part occur at exactly the same spot on each staff. We call this a unison passage — a passage in which all instruments play the same notes. If you think back to how *Eine Kleine Nachtmusik* starts, you'll remember that you could also hear all instruments playing the same notes. And that's it. You've just read your first score.

When you want to follow a score, remember that each black note on the page corresponds to a single played note in the music. Every time you hear a new note, you should be reading the next black dot on the page. As well, every written note corresponds to a single musical pitch; when the musical sounds go up, so do the printed notes, and vice versa. It is also helpful to know that all the notes in the musical scale have names. They could have been given numbers, but instead they are named after letters of the alphabet — A,B,C,D,E,F,G, going up the scale. Once you get to G, though, you stop and the next note up is called A. The notes above that one are called B,C,D and so on up to G again.

Going back to the score, each note has its own spot on the staff. In the treble clef (that is, in musical lines that start with this sign —
𝄞) the note A always sits in the second space from the bottom of the staff, B is written on the line above that space, C appears in the next space up, D appears in the line above that and so on. In the alto and bass clefs, the same notes show up in slightly different places. The positions where all the notes appear in all the clefs that appear in this book are shown on the facing page.

There are other simple kinds of communication a score contains. It tells you how fast a piece should be played (Allegro for *Eine*

treble clef

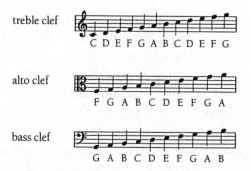

C D E F G A B C D E F G

alto clef

F G A B C D E F G A

bass clef

G A B C D E F G A B

Kleine, meaning "lively" in Italian). It tells you how loud to play various sections (the *f* — forte "loud" in the first bar). The sharps (♯) or flats (♭) at the beginning of the piece tell you which seven of the twelve possible notes of the Western scale this piece is made up of (the key signature). Every piece of Western music also begins with a time signature: an indication of the meter the composer has chosen for this specific piece. In *Eine Kleine Nachtmusik*, the time signature is that " c " in the middle of the staff of the first bar. The " c " is short for "common" time, which could also have been written "4/4." The top number in any time signature tells you how many beats there are to the bar, or the meter the composer has chosen for the work. 4/4 means four beats to the bar, the Hup-two-three-four meter. 2/4 would have meant two beats to the bar, the left-right meter. The bottom number in a time signature designates which time value has been chosen to get a single beat. In a 4/4 time signature, the quarter-note gets a single beat.

Every score has one other visual reminder of the meter of the piece: the bar line. Those vertical lines drawn right through the score, through every part, divide the music into equal bars, or measures. In *Eine Kleine Nachtmusik*, each of those barred measures contains four beats; each takes an identical length of time to play. The bar line also reminds the musician which beat, which note should get an accent. The first beat in every bar is the one that must be accented and it is easy to spot because it always comes right after a bar line.

Those bar lines are more than a performer's convenience, as we shall see. Composers like Mozart conceived of their musical ideas in terms of bars and symmetrical numbers of bars. The regularity of the bar, its metric inevitability, was a crucial feature of Mozart's musical language. Without the bar, and the order it represented, Mozart's music would be unthinkable.

You can see this for yourself if you look at how Mozart deals with meter and rhythm in *Eine Kleine Nachtmusik*.

Either play, listen to or sing to yourself the opening of the piece. It opens with that famous unison fanfare which we've already briefly looked at. As you listen to it again, start tapping your foot to the music. Can you feel the regularity of the meter that your foot is tapping out? Even though the rhythm of the opening is quite lively, that steady four-beat meter continues through the phrase, like a little metronome. And note as well the slight accent that you put on the first beat of every bar; the meter ensures that you will do that.

Here's the second phrase of *Eine Kleine*, which comes right after the first one:

The rhythm of this phrase is quite different from the rhythm of the first. For one thing, the instruments are no longer in unison. The melody is carried only by the top line, the first violin; the other instruments are providing an accompaniment for that line. But once again, as you sing or listen to this phrase, keep your foot going. Although the second phrase is quite different from the first, the meter has not changed at all and the first beat of each bar has the strongest accent.

We have come up against one of the important aesthetic principles of Mozart's music in this little analysis. The essence of Mozart's style is his ability to create music that is two things at once. The rhythms of the first two phrases are quite different from each other, yet they are connected by a unifying meter. We hear continuity in the meter but variety in the phrases, and so we get a small dose of classical music pleasure. Let's see what happens when we add the third phrase:

This phrase is only two bars long, not four, and once again, its rhythm is different from that of either phrase 1 or phrase 2. But check your foot. It hasn't varied an iota — it's still marking out the same, steady four-beat meter.

The next phrase in *Eine Kleine* sounds at first like it's from a different piece:

For the first time in the piece, Mozart has stopped the rush of notes and written two slower notes (bar 11), which begin a more leisurely phrase. But has the meter changed? No; despite the slower pace of this phrase, the meter continues unabated. There is really no end to the variety of phrases and rhythms Mozart is able to compose within the confines of a single meter. This was one of his great skills as a composer: he was never at a loss for the new rhythms he needed to create musical interest in his work. Had he not kept introducing rhythmic variations, the regularity of the meter in a piece like *Eine Kleine* would have dominated and deadened the vitality of the work.

To understand the creative tension between unchanging meter and constantly changing rhythms, try this exercise. Start your foot again to establish the meter of the piece. Then speak out loud or clap the rhythms of the first four phrases. As you do this, you'll be able to appreciate just how well the rhythms fit together, despite the fact that they change radically every four bars or so. The regularity of your foot contrasted with the ever-changing patterns of your hands is the essence of the relationship between rhythm and meter in classical music. The meter is the beat that never changes; it is like an inaudible metronome that keeps going in the background, establishing the tempo of the music, driving it forward, giving it a sense of pace and pulse. The rhythms are ever-changing, but never out of harmony with the meter.

If you're still with me, let's keep looking at these rhythms from another angle, and see if we can discover some of the compositional tricks Mozart is famous for. Clap the first phrase again, this time noticing the rhythmic symmetry Mozart has built into this piece. It's almost too obvious to point out that the rhythm of the second part of the phrase (bars 3 and 4) is exactly the same as the rhythm of the first part of the phrase (bars 1 and 2). As we investigate all the musical elements in the opening of *Eine Kleine*, we will see just how much symmetry Mozart managed to pack into those first few bars. It affects every element of the composition, but it begins with the rhythm.

And just in case you think that all the phrases have this kind of rhythmic balance, let's clap the second phrase again. Here Mozart does repeat a rhythm, but he repeats it in every bar, not once every two bars. Bars 6, 7 and 8 have exactly the same rhythm, and the rhythm of bar 5 is very similar. In effect, Mozart is speeding up the pattern of rhythmic repetition. In the first phrase, a two-bar pattern is repeated. In the second phrase, the rhythm of a single bar is repeated. Keeping this in mind, can you guess what Mozart is going to do in the third phrase?

Take another look. As you might have suspected, Mozart has repeated the rhythm once every half-bar in this phrase:

The rhythm of the first half of bar 9 is repeated once in the second half of bar 9, and again in the first half of bar 10, to be followed by silence, always the most dramatic effect in music. The sense of rushing forward that audiences have noticed in this music for centuries is created by the little rhythmic trick we've just discovered. The rhythms of the first few phrases repeat themselves more and more quickly all the time. Although the meter never changes and even the phrase lengths do not vary that much, there is an unmistakable sense of moving forward. It is no wonder that Mozart, ever cautious not to overplay an effect, completely changes the rhythmic pattern in the fourth phrase, and slows the music to a walk.

The music of Mozart is full of rhythmic effects like this one, subtle changes in the patterns of note lengths and beats that create significant musical differences. When you listen to Mozart, you should be alive to these effects, and to the emotional weight they carry. But none of this brilliant rhythmic play would work without the constant meter. That regular pulse is the framework that holds the whole piece together and allows a variety of rhythms to coexist happily without degenerating into musical chaos. Meter is the key to the kind of rhythm classical composers created.

Composers at different times in our musical history have dealt with the notion of meter in different ways. In the Baroque era, the era just before Mozart, meter gave music an unending quality, and rhythmic repetition was the chief technique used to create a vast emotional panorama. If you think of "Jesu, Joy of Man's Desiring" again, you can hear how the repeated rhythmic figure, based on the underlying meter, helps give the piece its transcendental emotional character. At the other end of the scale, in the Romantic era, the era that followed Mozart, meter was seen as a hindrance to the expression of deep emotion. Some pieces would change meter in the middle; sometimes the meter would seem to disappear altogether. Composers worked hard to ensure that the arbitrary patterns of 1-2 or 1-2-3 did not disturb the expressive laws of their compositions.

Mozart, as in so many things, stands exactly halfway between the Baroque and Romantic eras in his approach to meter and rhythm. Rhythmical balance and symmetry are of crucial importance to Mozart's style and personal sense of beauty. He can hardly write a phrase that does not contain two perfectly balanced halves or a series of exquisitely balanced sections. The regularity of the meter provides the constantly moving pulse that allows individual phrases to occupy just the right amount of time and number of beats. Without that imaginary metronome in the background, Mozart's style of composition would be unworkable.

In fact, the consuming interest of composers like Mozart in the aesthetic principles of metric regularity and balance gave rise to the term "Classical" to describe their music. Yet another term borrowed from another art (this time from architecture), "Classical" described the style, current at the end of the eighteenth century, which valued balance and symmetry above all else. If you can imagine one of those Classical façades, where rows and rows of windows of identical size are arrayed in perfect balance and harmony, you are creating the architectural equivalent of a series of measured and balanced musical phrases, the kind that Classical composers like Mozart delighted in creating.

In keeping with their emphasis on balance and symmetry, Classical composers were also careful not to let one musical element overwhelm the others. Balance between elements was as important as balance within any one of them. In most Western music, the two musical components that balance each other most completely are rhythm, based as it is on the regularity of a constant pulse, and melody, which focuses on the unique line, the one-time-only combination of notes that expresses a specific emotion.

Mozart himself placed high value on melody writing. It was, he once wrote, what distinguished the "packhorses" from the "thoroughbreds." Mozart was certainly a thoroughbred in this world; his works sparkle with dozens of highly polished melodic fragments, ranging from the merely charming to the deeply moving.

However, what Mozart called melody and what we know as melody are two different things. Our notion of this musical element was bequeathed to us by the nineteenth century — a long, complete, musical sentence that has a form and structure all its own. Mozart never wrote a melody like that. His melodies were actually short phrases, generally four or eight bars in length, which were always heard in combination with other, similar phrases. The musical effect is something akin to a mosaic, with individual pieces joining together to create a beautiful whole, as opposed to the expressive and highly charged melodic lines of Romantic composers like Tchaikovsky and Chopin.

Nonetheless, the same techniques apply to writing successful melodies, whether they are by Chopin or Mozart, Bach or McCartney. Although melody writing is the most mysterious aspect of music — the aspect that is almost impossible to teach — there are some basic techniques worth listening for.

Let's take an example of a simple melody so we can see how the techniques work. Except we won't take a melody by Mozart, we'll use one by George Gershwin. Let's do a little creative analysis of one of his first big hits, "I Got Rhythm," and then apply the same analysis to the opening bars of *Eine Kleine Nachtmusik*.

"I Got Rhythm" is one of Gershwin's most enduring tunes, but the song couldn't be simpler, or so it seems. The entire melody is based on two simple musical ideas. The first one, which is repeated more than a dozen times in the piece, consists of the four-note pattern we hear at the beginning of the song, the notes that go with "I got rhythm." It seems an awfully slim bit of music to build an entire song on, but notice a couple of things about it. First, it has a definite rhythmic punch, a highly identifiable character that will allow us to recognize the phrase by its rhythm alone whenever it reappears, even if its notes are not exactly the same. This is a key element of melody writing — creating ways for listeners to link phrases and elements that are not exactly the same. Mozart does it as often as Gershwin.

Notice also that the four-note phrase goes up when it is first introduced, with a big accent on the third note. Because of the meter of the piece, that note gets an extra little push: I got RHY-thm. Now hum the second line of the song. It is really a second version of the first: I got MUS-ic. One phrase goes up and the other down, but the rhythm of the two lines is identical. Moreover, they are made up of exactly the same notes. You can listen to "I Got Rhythm" several times without realizing that line 2 is line 1 played back-wards. Listen again for yourself.

The reason you don't immediately hear the connection is that Gershwin has disguised it. On the way up, the meter and accent structure of the piece provides a push on the third note of the sequence (1-2-3-4). On the way down, it is the second note that gets the push (4-3-2-1). This fools us into hearing the two lines as more different than they actually are. Gershwin has created the ultimate melodic success; using an economy of means, he has still managed to create variety.

To truly appreciate music — Mozart's, Gershwin's or any other composer's, it is vital to be alive to these little melodic devices. They are wonderful examples of the composer's art and can be found everywhere if you learn to spot them. But they have a musical significance as well. Composers try to fashion their pieces out of the fewest possible building blocks. If there are too many melodies, too many rhythms or too many different chords in a piece, the listener gets confused and eventually bored. On the other hand, of course, if there are too few, the listener is numbed by the excessive repetition and also gets bored. The balance between unity, which creates comprehensibility, and variety, which prevents boredom, has bedevilled every composer who ever sat down at the piano or in front of a blank sheet of music paper. It is a constant struggle to balance these two contradictory elements, as much for Mozart as for George Gershwin. Consequently, these first two lines of "I Got Rhythm," which have both unity (they are made up of the same notes and have the same rhythm) and variety (one goes up, the other down; one accents the third note of the sequence, the other accents the second) are what music is all about. The success of the composer and the eventual enjoyment of the music depends greatly on the cleverness of the techniques used to balance unity and variety.

Eine Kleine Nachtmusik doesn't seem to have much in common with "I Got Rhythm," yet the two pieces contain many of the same melodic techniques. Here, again, is the opening phrase of *Eine Kleine*. Hum the melody to yourself.

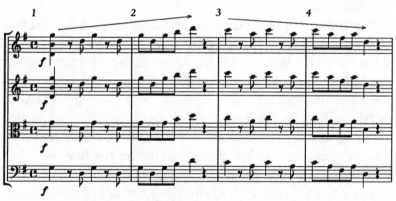

The first thing to notice about the opening phrase is the way it bounces around in the first two bars. Melodies often move carefully, step by step, one note at a time, but this one jumps up and down all over the place. The effect on the listener is one of openness and excitement; in a way, we psychologically follow the compass of a melody. Where it moves boldly around the staff, we feel a similar boldness; where it has a narrower compass, the effect on us is more subtle.

We have already noted the balance in rhythm between the two parts of the first phrase; the rhythm of bars 3 and 4 is an exact replica of the rhythm of bars 1 and 2. Now look at the melody; you can see that it is also divided into two parts. And they are balanced in almost exactly the same way that Gershwin balanced the opening to "I Got Rhythm." Where the melody of the first half of the Mozart phrase tends to go up, the melody of the second half tends to go down. The first half of the phrase ends on a high D (the last note of bar 2). The second half of the phrase ends on a low D (the last note of bar 4), exactly one octave lower. Mozart delighted in writing these "question and answer" openings to his pieces, but few are as perfectly balanced as this famous opening to *Eine Kleine Nachtmusik*. An almost perfectly symmetrical phrase is created with the unison texture, the balance of rhythms, the opposition in melodic movement of the two halves of the phrase and the wide compass within which the melody moves.

Let's leave Mozart for a second, and head back to the Gershwin to see what other tricks he had up his sleeve as he wrote "I Got Rhythm."

Remember that he used exactly the same notes in the first two phrases: first going up, then going down. The third fragment in the stanza is the first one all over again, exactly as it appeared in line 1, same notes, same rhythm: "I got MY man." Then, to change the pace, the stanza finishes with the only other melodic idea Gershwin uses in the piece, to the words "Who could ask for anything more?". The rhythm of this second idea is completely different from the rhythm of the first; it does not have the extra push on the third beat and it goes a lot faster. Sing the whole stanza to yourself, and you'll see how effectively that last phrase balances off the first three:

I got RHY-thm
I got MUS-ic
I got MY man
Who could ask for anything more?

Gershwin writing in the 1930s had the same sure-fire instincts as Mozart writing in the 1780s. If he had used the stop-and-start rhythm of the first three lines one more time, a clever musical idea would have turned repetitious. Gershwin, like Mozart, knows exactly when to give us a completely different rhythmic and melodic idea.

At the same time, Gershwin maintains the up-down balance between lines with his new idea. Line 3 goes up, as did line 1. Line 4, although it takes a little detour or two, goes down, as does line 2. Notice as well (there's more to notice in this simple song than you might have thought) that the highest note of the stanza occurs on the word "Who" at the beginning of the fourth line. The highest note of any grouping is very important for the ear; for some reason, it registers a significant emotional effect on the highest note and composers have learned to place that highest note carefully within a grouping. Gershwin, to achieve maximum balance between the fourth line and the first three, places the highest note where you least expect it, at the beginning of a brand-new phrase. The impact is even greater because you are expecting line 4 to go down (to correspond with line 2). Instead, line 4 begins at the melody's highest spot, which is a surprise, giving maximum value to that treasured position.

Let's return to *Eine Kleine Nachtmusik* again to see how Mozart's follow-up of the first musical idea compares with Gershwin's. Although the means Mozart uses are a little more complicated than Gershwin's, the basic principle is the same. That principle is balance. The difference is that where Gershwin can construct a whole song out of two small fragments, Mozart uses an abundance of ideas. The first two pages of *Eine Kleine Nachtmusik* contain no fewer than ten separate musical ideas, in music that takes less than ninety seconds to perform. We will see later how Mozart manages to avoid musical chaos with so many ideas, but for now, let's see how many we can identify.

The second musical idea in *Eine Kleine* is the idea that begins in bar 5, after the opening. We noted it when we looked at the rhythms of the piece. Let's take another look (see the music on the next page).

In contrast to the wide leaps in the first phrase, Mozart has created a little idea here whose compass is considerably narrower. There is more movement by step in the melody, although there are slight echoes of the melody of the first phrase in the little three-note figure that comes at the end of bars 6 and 8.

In the next melodic idea, the two-bar idea found in bars 9 and 10, virtually all the movement is by step:

And in contrast to the second idea, which balanced off up-and-down melodic movement, his third idea constantly ascends — ascends, in fact, to the highest note on the page, a high D. This note marks the end of the third phrase and the end of the speeding-up motion that characterized the rhythms of the first three phrases. It is followed, dramatically, by silence. To heighten the drama, Mozart places the highest note of the page just before this brief silence. A rhythmic and a melodic effect coincide. These are the kinds of techniques that composers spend their days and nights thinking about, discovering how to use the laws of musical psychology to create artistic effects.

Although the artistic motivations of a Mozart and a Gershwin are different, their understanding of musical psychology is often similar, as we have already seen. Among the musical tricks they both used is the element of surprise. Let's return to "I Got Rhythm" one more time to see how Gershwin, within the limitations of the popular song, used surprise to complete his artistic arsenal.

As is common in popular song, and not infrequent in classical music, the second stanza in "I Got Rhythm" is an exact repetition of the first, so you can get used to the melodic fragments that have gone into the making of the piece:

I got DAI-sies
In green PAS-tures
I got MY man
Who could ask for anything more?

The third stanza in the common four-stanza song is called the bridge, usually a form of traveling music that breaks the pattern of the first two stanzas, to relieve the boredom, but which often does not contain very interesting music of its own. For the bridge of "I Got Rhythm," Gershwin tries a daring experiment. He takes the first melodic fragment that we identified and repeats it, not three times, as he did in the first two stanzas, but four times, offering no relief through a contrasting bit of music. However, to use the bridge as a bridge, that is, a time to relax the ear, he reduces the melodic interest of the fragment almost to nil. Rather than outlining a little melodic movement, it stays nearly stationary. But because the rhythm is the same, we know it is the same fragment that we heard in the first two stanzas of the piece. Once again, unity and variety are equally served. And to complete the picture, Gershwin starts the fragment, and the stanza, on a note in between the opening of the other two stanzas and that note we identified earlier as the highest note (so far) of the piece, to give this bridging stanza a little extra musical interest.

> Old Man TROU-ble
> I don't MIND him
> You won't FIND him
> Round my door.

The bridge now over, Gershwin heads home with his last stanza. It starts out exactly the same as stanzas 1 and 2 note for note:

> I got STAR-light
> I got SWEET dreams
> I got MY man . . .

And then Gershwin throws us a carefully premeditated curve. Rather than repeating the "Who could ask for anything more?" line that everyone is waiting for, he breaks his pattern and writes us a new line, based on the rhythm of that second idea (in fact, using the same words as that idea), but which heads upwards instead of downwards, establishing a new highest note for the piece. To balance off the excessive use of that four-note idea, which was heard three times in stanzas 1 and 2 and four times in stanza 3, Gershwin has created this wonderful counterpart: an unexpected extra line, taking off in an unexpected musical direction, which then settles back to the normal pattern of the piece. "Who could ask for anything more?" is then repeated again, exactly as it appeared in stanzas 1 and 2, and the piece comes to an end.

To appreciate the significance of that extra "Who could ask for anything more?", try singing "I Got Rhythm" without it, with a normal four-line last stanza. The piece just lacks something. With the extra line, it has balance, surprise, freshness. Without it, it lies a little flat, it's a little boring. It took the special talent of a great composer like Gershwin to find a solution to his musical problem that might have escaped many other musicians. Great composers do that — find just the right combination of elements to make their music work.

Of course, Mozart was more than a great composer, he was a genius. We could spend the rest of this book analyzing the melodies that Mozart used in *Eine Kleine Nachtmusik*. Each one of them is a little bit of perfection, full of surprise, balance and compatibility with its neighbors. Look at the little melody that follows the third phrase of the piece:

Remember this musical idea? Notice its inevitable downward motion, which balances off the upward motion of the phrase that precedes it. Notice, as well, its internal balance, always a part of Mozart's music. The phrase goes down for three bars, and then up for the final bar.

There is one exception to this pattern, however. The second note of the phrase goes up instead of down. This is a bit of a Mozart joke. We have just left the phrase that ended with the high D followed by silence, and so would expect a phrase that would balance off this upward motion by starting lower down and continuing on down the scale. But right after the first note, the phrase goes up a note before it goes down. It's not supposed to do that; if you can imagine the phrase in bar 11 starting an octave higher, that second note would be the highest note of the piece, one-upping the high D that ended the previous phrase. It is a subtle jest, but a jest nonetheless. Learning to understand the jokes is an important part of learning to understand Mozart's musical personality. It was not just in his personal life that he loved to play tricks.

The melodies in Mozart are always fresh, and there are always a lot of them. Here's a little fragment that takes on some importance in *Eine Kleine*, the idea that starts in bar 28.

Here, as in the other melodies, balance is crucial. The first bar of the melody features a little triplet figure; it is balanced off in the second bar by three detached notes. And, as usual, the first two bars are balanced off by the last two. This is Mozart; you'll find time and time again in his music that when one idea is put forward, a contrasting notion is immediately put beside it. Everything is even, and even-tempered. Elegance and decorum rule his musical universe.

We have looked now at three of the basic elements that go into classical music — texture, rhythm and melody. Our last element is harmony. We saw in the Gershwin example that the form of the piece, its division into stanzas, and into lines within those stanzas, was basically tied to melody. In Mozart's music, it is not melody that determines the form, but harmony. So we will reserve most of our discussion about harmony for the next chapter, when we talk about form. But here let's spend a little time on this, the fourth basic element that goes into making Western music.

Harmony is the psychological effect that is created when two or more notes are sounded simultaneously. Early in our musical history, composers realized that harmonies had enormous potential for emotional impact and that different harmonies could create widely varied impressions. We can easily sense that for ourselves.

If you can play together the notes C and E, a grouping we call a major third, you'll realize that this interval expresses a positive feeling, a feeling of confidence and joy. Changing the notes ever so slightly, play a C and an E flat together (a minor third). This interval gives the listener an overwhelming sensation of sadness, incompleteness, instability. A difference of half a tone can cause enormous shifts in emotional reaction.

Over the centuries composers began to use different intervals, chords and combinations of chords to evoke different emotions. Although we'll spend more time investigating these combinations in the next chapter, for the moment it is most important to know that composers eventually discovered two chords that had the most interesting and varied relationship. In any key, these are the chord built on the first note of the scale and the chord built on the fifth note of the scale. In musical terminology, that first chord is called the tonic and the second one, the dominant. The relationship between these two groupings of notes became one of the most important features of the classical style of composition.

The most common chord used in the music of the Classical era was the triad, a grouping of three notes, arranged in thirds. C-E-G is a major triad; C-E-flat-G is a minor triad. Triads were named for their lowest note, so the grouping C-E-G is called the C major triad. If a piece of music was in C major, the C major triad would be the tonic chord: the one you will hear most often in the piece. So in *Eine Kleine Nachtmusik*, which is in the key of G major, the G major triad is featured most prominently; that chord is made up of the notes G-B-D.

Harmony is created when notes sound together. However, it is important to realize that the effects of harmony work not only when the notes of the interval or chord are played simultaneously, but also when they are played successively. If you play C and E together, or sing the same notes one after the other, the effect is about the same. That is why composers could use harmony, and the chords that harmonies are made up of, in melodies as well as in the supporting harmonies themselves.

Let's see how this works in practice in *Eine Kleine*. Once again, let's take a look at that opening phrase (see next page).

Let's name the notes that the first violin is playing in the first two bars: reading from the beginning, they are G - - D-G - - D-G-D-G-B-D. In other words, the first two bars do nothing but outline a G major triad; every note in the two bars comes from the chord. Let's continue, and look at the notes in bars 3 and 4: they are C - - A-C - - A-C-A-F#-A-D. What those notes outline is a chord based on the dominant, D (D-F#-A-C). (It is called a dominant seventh because it is made up of the dominant triad plus C, which is seven notes above the bass note, D.) What Mozart has done in the first four bars is provide us with the two most important chords in the piece, the tonic and the dominant. So in yet another way, the four bars are perfectly balanced. Two bars based on G are followed by two bars based on D. Now watch what happens as the piece progresses.

In the second phrase in *Eine Kleine*, the parts are not in unison, as we mentioned before. Take a look at the phrase again:

G major   D major   G major   D major

When you're trying to determine the harmony of any section in a classical work, it's sometimes easier to look at the middle parts than at the melody in order to determine what's going on. So let's take a look at the second violin part for this phrase. The second violin begins the phrase (in bar 5) by playing the repeated notes B and D (the cross-hatching on the stems of the notes means "repeat"). B and D are the top two notes of the G major triad, so it seems as though the harmony of G major is being re-established here. Now look at the bottom two staves (the viola and the bass and cello lines). There you'll find the missing G to complete the triad — which confirms the feeling of G major.

Now look at the second violin part in bar 6. The second violin has started playing the notes C and D, two notes from the dominant seventh chord. Again, the viola fills in the missing notes of this chord, in the second half of its bar. In bar 7, the second violin returns to B and D (of the G major triad). In bar 8, we're back to C and D. What Mozart is doing in these four bars is similar to what he did in the first four. He is alternating harmonies, between G major and D major. In the first phrase, he changed harmonies every two bars; in the second phrase, he changes in every bar.

Now let's take a look at the first violin part for this phrase to see how Mozart uses harmony in his melody. Mozart has to be careful here; this regular alternation between tonic and dominant could become quite predictable, if not balanced off by some other element. As expected, the notes of bar 5 in the first violin part are almost exclusively derived from the G major triad. They are: G-G - - B-A-G. Only that middle A between B and G is not from the G major chord. How about bar 6? Here the harmony is derived almost completely from the dominant chord, with one exception (although it's an important exception). The notes are G-F#-F# - - A-C-F#. Only the beginning G is not part of the dominant seventh chord. It is out of place, but what an out-of-place note it is. Because it is the first note in the bar, that "wrong note" G is heard very prominently. Mozart has done this on purpose. He has created the impression that the first violin somehow forgot to change the harmony at the right time, and is still in G major at the beginning of bar 6, when it should be in D major. He does exactly the same thing in the next two bars. The first note in bar 7 (a bar based on the G major harmony) is an A, left over from the bar before; the first note in bar 8 is a G, left over from bar 7.

This little device is enough for Mozart to disguise the regular alternation of harmonies in the supporting instruments. By delaying the first violin as he does, he creates a wonderful sense of ambiguity for the ear. For a fleeting moment in each bar, we seem to have two different harmonies at the same time. If you listen to that phrase again, you'll hear a bit of friction, of dissonance at that point. It's there to provide musical interest.

Harmonic effects like these are common in Mozart; he was one of the great masters of harmony. Yet again, we must alert ourselves to be sensitive to a part of the composition which we might otherwise have totally ignored. If we continue our harmonic analysis of *Eine Kleine* for just one phrase more, we will see yet another use of the alternation between the G and D harmonies:

We have been noting as we analyzed this fragment that it is only two bars long, rather than the normal four, but we've never said why. Taking a look at the harmonic underpinning of the bar might give us an answer. Look at the bass line. This is often the line that tells us most clearly the harmonic basis of any bar or phrase. In bars 9 and 10, the bass plays the following series of notes: G-G-A-A-B-B-F#-F#-G-G-A-A-B (rest). What this series represents is the same old alternation between tonic and dominant harmony, but an alternation that now takes place every beat, every second note.

Mozart started the piece alternating these two harmonies every two bars. Then he alternated them every single bar. Now he is alternating them on every beat, four times a bar. Now you know why you can sense a musical compression in this opening; we saw it rhythmically and melodically, and now we see it expressed harmonically. This phrase is shorter than the others because our ear can only take so much rapid harmonic change. There are seven harmonic changes in these two bars, and that's enough to balance off the four changes in the previous four bars, and the two changes in the opening four bars. Two, four, eight (seven actually, because one beat is a rest): you can see why Mozart has been labeled a composer obsessed with symmetry, balance and form. Hidden in this innocent opening section of *Eine Kleine Nachtmusik* is writing of the most fabulous complexity and purest symmetry.

Are we supposed to hear all this subtlety under the surface of Mozart's music? Must we hear all of this to fully appreciate his works? The answer is yes, and no. Some of these effects Mozart clearly wanted disguised; others he probably hoped his listeners would hear. Like the man himself, Mozart's music always remains somewhat mysterious. He took such pains in his art, almost unbelievable pains, to create the most satisfying and rewarding music for us, his listeners, yet he hid away some of his most beautiful effects behind veils of subtlety and reserve. The more we can pierce some of those veils, without losing sight of the surface that Mozart so lovingly created, the more we can hope to understand the true significance of the extraordinary art this great man created.

CHAPTER THREE

———◆———

Patterns of
the Sublime

Y OU ARE probably starting to get a sense of how Mozart crafted his music, and of the ways you might want to listen to his works in order to hear everything there is to hear and enjoy. Now that you know something about Mozart's use of texture, rhythm, melody and harmony, listen again and again to some of the Mozart works that you like — then listen to some you do not like so well. As you familiarize yourself with a work, listen once for the texture only, concentrating on details of orchestration or tone color. Listen again for the rhythm and the melodies, and then again, if you like, for the harmonies. A composer like Mozart will repay repeated listening, because of the wonderful complexity of his musical language. As I mentioned in the last chapter, it may take a little while to grasp all the details of this language. Don't worry if it does; the music isn't going to go away. You can take all the time you need to get used to the ways in which classical composers used musical structures, small and large, to get their messages across.

Once you have become accustomed to the language of classical music, you will be ready to take the next step and listen to a piece of music for its form, its organization. As you read the upcoming discussion of form, don't worry if you need to stop every so often to get your bearings. If the explanation gets a bit confusing or if you find yourself getting a bit lost, don't feel you must press on. Re-read a passage, move on to another part of the chapter, even move on to another chapter if you like.

Eventually, however, you'll want to come to grips with form and organization to truly understand Mozart's music. For many composers after Mozart, and for even a few before him, form was not so important. Each one of their pieces had a form, certainly, but the nitty-gritty of the composer's message was communicated through other elements of the music.

Mozart is different. The way he played around with the formal patterns he inherited and created were very important for him. Unless you understand those patterns and can hear how they work in the music, you'll miss a lot of Mozart's sense of humor and much of his way of creating musical drama — two vital features of his art. Even if it takes a little time to understand form, it will certainly be worth it. And again, listen to the music as you read. That will help your understanding immeasurably.

Think of form as if it were the plot of a play. In Classical music, as in a play, something is happening all the time, every event has been preceded by another, and leads to another. To truly appreciate the music, you need to understand its overall shape and how each individual part fits into the whole. As you learn to hear the form of the piece, along with the details of rhythm, melody and harmony, you will be communicating with the composer in the way he wanted to communicate with you.

Form was important for all classical composers, although in differing degrees, as mentioned above. They lavished a great deal of attention on the organization of their pieces and spent a lot of time perfecting their construction. They saw the manipulation of form as the pinnacle of their art. However, composers do not invent new forms every time they put pen to paper. Each musical era develops standard patterns which become the basis for most of the music written at any given time.

The Classical period — Mozart's era — coincided with the political upheavals of the French Revolution, and the two were closely linked. As polished and restrained as Classical music might seem today, it is important to remember that it was revolutionary in its own time. It created a revolution for simplicity, for direct communication, for common humanity against aristocratic exclusiveness in music.

Think back to *Eine Kleine Nachtmusik*. Yes, we agreed, it conjured up images of an aristocratic setting. But the music speaks joyously to our common humanity. We hear it this way today; it still appeals to the sense of musical joy shared by all people. Compare the lightness and charm of *Eine Kleine* with any piece you know by a Baroque composer, like Johann Sebastian Bach, and the difference between the two pieces becomes immediately apparent. Baroque music represents a world of opulence, stability and emotional evenness, downplaying drama and unpredictability. It was the music of a feudal aristocracy. Classical music, on the other hand, belonged to the emerging middle class — it was less pompous, less noble, more down to earth. However, that is not to say it was less powerful than its Baroque predecessors. In fact, just the opposite was the case.

Although Mozart eventually became one of the chief exponents of the new kind of music, later to be called "Classical", he did not invent the style. In fact, no single composer completely invented the style, but Franz Joseph Haydn, twenty-four years Mozart's senior, came close. It was his musical experiments in the late 1760s and throughout the 1770s that brought drama and suspense into the world of purely instrumental music, creating the Classical style. It was Haydn who first invested the forms of the symphony, the string quartet and the concerto with great musical power. Although all these forms had existed long before Haydn started to work with them, it was in his hands, and those of Mozart and Beethoven, that they became the most profound musical vessels ever created in the Western tradition. Our sense of the symphony as the repository of a composer's most powerful thoughts and of the string quartet as the medium for his most intimate utterances dates back to Haydn.

Until the mid-eighteenth century, musical power and drama had been confined to the operatic stage. Instrumental music only provided pleasant entertainment, in the form of the Baroque suite, based on a series of dances, the early sonata or serenade, or the early symphony. So Haydn was doing a revolutionary thing when he freed musical drama from reference to the stage and mundane human action. He allowed it to take hold in the imagination, where the depths of human emotion and heights of human understanding could be registered. By creating a dramatic sense that needed no reference outside the music itself, Haydn stumbled onto an artistic power unequaled, many would say, in the history of any art form. If it was not until the symphonies of Beethoven that the full power of the Classical style was unleashed, its potential was first discovered by Haydn and developed by Mozart.

With the sense of drama came the sense that music should be uni-directional, constantly propelled in a single forward direction. For the first time in the history of instrumental music, the key questions for the listener became "What comes next?", "Where is the composer taking this idea?", "How is this concept being developed?". No longer was music judged solely on its ability to conjure up a single emotion and represent it perfectly, or to express beauty complete in itself, as it was in the Baroque era. Music now became statement; it was judged on the quality of its musical ideas, on its power to move, to create emotion and above all to create and resolve artistic tension.

How did Haydn fashion this musical revolution? He did so by concentrating on two principal musical ideas — one small, the other large. On the large scale, Haydn refined a new formal organization called "sonata-allegro" form. On the small scale, he emphasized a simple device called the four-bar phrase. So named because it was a musical miniature that normally took four bars to play, it was a tidy little musical statement, well-defined melodically and rhythmically, which appeared and reappeared in a piece.

These four-bar ideas became the "characters" in the musical drama of the Classical style. The listener had to recognize them because things were going to happen to them in the course of the work. As you listen for the four-bar phrases in Mozart's works, think of them as if they were building blocks. In one formation, they make a certain kind of pattern; however, if you rearrange them, the pattern can change substantially, even though the blocks are identical. They are the pieces with which the composer creates the work. The development of these building blocks became one of the features of the drama in the music; it was essential that each idea be presented clearly and separately from its neighbors, so it could be identified by the listener.

Even though Haydn — and Mozart — took pains to do this, when you actually listen to Classical pieces, the feeling of continuity in the music is often so strong that you tend to hear these separate phrases as part of one big musical idea. But the first step in truly unlocking Mozart's deeper secrets is to separate these musical ideas from each other and register the most prominent of them in your memory. One trick is to mentally count to four while you're listening to a Mozart work. By and large, although not exclusively, a new musical idea will appear every time you reach "one" again. (What you are actually counting are downbeats, those extra-strong beats at the beginning of each bar.)

You need to have a strong sense of where each musical idea begins and ends, because Mozart is going to throw you a few curves before the piece is over. He is going to repeat his little phrases, but conceivably in a different order, combining two ideas that were first presented separately. He may also change the character of his phrases — by having them played in a minor key rather than a major, for instance, or by shortening some and lengthening others. If you have been listening to recognize the individual elements, you won't miss the point when Mozart engages in a little compositional legerdemain.

Once you get the hang of it, listening for those four-bar phrases — those building blocks — is relatively simple, because they are right on the surface of the music. Just to remind you, the first building block in *Eine Kleine* was that opening fanfare, a little musical package with its own rhythmic, harmonic and melodic pattern. Then came the phrase that followed that unison fanfare. It also had its own internal unity. Then came the two-bar building block and another, slower, four-bar component. Each of these phrases is a different musical idea; build them up, one after the other, and you can create a massive musical structure — a symphony, for example, that can last forty minutes. Every time you listen to one of Mozart's works, especially one unfamiliar to you, start listening for those four-bar phrases right away. They are the key structural components Mozart used to create his music throughout his career.

Classical composers put themselves in a dangerous position, however, when they made the four-bar phrase the cornerstone of their musical language. For the dramatic success of their works, they had to make sure that listeners would hear those building blocks as different, because if they did not, they would never understand the dramatic devices that would be applied to them. On the other hand, if each succeeding four-bar phrase were totally independent of the others, the music would degenerate into chaos, a series of musical non-sequiturs. So the challenge that Mozart and his colleagues faced was to create a series of phrases that sounded both different and related at the same time. Unity and variety — both had to be satisfied.

It is here that Mozart the magician makes another major appearance, the Mozart of subtlety and complexity. The means by which he creates unity in his works are so varied and well hidden that some musicologists have rebelled at the attempts of their colleagues to find relationships between musical ideas in his works, claiming that the experts are creating links of which the composer was unaware. This is almost assuredly untrue. There are so many connections in the music of Mozart that they cannot be accidental or spontaneous.

Let's return to the opening page of *Eine Kleine Nachtmusik* one more time to look at these connections (see the score that starts on the next page). Although the musical connections are carefully concealed, virtually every bit of music in the first thirty-five bars comes from one single idea. To see how the links are formed, let's look again at the very first phrase. In the first violin part, the last

Serenade
Eine Kleine Nachtmusik

W.A. Mozart
1756-1791
Köchel No. 525

56   Development - Main theme in dominant _ _ _ _ _ _ _   Idea from bar 35

61

65

69

Recapitulation - Tonic section

"Second theme" - now in tonic

three notes in the second bar outline the triad of G major: the notes G, B and D. To create unity, Mozart writes echoes of these three notes, or some form of them, in every phrase of the piece. Let's look at the phrase that begins in bar 5, for instance. The echo is weak, but it is there: we start again on G, and the next different note we hear is B.

Now look at the phrase that begins in bar 9, the two-bar phrase we've mentioned before. The G-B-D pattern of bar 2 is easier to find here. The G occurs on the first and third beats of bar 9; the B appears on the first beat of bar 10, the D on the third beat. This echo of the last three notes of bar 2 is no accident and both the high Ds are purposely followed by rests to accentuate their high pitch.

A completely different kind of phrase begins in bar 11 with those two long notes, but even that phrase ends with another echo of the three notes of the opening: the three notes G, A and B, in bar 14. Now, the notes are not G-B-D as we might expect, but the similarity between the two phrases is unmistakable. Both begin on a G, both include a B, and both go up. It is as though the little phrase in bar 14 didn't have quite enough power to leap up a third note by note, but could only move step by step. Even though the notes are slightly different, the two phrases seem somehow to be trying to achieve the same musical end.

And to further accentuate those three notes from bar 2, look at the transition phrase that begins in bar 18. The first notes of bars 18, 19 and 20, all heavily accented because they are first beats, are — you guessed it — G, B and D. Once again, Mozart has linked these apparently separate ideas by making them echo each other in the most subtle ways.

The effect of these correspondences may not be clear to your conscious mind as you listen to these phrases — after all, the music we've just described takes less than a minute to perform — but they are heard by your musical subconscious. Your ear registers these correspondences if only lightly; they help create the overall atmosphere of a work and define your basic response to it. You probably feel the music belongs together somehow even though you can't say exactly how it all fits. The extent to which Mozart hides these relationships is almost unique to him as a composer. Most other composers wanted you to hear how clever they could be; Mozart preferred to let these relationships hide in the shadows of his work, so that sometimes you think you hear something familiar, but it passes before you can be sure.

The emphasis on the four-bar phrase and the development of these phrases was the small idea that helped forge the drama of Classical style. These phrases became the characters in the musical drama that was about to unfold.

But you need more than characters to create an overall dramatic effect. A set of circumstances or ideas has to be established, challenged and re-established. This three-part chain holds all drama together, from the earliest Greek tragedy to the silliest *opéra comique* to the noblest Shakespearean play. It was Haydn's great achievement to create drama by developing a musical form that followed this pattern. In his works, the something that was established, shaken and eventually re-established was strictly musical. It was not a situation, but a key, a tonality. If the four-bar phrases are the characters in the musical drama, the harmonic framework is the scenery in front of which they act out their drama — and changing the harmonic setting adds to the drama of the work.

We mentioned in the last chapter that harmony exists in music on two quite separate scales. We looked at how small-scale harmony has a profound emotional effect on us as listeners. As composers like Haydn began to experiment with longer formal structures, they realized they could create emotional meaning in a piece using large-scale harmonic patterns as well. Composers from about the year 1600 on realized that not only did certain intervals bond together well, but whole series of chords could also create coherent patterns. A feeling of a home key could be established, strayed from and re-established. The concept of home key and the relationships that various chords could have to this home key is called tonality. In other words, it is the large-scale harmonic plan of the piece, which consists of a series of chords and harmonies that take it from the home key at the beginning back to the home key at the end.

Almost every piece of Western music written between 1600 and 1900 is in a definite key. *Eine Kleine Nachtmusik*, we saw, was in G major, as it started with a G major chord. If we looked to the end of the work, we'd see that it ended with a G major chord as well. In each key, there are seven main triads (three-note chords) that can be used to build its harmonies: these are the triads constructed on each note of the scale. Other triads can be used too, but they will lead the piece into other harmonic regions, away from the security of "home base." The more the seven main triads are repeated, in varying formations, the greater the sense of a coherent structure; the more often other triads are used, the less powerful is the sense of coherence and the more mysterious and evocative the music can become.

Composers in the Classical era began to create musical forms by exploiting the dramatic implications of different combinations of harmonies: a period of relative harmonic coherence, in which the music stayed close to the harmonic base, was followed by a section of harmonic turmoil, in which the composer would intentionally write harmonies that ranged farther away from the harmonic base. All this was followed by yet another section of calm. The harmonic tension thus created in a work became the key dramatic element in its development.

There was one harmonic progression in Classical music that outshone all others for its structural importance. If you think of the opening harmonies of *Eine Kleine Nachtmusik*, you'll remember that Mozart basically used just two chords to construct most of the first page of the piece. These were the tonic and dominant chords of G major (G and D). These two chords are always the most important in any piece of Western music.

For reasons which we honestly do not know, these two chords act as polar opposites in any given piece. Movement from the tonic to the dominant and back again, whether within a single phrase, as we saw in *Eine Kleine*, or within an entire piece, seems to create a sense of balance and satisfaction in us as listeners. Over and over again, as we look at Mozart's large-scale orchestral works, we will talk about this opposition of tonic and dominant. It is one of the fundamental organizing principles in Classical music, and one which Haydn, although he did not invent it, was the first to exploit consistently for dramatic purposes. Tonic and dominant are the twin harmonic poles around which all the other chords and harmonic relationships of a piece revolve. All Classical forms are based on the drama inherent in this opposition.

We mentioned earlier that Haydn inherited forms called symphonies and string quartets when he began to experiment with his new dramatic techniques in the late 1760s. Actually, they had been around for decades before Haydn started composing. What Haydn did was to take these older forms and give them a new lease on life, a new dramatic urgency. In the late 1770s and beyond, most Classical works began to take on a similar formal plan.

The pieces were divided into sections, called movements. Movements are like acts in a play; they are intended to follow each other in a logical sequence, creating a dramatic effect similar to that of the theater. Generally, Classical pieces were in three or four movements. The first movement of the work stated the basic ideas and emotional character of the piece, whether it was going to be happy or playful or tragic. The second movement was always slower, providing a balance to the musical action of the first. The third movement, in those compositions that included it, was a minuet and trio, a shorter movement intended to provide a bit of relief after the musical depth of the first two. The final movement was an energetic, lively section providing resolution and joy at the end of the work. Symphonies and string quartets used all four movements of this plan; concertos and sonatas eliminated the minuet and trio movement.

It was the organization of the first movements of these pieces that became the most complex and sophisticated. It came to be known as first-movement form, or sonata-allegro form, because it appeared in the first movements of sonatas, which were almost always marked "allegro." The whole organization is based on the opposition of two themes, or two groups of themes, one of which is played in the tonic, or home key, of the piece, the other of which is heard in the dominant.

Movements in sonata-allegro form have three sections (see the diagram on this page). In the first section, which is called the exposition, the two themes or groups of themes are exposed (or stated) for the first time — the first group in the tonic, the second in the dominant.

The second section is called the development, because that's exactly what happens in the music. The development is a free section of the piece where composers got a chance to play around with the musical phrases they introduced in the exposition. Often the music is quite wide-ranging, both melodically and harmonically. The point is to heighten tension and suspense in the work, to increase the dramatic possibilities of the form.

SONATA-ALLEGRO FORM

Exposition ⟶

First Theme (Tonic) ⟶ Second Theme (Dominant) ⟶ Coda (Dominant) :‖

Development ⟶

Development of Themes (free harmonies)

Recapitulation

First Theme (Tonic) ⟶ Second Theme (Tonic) ⟶ Coda (Tonic) |

The development leads into a third section, the recapitulation, in which the themes from the exposition are presented again, except this time they are both written in the tonic key. The opposition between tonic and dominant disappears. It is as though the free-wheeling harmonies of the development needed to be balanced by an extended section in the home key of the tonic. The recapitulation is the happy ending of sonata-allegro form; the opposition of the first theme and the second theme, expressed by their original introduction in different keys, is resolved. Everything is now played in the tonic — both the first and the second theme.

Sonata-allegro form is a mini-drama in pure music. Two groups of themes are set off in opposition to each other, then they vie for prominence in the development and are finally reconciled in the recapitulation. The music constantly moves forward; we are always listening for what comes next in the piece, where it is going. At the same time, it is an organization with a certain amount of formal balance. Exposition and recapitulation act like bookends, with the highly charged development in the middle. The exposition itself is divided into two balanced sections, one in the tonic, the other in the dominant. It is no wonder that a composer like Mozart who adored both formal balance and the dramatic in music would love composing with this form. It allowed him to indulge every one of his artistic whims.

Now let's take a deep breath and see if we can hear this important form when we listen to Mozart's music. We are lucky in one respect. *Eine Kleine Nachtmusik*, even though it is not a symphony, is written as though it were. Its first movement is a perfect miniature of the same sonata form that Mozart used time and again in much larger compositions. If you can learn to hear the form in *Eine Kleine*, you will find it easier to hear in Mozart's mature symphonies, string quartets and piano concertos. Eventually, if you listen to enough music, the form will become second nature to you. You'll get to the point where the various sections of the work become obvious to you. Don't worry if you're not quite sure where everything is at first — it does take a little bit of practice.

We already started our formal analysis of *Eine Kleine* without being aware of it when we identified all those four-bar phrases at the beginning of the work. As we've said, the four-bar phrase is the building block with which Classical composers created their structures. Now it is time to see how Mozart builds a form with them. Keep those individual ideas in mind, though. If you can hear them, you will eventually be able to hear the form they make up.

The first bit of music you hear in a sonata-allegro movement is the single most important bit of music in the piece. A composer must establish two things right off the bat. First, there must be a highly identifiable theme that we'll recognize each time it reappears. If we can't recognize that opening theme, we're going to miss the point when it returns in the recapitulation. The composer must also establish the harmony of the opening quite clearly in our ears so we can tell when it changes midway through the exposition.

Mozart is successful on both fronts in *Eine Kleine Nachtmusik*. His opening idea — that unison fanfare we talked about earlier — is one of the most famous openings in the history of music. Because of its texture and rhythm, we'll know it in a second when it reappears. Not every composer would have been able to do that. Often, a less successful composer will open a piece with an idea that sounds too much like other ideas in the work. So when that first idea reappears, we can't quite remember what it is. As Mozart got more experience in using this form, his first ideas became easier and easier to identify.

Mozart also helps us hear the home key of the movement, G major, in the opening few measures of *Eine Kleine Nachtmusik* by making sure the entire first page is based, one way or another, on the G major chord, both melodically and harmonically. Do you remember this from the last chapter? Now we realize why Mozart went to so much trouble to establish the sound of that G major triad in our ears. Despite the fact that there are five different musical ideas in the first twenty bars of the movement, Mozart wants us to hear the uniform G major sound they all share. It is central to the artistic success of this movement that we get a strong sense of the home key right at the beginning.

As we mentioned in the last chapter, one of the easiest ways to guess the key of any section of a work is to check the bass line, the bottom line of the score. Often the note the basses are playing is the tonic note of the section. Looking at the first page of *Eine Kleine*, you can see how often the basses play nothing but a repeated G. Even when they desert the note G, they don't stay away long. This is further confirmation that the home key is G major.

Listen to the opening of the movement again for that common harmonic foundation. We know that the musical phrases are differentiated by their melody and rhythm, but for the form's sake, we must hear them as part of a single section. The ideas certainly contrast with each other, but they are all based on the same harmony.

Every sonata-allegro movement in Mozart begins like this one, with a strong opening phrase in the home key, followed by a series of complementary ideas, all sharing the same harmony. There might be four or five ideas in this section, as there are here, or more than a dozen, as is quite common in some of Mozart's bigger compositions, but the principle is the same. The piece needs a strong section in the home key.

In every sonata-allegro movement, there also comes a point where the music starts to transform into the dominant key (the official term is "modulate"). This is the second critical point in any sonata-allegro movement. The move to the dominant must be made smoothly, but obviously enough so that we can be alerted to the fact that the work is moving into a new section. At one point, our ears must realize that something is about to happen.

In *Eine Kleine Nachtmusik* the harmonic scenery begins to change just after bar 18. In bars 18 to 20, the piece is definitely in G (check out all those Gs in the bass). However, the harmonic ground starts to shift in bar 21. Here is where the movement to the dominant key of D major begins. Do you see that C sharp that sneaks in at the end of bar 21 in the first violin part? C sharp is a note that is not part of the scale of G major, that does not occur in the key of G, but it is part of the key of D. In fact, it is the only note in the key of D that is not also in the key of G. So when the ear hears that C sharp, it starts to shift its harmonic focus involuntarily. It starts to think in the key of D instead of the key of G. And just to make sure, Mozart repeats that C sharp over and over again in the next few bars (bars 22 and 23, bars 26 and 27). The ear is held captive and is forced to say goodbye to the relative safety of the home key, following the composer to a new harmonic region.

Listen to that section of the piece, perhaps several times. Can you sense how a different "color" has entered the music? It is important to be able to spot transition passages like this one when you hear them because they announce new sections in the form. There are a few hints to help you. Because transition passages are there strictly to move from one harmonic region to another, they usually have limited melodic or rhythmic interest. Often there are a lot of repeated notes in these passages, hammering away the transition to the new key. Almost all of them come to a definite end on a feeling of anticipation. When you hear one of these passages (and with a little practice, you'll be able to spot them a mile away), they are a giveaway that the piece is moving into a new section. They are written as signposts to help you follow the form.

The transition passage leading to the dominant section of the exposition ends in bar 27 with a rest, and a new group of themes — in the dominant — begins in bar 28. The first theme in this group is often called the "second theme" of the piece, even when it is far from the second musical idea exposed in the work.

Here is another place where a composer must be sure to create just the right kind of music. Sonata-allegro form is based on us listeners making a distinction between this new group of themes and the set of themes that appeared at the very beginning of the movement. It is crucial that the first theme we hear in the dominant section be as clearly defined as the first theme we heard in the tonic section. Composers had to make sure that its character firmly contrasted with that of the opening theme of the work, so listeners would understand that it was announcing a different section. When you listen to a movement in sonata-allegro form, keep your ears open for that "second theme." Next to the opening, it is the most important musical idea in the piece.

In *Eine Kleine Nachtmusik*, Mozart gives this phrase its own character by using a rhythmic trick: the triplet figure that shows up in bar 28. This is the first time in the piece that we've heard this specific rhythm, and it's enough to fix the idea in our memories.

The "second theme" is followed by two other musical ideas, both in the dominant, both wonderfully charming. First, in bars 35 to 38, Mozart gives us an idea based mostly on a repeated note that acts as a balancing feature. Then another idea is presented (in bars 39 to 40). Both of these ideas are repeated before Mozart rounds off his exposition with a little coda, or ending, which begins in bar 51.

The opening section of *Eine Kleine* is a perfect miniature of an exposition: the tonic is established, the piece modulates to the dominant, a second group of themes establishes the new key in our ears and a short coda rounds off the proceedings. Listen to the whole thing again to establish the various components of the section in your memory. Virtually every musical idea is there for a reason; you shouldn't overlook any of them. Generally, in sonata-allegro form, the exposition is repeated, to make sure that the audience has had a chance to fix all these ideas in its mind.

If the exposition is the establishing section of sonata-allegro form, where the basic themes of the piece are presented and the opposition between tonic and dominant is displayed, the development is the transformation section, where the music can change dramatically.

Sonata-allegro movements always begin in the home key before they modulate to the dominant. But contrary to what you might expect, they don't go back home at the end of the exposition. The piece is still in the dominant key at the end of this section, still in a state of suspended harmonic animation. (Notice the three repeated Ds, not Gs, in the bass part of bar 55.) We know that before the movement is done, it will return to the home key, but to do so, it will have to travel through the harmonic wilds of the development.

The development is the most exciting part of sonata-allegro form. Anything can happen in this section. Composers will range far afield harmonically, rhythmically and sometimes melodically. Thematic material which first appeared in the exposition can pop up here in the most surprising disguises. As the Classical era progressed, the development section took on a more and more important role within the first movement of symphonies, concertos and sonatas. It became the most dramatic part of the piece, the section that contained more and more of the musical and emotional impact of the work. For Beethoven, the most dramatic of all composers, the development played a central role, for this was where drama, suspense and surprise could be played out to the full. Mozart, as we shall see, was less interested in exploiting the element of surprise in his development sections than in using the whole section to establish the formal balance of the entire movement, although he's not afraid to give us a few surprises as well.

The development section in *Eine Kleine Nachtmusik* is only twenty bars long (from bar 56 to bar 75) but it demonstrates what development sections are all about. Mozart begins the section by returning to that unison phrase we heard right at the beginning, but now it is in the dominant key, not the tonic. It is a D major triad that is outlined in bar 56, not a G major triad. And watch what he does from there. If Mozart were to completely match the opening of the piece here, the answering phrase to the one outlined in bar 56 would be in A major (five notes higher than D). But he starts the answering phrase on the same note as the one the first phrase ended on, rather than the note one step lower. With this tiny change, Mozart actually writes this answer not in A major, but in B major, a completely unexpected chord and key. And what he does next is even more interesting. The next phrase (the one that begins in bar 60) is not what we expect at all; it comes from the musical idea that began in bar 35, in the second section of the exposition, not the first. Two phrases that appear thirty-one bars apart in the exposition are juxtaposed in the development. This is a common Mozartean maneuver but a wonderful one nonetheless — joining two ideas together which were originally presented separately, and in different contexts. If you've listened carefully to the exposition, you'll realize the trick; an apparently unimportant musical idea from the exposition is promoted to prominence at the very heart of the piece.

And look what Mozart does with that little idea. It is given the principal role in the development as it is repeated again and again (five times in all — bars 60 to 70), each time with a more complicated harmony supporting it. We saw that Mozart sneaked into B major in bars 58 and 59, just before he introduced this idea. B major is generally a prelude to a bar in E major. Instead, Mozart gives us the last chord we would expect in bar 60, a C major chord (check the bass note) — the first time this chord has appeared anywhere in the piece so far. Can you hear how different that bass note sounds? And in the next few bars, Mozart repeats this phrase in E major (bar 65), in A minor (bar 66), in D major (bar 67) and then, taking us totally by surprise once again, in E flat major (bar 68). The net effect of all these new chords, and surprising ones at that, is to make us feel a little lost harmonically. We're not sure where we're going, and although none of us can remember what the home chord G major sounded like, we sense that we're getting a long way from home.

Mozart was probably the greatest master of harmonic change in Western musical history. Those chord changes in the development of *Eine Kleine* seem so simple and effortless, but it would take five pages to analyze the harmonic complexity they represent. Mozart's own ear was so acute that he could hear the various relationships between chords, and ways of linking new chords with old ones, better than any other composer. Once you get used to the language, listening to Mozart manipulate harmony is one of the great joys you can experience in his music. It's like being on a musical roller coaster. You thrill to the various ups and downs, secretly knowing that you'll somehow get home safely.

So how does Mozart get us back to G major? Simple. He takes a figure based on the coda of the exposition (bar 70 and on) and quickly unties all the harmonic knots he has created for us. The harmonic complexity of these few bars is monumental, though their apparent ease is absolute. But by bar 76, we are already safely back in the home key, ready to begin the recapitulation.

The development section of the first movement of *Eine Kleine Nachtmusik* is quite short, which befits the joyous character of the music. This would not be the piece to get deeply involved in complex, unsettling harmonic sequences. But imagine what happens in those pieces where there are no such restrictions. In those cases, the development is where the composer can take the gloves off and move the piece throughout the musical spectrum, harmonically and melodically. You must have your ears about you in developments like that. It is the place where some of the most wonderful surprises of Classical music occur, as well as some of the most profound music. The composer is trying to trick you and by tricking you, move you as well. The clear musical sky of the exposition can darken quickly in the development. It is the dramatic climax of the piece. If a composer has done the work successfully, we listeners should welcome the recapitulation like the sight of an old friend.

There is always a sense of triumphant return when the opening theme is restated at the beginning of the recapitulation. We are back firmly in the tonic, never to leave it again. We have been pushed and pulled by the harmonic range of the development; our musical anxiety has been increasing. Now we are on familiar territory, and the joy at that familiarity is part of what the recapitulation is all about. You should hear that sense of joy in the music.

Once we realize we have returned home musically, the tonic section of the recapitulation sounds almost exactly the same as the tonic section of the exposition in *Eine Kleine Nachtmusik*. Then, around bar 95, Mozart seems to begin a transition section as he did in the opening, except this time, the transition is never made. Even though he still introduces those C sharps that we said were a tip-off that the music was heading towards a new key, in the recap he never takes the piece into the new key. (Mozart accomplishes this by cleverly cutting the transition section short by a couple of bars.)

We've worked too hard, emotionally, to get back to the tonic in the recapitulation to be willing to lose home key again. The strength of that feeling of permanence forces the second group of themes into the tonic for the recapitulation; they are not permitted to stray into the dominant. Compare the "second theme" in the recapitulation (bar 101) with the "second theme" in the exposition (bar 28), and you'll see that the music is five notes lower in the recap. The "second theme" is in G this time, not in the dominant key of D, as it was in the exposition.

This is the last important feature to listen for in sonata-allegro form. Although we are not as sensitive to keys as audiences were in Mozart's day, we should learn to recognize the slightly different sound the "second themes" have when they are played in the tonic. The timbre, the tone color of the new notes, is often different, as they are five notes lower than they were originally.

Mozart continues his recapitulation in the tonic key following the patterns he established in the dominant part of the exposition, and then adds a short coda to the piece to tidy up the movement (bars 127 to the end). And just to reiterate the point, look at how firmly he establishes the sound of G major in the last six bars; virtually every part is playing some form of the G major triad in all these bars.

One hundred and thirty-seven bars make up this exquisite movement; one of the finest miniatures in the history of any art. Although the movement is short, its structure is similar to the larger versions of the same structure that he used in all his mature works. If you can understand it here, you can understand it anywhere.

Sonata-allegro form is complicated, and it will take a little while for you to get used to it. Listen again to the opening movement of *Eine Kleine*: follow the score if it helps. Eventually, you will learn to hear the various sections in the piece almost by second nature. And when you approach a new piece, you'll find yourself automatically listening for the form as you listen to all the other elements in the work.

The great advantage of sonata-allegro form is its extreme flexibility. It is such a complex and interesting form of organization that it can be used again and again without ever repeating itself. Mozart wrote over a hundred movements using this organization, and no two are alike. In some the first theme is developed immediately; in others the development is extremely long; in yet others new material is introduced in the recapitulation. Each time a composer used the form, it was the internal balance of the various elements that determined the overall shape of the piece.

Although nowadays sonata-allegro form is often considered a highly regimented way of writing music, in Mozart's day it was a living artistic organism, adaptable and constantly changing. For Mozart, it was the most important aesthetic organizing principle in his career. Every artist needs a form in which to work, through which to express artistic ideas. By the end of his career, sonata-allegro form was as much a part of Mozart's musical language as the four-bar phrase and symmetrical rhythms. It became the way he thought about music. If we want to understand Mozart's music as he understood it himself, the principles of sonata-allegro form have to become part of our language, too.

As important as sonata-allegro form came to be in Mozart's music, his love affair with this kind of musical organization did not begin until about the middle of his artistic life. At the beginning of his career, he was known not as a composer but as a performer of musical feats that are still unsurpassed. Mozart, the child prodigy, became a legendary figure in the history of music and it is to his childhood exploits and adventures that we now turn.

CHAPTER FOUR

——◆——

The Prodigy
from
Salzburg

MOZART'S musical genius was unparalleled in the history of music; even today, it strikes us as not quite believable. At three, he spent hours picking out intervals of a third on the family piano and registering his pleasure at his accomplishment. At four, he could learn in thirty minutes pieces that normally took practiced musicians weeks to master. He had a superhuman musical ear and could distinguish between two notes an eighth of a tone apart (most musicians can only distinguish between notes a half-tone or more apart). What is more, the two notes Mozart heard were played over a two-day period. This is the equivalent of someone telling you on Wednesday that the dinner they were eating was half a degree hotter than the dinner they'd had on Monday — and being right.

The sensitivity of his ear was legendary, even in his own lifetime. Until he was nine, he had a pathological fear of trumpets, because of the amount of sound they could make. "Merely to hold a trumpet in front of him was like aiming a loaded pistol at his heart," wrote an observer at the time. In a misguided attempt to cure his son of this phobia, his father once asked the court trumpeter in Salzburg to play the instrument in Wolfgang's presence. Remembering the scene years later, the trumpeter André Schachtner said, "My God! I should not have been persuaded to do it; Wolfgangerl scarcely heard the blaring sound, than he grew pale and began to collapse, and if I had continued, he would surely have had a fit."

His musical memory was just as fantastic as his ear. By the time he was in his early teens, he could write out any piece of music perfectly, note for note, however complex it was, after hearing it only once. When he traveled to Rome with his father in his teens, he heard a famous Baroque piece called the Miserere, which no one outside St. Peter's was allowed to perform. After each presentation of this long and complicated contrapuntal work, the parts would be collected and locked up so that no other group of musicians could ever perform the work. Wolfgang heard it, returned to his hotel later that day and wrote the whole thing out — every part, every note. His father was terrified that the copy would be discovered and he would be excommunicated for stealing the piece. No one would ever have believed that anyone — let alone a boy of fourteen — could have written the piece out from memory after just one hearing.

Mozart's prowess at the keyboard and with other instruments was equally astonishing. Somehow, instinctively, he just knew where to put his fingers to make the right sounds. He could play immediately any piece of music plopped down in front of him. Without even pausing to look the work over, he would play the piece as though he had been practicing it for months. More incredibly, he could play instruments on which he had received no instruction at all.

Events in the Mozart household must have been nothing less than fantastic in Wolfgang's youth. André Schachtner witnessed one in the early 1760s, which he related to Nannerl, Mozart's sister, just after Wolfgang's death. Imagine, if you can, the following scene:

In the days after your return from Vienna [i.e., when Mozart was five], Wolfgang having a little violin that he got as a present in Vienna, our former very good violinist, the late Herr Wenzel, came to us. He was a beginner in composition, and brought six trios with him, which he had written while your father was away and asked your father for an opinion on them. We played the trios, Papa playing the bass with his viola, Wenzel the first violin and I was to play the 2nd violin.

Wolfgang had asked to be allowed to play the 2nd violin, but Papa refused him this foolish request, because he had not yet had the least instruction in the violin, and Papa thought he could not possibly play anything. Wolfgang said: You don't need to have studied in order to play 2nd violin, and when Papa insisted that he should go away and not bother us any more, Wolfgang began to weep bitterly and stamped off with his little violin.

I asked them to let him play with me; Papa eventually said: Play with Herr Schachtner, but so softly that we can't hear you, or you will have to go; and so it was. Wolfgang played with me; I soon noticed with astonishment that I was quite superfluous, I quietly put my violin down, and looked at your Papa; tears of wonder and comfort ran down his cheeks at this scene, and so he played all six trios.

When we had finished, Wolfgang was emboldened by our applause to maintain that he could play the 1st violin too. For a joke we made the experiment, and we almost died for laughter when he played this part too, though with nothing but wrong and irregular positioning, in such a way that he never actually broke down.

Once Mozart discovered music, there was time for little else in his life. He would only play games if they were somehow connected to music. In every free moment, he was at the piano or playing the violin. By the time he was five, his whole life was centered around music. Other influences on the young prodigy during these formative years remain something of a mystery to us. Already Mozart the person was being obscured by Mozart the musician.

We know frustratingly little about Mozart's relationship with his mother. Maria Anna Pertl was orphaned at an early age, and seems to have been a typical Salzburg housewife of the mid-eighteenth century. That meant that she loved to have fun, to gossip, to appreciate the odd vulgar joke and to stay in her husband's shadow. Perhaps Mozart inherited his love of practical jokes, of wordplay and of vulgarity from her; it's hard to know. The part played by Maria Anna, senior, in Mozart's life was never recorded — apart from a trip she and Wolfgang took together to Paris when her son was in his early twenties.

We know a little bit more about Mozart's relationship with his sister, Maria Anna, junior — affectionately known as Nannerl. Nannerl was four years older than Wolfgang, and was his first companion and friend. She studied music and toured Europe with him, she joked and played with him in their Salzburg house. When they toured together, Wolfgang made up an imaginary kingdom called "The Land of Rücken" for their amusement. The kingdom was so vividly described that their traveling servants drew maps of it for them. When Mozart entered his teens, Nannerl became the first recipient of the bantering and comic letters he would write all his life.

Milan, 18 December 1772

I hope that you are well, my dear sister. When you receive this letter, my dear sister, that very evening my opera *[Lucio Silla]* will have been performed, my dear sister. Think of me, my dear sister, and try as hard as you can to imagine that you, my dear sister, are hearing and seeing it, too, my dear sister. That is hard, I admit, as it is already eleven o'clock . . . . That reminds me. Have you heard what happened here? I will tell you. We left

Count Firmian's today to go home and when we reached our street, we opened the hall door and what do you think we did? Why, we went in. Farewell, my little lung. I kiss you, my liver, and remain as always, my stomach, your unworthy

frater

Brother WOLFGANG

Please, please, my dear sister, something is biting me. Do come and scratch me.

In the original of this letter, every other line is written upside down.

Nannerl seems never to have completely understood her brother, and there is virtually no evidence of her joining in the fun and silliness that was directed her way. Her teenage letters back to Wolfgang are always safe and conventional, and she seems to have remained this way throughout her life. Perhaps for the first but certainly not for the last time in his life, Mozart received no response from a quarter where he desperately needed a companion, a sympathetic spirit. Although he grew up with his sister, traveled with her, performed with her and clearly loved her, her response to him seems muted, distant and slightly disapproving.

We can only speculate whether Nannerl's distance from him hurt the young Mozart, as we must speculate whether he would even have noticed it. Early in his life, whether because of his almost total absorption in his music, or for some other reason, Mozart began to live in a world of his own making. It was a wonderful world, full of the indescribable joy he felt in listening to and making music, and it was not entirely separate from the world his contemporaries inhabited. But it was different enough that Mozart did not always react to the world in ways that world expected. Perhaps it is the curse of the artist to live in a parallel universe — a world made up of the same objects, events and situations as everyone else's, but felt and interpreted in a different way.

If the connections between Mozart and his mother and sister remain shrouded in mystery, the one relationship we can speak of with certainty in Mozart's life is the complex emotional bond he formed with his father. Leopold Mozart controlled almost every aspect of his son's life until Wolfgang was in his twenties. He acted as his son's teacher (Wolfgang never attended school of any kind), his musical adviser, his agent, his impresario, his guidance counselor, his spiritual mentor. The relationship between the two was at the same time loving, exasperating, angry and emotionally overwhelming. If Wolfgang Mozart continues to remain an enigma to us, Leopold Mozart stands etched in the clearest detail.

Leopold was thirty-eight when Wolfgang was born. He was himself a professional musician — a violinist, composer and teacher in the employ of the Archbishop of Salzburg, the absolute ecclesiastical lord of Leopold's adopted city. Leopold's musical talents — much to the delight of future generations — were considerably more advanced as a teacher than as anything else. He was a mediocre performer and composer and was never successful, despite forty-five years of trying, in getting a more important position than that of Assistant Kapellmeister in the Archbishop's musical retinue.

But he was a good teacher. He had an inquiring mind, a keen perception and an excellent knowledge of music and musical styles. In fact, had Leopold not been the father of Wolfgang, he would still be remembered today for his *Violin Method*, a book which remained the classic textbook on the subject for generations.

Leopold's life and career were transformed by his son's unbelievable musical abilities. From the time Wolfgang was four, Leopold's every thought centered around his son — how to teach him, how to tour with him, how to provide him with the necessary advantages to allow him to make his fortune in the world. And Wolfgang, an unnaturally sensitive child to begin with, obviously responded to the overpowering affection his father lavished on him. Wolfgang made up a ritual for going to bed when he was four or five; he would stand on a chair, kiss Leopold on the nose (it had to be on the nose) and then sing him a nonsense song of his own making. This continued every night until Wolfgang was nine. Twenty years afterwards, both Leopold and Wolfgang could remember the words to the song.

Leopold's influence on Wolfgang had many benefits. He taught his son well and exposed him to the widest possible range of musical influences. His intelligence and worldliness were an important starting point for young Wolfgang.

But there was a darker side to Leopold as well. He was a thoroughly distrustful individual, always suspicious of others, with a skepticism that often bordered on the cynical. He would have called it realism, and undoubtedly the social setting into which Leopold had been born fueled his attitudes. Leopold thought of himself as a musical servant of his Lord, as all Europe thought of musicians throughout most of the century. The nobility were to be feared, outwitted, manipulated, but never to be trusted. Leopold constantly tried to pass on these attitudes to Wolfgang.

He was up against something greater than he knew. Leopold's message of caution and distrust could not have fallen on less receptive ears than those of his son. Born with an open and easy nature, innocent and unsuspecting, Wolfgang could never have acted in the manner Leopold took for granted. For one thing, the spirit of the age was challenging the inevitability of the master-servant relationship, and Wolfgang refused to kow-tow to the aristocracy in a manner which had become second nature to his father. But, more to the point, Leopold failed to understand that the artist he loved and admired in his son could not be separated from the seemingly irresponsible individual who never quite cared enough about political maneuverings at court. The same innocence and unworldliness that Leopold hated in the man were precisely the characteristics that made the artist so remarkable. Fundamentally, and tragically, despite the tremendous love that obviously existed between the two men, Leopold Mozart refused to accept his son as he was obviously destined to be. And as Wolfgang got older, Leopold's frustration became more impossible for either father or son to ignore. But his influence on Wolfgang was sizable, and never so strong as during Mozart's youth, when he and his sister became the musical sensation of Europe, dazzling audiences in half a dozen countries.

The Mozart tours have become a standard part of the Mozart legend, alongside the stories of Wolfgang's superhuman musical feats. For the better part of a decade, Leopold dragged Wolfgang, sometimes with the rest of the family, sometimes alone, from one city to the next, exhibiting his son's talents in palaces, country estates, city homes, wherever a noble audience seeking a little novelty would assemble. Mozart played for kings and queens, emperors and empresses, as well as for the ranking nobility in two dozen principalities and cities.

A great deal of controversy has swirled around the propriety and advisability of Leopold Mozart exhibiting his two children on demand and subjecting them to the rigors of constant journeys to distant cities. Getting around in mid-eighteenth-century Europe was a pretty primitive affair — as dozens of passages in Leopold's letters attest. Travel was by coach with or without a source of heat, over roads that were sometimes there and sometimes washed out or made impassable because of mud or snow. The travelers stayed at inns that could be filthy, cold or dangerous: Mozart contracted scarlet fever, rheumatism, typhoid and smallpox over the course of four years on the road.

Leopold was convinced, however, that these tours were worth the risk to his family's health and happiness. He pressed on despite the difficulties, secure in the belief that he had a moral duty to show the world the gifts his son had miraculously received from God, as well as a domestic duty to try to make enough money from the exhibition of his son's talent to secure his family's financial independence. Although he failed in the latter — his financial mission — he certainly succeeded in the former.

Mozart created an unbelievable sensation wherever he appeared. This seven-year-old boy, decked out in a miniature wig with a miniature sword by his side, would sit down to a harpsichord considerably larger than himself and begin to play like the most accomplished virtuoso. His technical prowess was phenomenal, although his hands could hardly stretch five notes across the keyboard. But that was only the start. He also composed on the spot, fitting an accompaniment to a melody that someone would give him, and then fitting another accompaniment to the same melody, and then another. He would be given pieces of music with some of the parts missing. He would play through the work, filling in the missing parts, exactly as it had been originally written.

Few musicians in Europe could have put on anything resembling this kind of display, no matter what their experience or ability. For a child of seven to do it verged on the supernatural. His ability was truly miraculous; no one really knows why or how his musical skill developed. Professional musicians could only marvel at Mozart's skill as he paraded across Europe. The nobility considered him a charming novelty, a plaything, yet another distraction in their weary life of pleasure and amusement. But none could remain unmoved by the experience of watching him perform. Baron Melchior von Grimm, who first saw Mozart in Paris in 1763, probably spoke for many when he wrote:

> I cannot be sure that this child will not turn my head if I go on hearing him often; he makes me realize that it is difficult to guard against madness on seeing prodigies.

Mozart's youth, though, was the crowning glory of his achievement, allowing him innocence of age combined with maturity of skill. When Mozart was in London, he visited the reigning master of English music, Johann Christian Bach, one of J.S. Bach's sons. We have this account of their meeting from one William Jackson, who witnessed it:

> When he was a mere infant he was exhibited as a great performer on the harpsichord, and an extraordinary genius for music. John Bach took the child between his knees and began a subject on that instrument, which he left, and Mozart continued — each led the other into very abstruse harmonies, and extraneous modulations, in which the child beat the man. We were afterwards looking over Bach's famous song "Se spiego" in *Zanaida*. The score was inverted to Mozart, who was rolling on the table. He pointed out a note which he said was wrong. It was

so, whether of the composer or the copyist I cannot now recollect, but it was an instance of extraordinary discernment and readiness in a mere infant.

What an exceptional life the young musician led during this time. Days of weary travel gave way to evenings of the most wonderful opulence and luxury. The kings and queens of Europe were Mozart's first audience; they marveled at his accomplishments, showered him with praise and occasionally favored him with a valuable gift. And Mozart seems to have reveled in it all. Although it would not have been surprising if the years of constant travel and performing took their toll on him psychologically as they clearly did physically, this does not seem to have been the case.

By all accounts, he enjoyed his traveling life immensely. The first Mozart letter we have, written weeks before his fourteenth birthday as he was beginning his travels to Italy with his father, was a hasty postscript he scrawled on a letter Leopold was writing back home:

Dearest Mama!
My heart is completely enchanted with all these pleasures because it is so jolly on this journey, because it is so warm in this carriage and because our coachman is a fine fellow who, when the road gives him the slightest chance, drives so fast.

Although this letter was clearly written in the excitement of the moment, there is no reason to believe that it did not accurately reflect Mozart's emotional life on the road. Unlike most prodigies, who burn themselves out early, or who are consumed by anxiety because they possess an enormous power which they do not know how to control, Mozart seems to have handled his travels extremely well. Despite the unusual hours, the constant performing and the circus atmosphere that sometimes surrounded his appearances, he remained merry and happy unless ill health prevented him from feeling buoyant.

His was the temperament of an artistic personality, and it emerged early. All his life, Mozart's soul was to be completely overwhelmed by his immediate experience. Whether it was a coach speeding down an Italian road, a new friendship he had just made, a beautiful woman he had just seen or a tragedy he had heard about or witnessed, Mozart would be completely overcome by the emotion of the moment. Much to the chagrin of his father, mother and eventually his wife, Mozart lacked that ability, common in more ordinary mortals, to put events and experiences in perspective. Mozart lived for the moment, loved the sensations of the moment, was happiest when he experienced the present.

Perhaps it was the personal joy he derived from his musical power that lay at the heart of this attitude. Mozart as a boy and a youth did not have to worry about the things that most of us worry about. He was a master in his chosen field without having to do anything about it, and was acknowledged as such; he was fêted by an entire continent and surrounded by adulation. He lived and traveled within a very tight family unit that provided him, at least in his childhood, with the love and affection he craved, as well as organizing his life for him. He loved music and spent his whole life absorbed in it.

Mozart also loved to perform and adored an audience. He learned to play to a crowd, to entertain and move them, to engage them emotionally. The more mundane business of gaining advantage over others, of presenting oneself in the best light, of manipulating others for personal gain, was beyond him. His was a spontaneous and open nature — at least it began that way. When Mozart finally came to realize that he needed more than openness to make his way in the world, he really couldn't, or wouldn't, adapt.

Mozart was doing more than traveling around as a performer during his journeys in the 1760s and 70s. He was also receiving an unparalleled musical education. Everywhere he went, Mozart heard new music, met new composers, was confronted with new styles and ideas. No other musician of his time received such a thorough musical education as did Mozart before he was ten. With his superhuman ear and astounding musical memory, even the slightest contact with a new style was permanently recorded in his mental catalogue of musical effects, sometimes to emerge years later. This education was critical to his development as a composer.

Mozart began composing soon after he began performing, as both he and Leopold realized that musicians made their true mark as composers, not as performers. His first compositions date from the time he was seven; by the time he was in his teens he was composing constantly. The early compositions were clearly written for his own performance: sonatas for violin and piano for him and Nannerl to play; little symphonies to open up his concerts; and eventually larger symphonies composed in imitation of the style of others. For Salzburg, Mozart wrote church music and the odd dramatic piece.

The styles in which Mozart wrote these early compositions were all copied or at least adapted from the many kinds of music he heard as he traveled through Europe. The period of the long journeys in Mozart's personal life was the period of maximum experimentation in European musical life; it was that period during which Baroque forms had largely disappeared but no clear new style had taken their place. Composers were trying out new ideas based on Italian opera buffa, writing music that was simpler than the Baroque, more tuneful, more accessible — in a style we now call "*style galant*." In the history of music today, it is seen very much as a transition phase between the high Baroque and the Classical style, and few composers apart from Mozart who were writing at the time are remembered today. But in their own day, *style galant* composers like Johann Schröter and Wilhelm Friedemann Bach were important musical figures struggling with a new musical aesthetic.

There are a few things to keep in mind when we listen to Mozart's early compositions. He lived in a time of transition, so he himself eclipsed the accomplishments of his youth in his later compositions. Mozart truly came into his own as a composer only as the Classical era emerged out of the Baroque. In concrete terms, this means that Mozart's works became interesting for all time, rather than just for his time, in the 1780s, after his move to Vienna. However, he composed over two hundred works before he got to

Vienna, and his genius showed in every one of them. There are a number of lovely moments in the early works that are worth listening to, even if the total artistic effect pales in comparison with the greatness of his later work.

What you'll find about the early works is that they are filled with charming phrases, lovely melodies and some interesting harmonies, but that those moments don't connect with each other with the impeccable musical logic that we saw in *Eine Kleine Nachtmusik* in the last chapter. Mozart was content in his early works to create inspired copies of the kind of music he heard around him, so the strengths of this music became his strengths; its limitations, his limitations. However, as Mozart the child became Mozart the teenager, more and more original touches enter his compositions. In a couple of works composed in 1773, when Mozart was seventeen, a new maturity starts to break through. His Symphony no. 25 in G minor, K. 183, is an extraordinarily dark statement for a young man to make, and one that seemed to tear out of him unexpectedly. The 29th Symphony, in A major, K. 201, is an elegant companion to the G minor Symphony. Where the G minor is anguished, almost violent, in its emotional tone, the A major portrays perfect restraint and elegance. As Mozart got older his works took on increasing sophistication and interest, but they still belong to a different intellectual and emotional world than the works of his true maturity.

By the mid-1770s, Mozart was no longer a child prodigy, because he was no longer a child. The teenaged Mozart was not a sensation; it was less striking for a sixteen-year-old to be able to do the kinds of things that Mozart had done at seven. The trips that Wolfgang and Leopold continued to make, primarily to Italy, were now made in search of a position for Wolfgang as well as for commissions for operas and other compositions from wealthy patrons.

Like his father, Mozart in his teens was making his living as part of the musical retinue of his home-town prince, the Archbishop of Salzburg. He had been formally attached to the Archbishop's court before he was twelve and was paid a small retainer to compose and to play the organ in one of the Salzburg churches. But both Mozarts, father and son, felt that, with Wolfgang's talents, it was increasingly absurd that he should hold such a minor position. Surely he could land a lucrative, high-profile position in one of the major courts of Europe — in Vienna, Munich, Mannheim, Paris or London. This desire to escape from Salzburg was intensified in 1772 when the old Archbishop died, and a new Archbishop, Hieronymus Colloredo, was installed.

Colloredo's relationship with the Mozart family has bestowed on him a sort of negative immortality. He was suspicious of, if not actually hostile to, the Mozarts, which meant that Leopold's frequent lengthy absences from the court became absences without pay. The Mozarts and Colloredo began a running battle that lasted for a decade. The Archbishop found the family uppity and disloyal; the Mozarts found the Archbishop cold, vain and insensitive. History, of course, has come down firmly on the Mozarts' side in this dispute; how could it not? But at the time, we might have more readily understood Colloredo's side of the story. The Mozarts, and especially Leopold, were constantly trying to outwit him. The family wrote long sections of their letters to each other in code so that the Archbishop (or Archbooby, as they called him) could not read them. Leopold was always plotting secret stratagems to find Wolfgang a position in another court without the Archbishop finding out.

In the end, none of the stratagems worked. As it turned out, the Archbishop was not the only member of the European nobility who was insensitive to the Mozarts and the genius of their son. At one point, the Governor-General of Milan, Archduke Ferdinand, a son of the Austrian Empress Maria Theresa, asked his mother whether he should engage the fifteen-year-old Mozart, who had just registered an operatic triumph in Milan with his opera *Ascanio in Alba*. Maria Theresa's reply is still chilling two hundred years later:

> . . . you ask me to take the young Salzburger into your service. I do not know why, not believing you have need of a composer or of useless people. If, however, it would give you pleasure, I have no wish to hinder you. What I say is intended only to prevent your burdening yourself with useless people and giving

titles to people of that sort. If they are in your service it degrades that service when these people go about the world like beggars. Besides, he has a large family.

Mozart didn't get the job. Nor, in the end, did he get any job, in Milan, Munich or Mannheim. Reluctantly, he made Salzburg the main focus of his activity as he matured into a young man at the end of the 1770s. And yet, as he reached his twentieth birthday, despite being stuck in Salzburg, he began to create some of the most joyous and free-spirited music of his entire career. The free and open youth of the 1760s had become a boisterous practical joker in the late 1770s. Full of boyish high spirits, uncontrolled emotionality and a decided taste for the vulgar and scatological, Mozart's personality began to crystalize in the last years of the decade. His immense love of life, and of sensation, are poured out in the music he wrote during this period. We will fail to understand the complexity of the fully mature Mozart if we do not understand his great love of pleasure and sensuousness and listen to some of the music written during this time that embodies those qualities most completely.

One of the best examples of this kind of music is the *Haffner* Serenade, composed in June of 1776 (just as Thomas Jefferson, a continent away, was composing his masterpiece, the American Declaration of Independence). Mozart was back in Salzburg that summer, composing music for the church and occasional pieces on demand, like this piece, which was written to celebrate the wedding of Elisabeth Haffner, daughter of a prominent Salzburger and a friend of the Mozart family. Serenades were meant to be performed outdoors and consisted of several movements; the *Haffner* has eight, including three minuets for the wedding guests to dance to.

The Serenade was performed on the evening of Elisabeth Haffner's wedding but was also popular enough to be repeated once in a while in succeeding years, quite a rarity for Mozart. Today, it is still an engaging work: it breathes charm, melody, inventiveness and generosity. It seems a true gift from Mozart to Elisabeth Haffner and, indirectly, to us as well.

The *Haffner* Serenade gives us a glimpse of Mozart just a couple of years before he was to emerge as a truly independent artist. Most of the features of his mature style are just waiting to blossom; many are there in embryo. In several movements of the Serenade, Mozart uses a loose version of sonata-allegro form, although it is clear the form occupies very little of his attention as an artist. The four-bar phrases and the beautiful melodies that Mozart wrote all his life are here in profusion, almost too lavishly presented. The *Haffner* can remind you of a teenager with too much energy and not enough control to focus that energy.

There is an abundance of musical material in this work; it is almost overflowing with melodic inventiveness. As Mozart matured, he tended to use fewer and fewer elements in his work, and linked them together more and more securely. But here the emphasis is on tunefulness, energy and the creation of an atmosphere, an atmosphere of celebration and joy. We are given eight movements of seemingly effortless melodies, wonderful sonorities and delightful combinations of instruments, all designed to please, to charm, to entertain. It was as if Mozart could not get his musical ideas on paper fast enough.

The opening movement of the *Haffner* Serenade is not as important to analyze as the first movement of *Eine Kleine Nachtmusik*, because the *Haffner* makes its impact in quite a different way than the later work. The effectiveness of the piece depends more on elements like texture and the melodies themselves than on any large-scale formal pattern. The texture of the piece is jubilant and airy; trumpets and drums abound in the first movement, a solo violin joins the piece for two of the movements, turning it into a mini-violin concerto. And the energy of the first and fourth movements is captivating; the music quite literally rushes along like a fast-moving river. The four-bar phrases, the little melodies with which the piece is made up, are charming and tuneful.

However, at least in the first movement, the linking of these themes, and the transitions from one theme to the next do not seem quite as inevitable as in *Eine Kleine Nachtmusik*. Let's ignore the slow introduction for a moment and just look at the first few musical ideas in the allegro.

Idea from
Introduction

Transition section

Second theme

You can refer to the score that starts on page 89 as you listen to the piece — or just listen if you prefer. The movement proper (after the slow introduction) starts with a unison figure, as did *Eine Kleine Nachtmusik*, this time with full orchestra. It is a rushing sort of figure that comes to a solid rest on the tonic note, D (in bar 3 of the first violin part). This idea is followed four bars later by a second figure that is made up of wide leaps, which contrast with the smoother unison opening (bars 5 to 8).

Now notice what Mozart does in the last bar of this figure (bar 8 of our example). He actually finishes off the second musical idea with a series of eight notes that look suspiciously like the first idea. This is not so much a linkage as a blurring of the distinction between the two ideas. Mozart had not quite got to the point in his stylistic evolution where the separateness of his musical ideas became all-important. He further blurs the distinction between ideas 1 and 2 by repeating idea 2 in bars 9 to 11 and the first half of bar 12. Things are a bit backwards here. The very first idea in the allegro section should be the most prominent music we hear in the piece. Somehow, it's gotten lost in this blurring of phrases; it is hard for us to remember exactly how that original idea went. This is not a "mistake" in the music; it is merely a different style, one that places more emphasis on the overall continuity of texture and meter and less on the delineation of specific musical ideas.

Mozart continues this technique in the next few bars. The musical idea that starts in bar 15 is something of a joke. Mozart has already given us this idea slowly in the introduction; now, without warning, it surprisingly appears in the allegro section. But Mozart does nothing with this surprise; the idea is presented once and then immediately supplanted by another idea (beginning in bar 19) that has nothing to do with anything we've heard previously. The mature Mozart would never have "wasted" such a neat musical trick. It would have been repeated and developed. This idea gives way to a relatively standard transition section leading us to the dominant, and the "second theme," which begins in bar 38. Can you sense the slight awkwardness in this movement? Ideas are presented which are not fully developed, or which bleed into the next; they come and go too quickly; the transition section is a bit long for what has preceded it. All in all, the overall effect of this music is based as much on its powerful sense of motion and sound as on anything else. All the ideas are certainly charming; but their combination is not quite as powerful as the melodic combinations Mozart was to write in later years. This is not to suggest that this is anything but a wonderful work; that would be absurd. However, the beauty of the work lies on a slightly different level than that of the *Nachtmusik*, for example.

You can listen to the rest of the movement for yourself to hear not only the wealth of beautiful ideas that Mozart has so generously spread throughout this work, but also the relatively loose continuity he creates between them. Remember to count to four if you want to hear where the ideas begin; the phrases are actually extremely regular in this movement. In the end, the first movement of the *Haffner* charms because of its wonderful energy and the beauty of its little melodies, which come and go like so many shooting stars.

Mozart had every right to take pride in his ability to compose these little melodic phrases. Within the limitations he created for himself (those of the four-bar phrase), he was one of the most successful melody writers of musical history. One can only wonder at the melodies Mozart might have composed had he been born into the Romantic generation, when melody writing was freed from the excessive rigidity of the four-bar system and obeyed only the laws of representing emotion. But Mozart was born when he was, and the *Haffner* is full of the little melodic gems that were his stock-in-trade.

The same divine melodic invention lies at the heart of the first andante, the second movement of the Serenade. Here Mozart introduces a solo violin to change the texture, but the emphasis is still firmly on the melodic. This andante is not as unlike his later slow movements as his opening allegro is unlike its successors. Slow movements were generally looser in structure, to provide for a more languid atmosphere, and the general looseness of the *Haffner* suits this movement perfectly. A dozen or so beautiful melodies are crowded into the nine minutes that it takes to play this movement. The solo violin is also featured in the fourth movement, a rondo, where the simplicity and tunefulness of the *style galant* is clearest. This is music to enjoy, purely and simply.

To balance off these movements, Mozart provides a little spice in his three minuets and trios. The harmonies of the first minuet, the third movement of the piece, are among the most daring he ever wrote. More than a decade would pass before Mozart would write anything as harmonically dense as the first dozen or so bars of this movement. Look at its opening bars (see the score on the next page).

To understand what Mozart is up to in these sixteen opening bars, we have to stop for just a moment to investigate something called chromatic harmony. A term borrowed from the visual arts, chromaticism refers to a fast-changing, wild array of colors, in this case harmonic colors. We've mentioned that composers discovered that certain combinations of chords could create a strong sense of completeness and solidity when played in succession. Chords are considered to be harmonically "close" to each other when they sound as if they fit closely together. Often, they are chords that share one or two notes.

Other chords are close to each other physically. If you think of the piano keyboard or a guitar, there are certain notes and chords that are right beside each other, like C and C#, or F and F#. It is

III

easy to move from one of these chords to the next as you play. What's interesting for the composer is that these chords, which are so close physically, are far apart harmonically. A C major chord and a C# major chord, for instance, have no notes in common. To play them in succession creates no harmonic unit at all.

Harmonies made up of chords that are close physically but distant harmonically are called chromatic harmonies. They are easy to spot in a score, since their chords always have lots of flats and sharps like the ones in bars 9, 10 and 11 of the minuet. The sharps and flats in the score are a tip-off that the composer is creating harmonies out of notes that don't belong in the normal scale of the piece. To the ear, chromatic harmony sounds like someone making their way gingerly down a flight of narrow steps. Only the best composers are able to handle these chords. They can provide a dramatic sense of dislocation in a piece, but they must be controlled by an even stronger sense of fitness.

Now let's return to the opening of the third movement of the *Haffner*. The first four-bar phrase outlines a solid, straightforward chord progression in G minor, which is the key of the movement. Look at the bass line. Bar 1 is based on a G minor triad, bar 2 on a C major triad (the chord four notes above the tonic), bar 3 on D, the dominant triad, and bar 4 on G again. Mozart has clearly outlined his basic harmony — he has had to, because it isn't long before the harmonies begin to wander far afield. In bars 5 to 8, Mozart outlines a harmony of no fixed address. Although the chords are in the key of G minor, the shifting melodic line in the second violins and the bassoons sends the harmony a bit out of focus. (Notice all the flats and sharps.)

Then, in bars 9 to 12, things start to get really complicated. This is one of the most densely chromatic passages Mozart ever wrote. Nine different chords are played in this four-bar phrase. And look at the close, chromatic movement. Run your eye over each part, and you'll see how many sharps and flats Mozart has created. Whereas most harmonic change moves by step in Western music, in these four bars, most of the changes move by half-step. The effect is one of almost complete dislocation for the briefest of moments —

the audience can't figure out where it is harmonically. There is a sense of almost physical discomfort. We do end up on the D chord in bar 12, which is back in familiar territory. But to keep the chromatic effect alive, Mozart finishes the section with two bars of ambiguous harmonies, where it is difficult to tell exactly what chords are being suggested. The effect is somewhat eerie and disturbing; Mozart is stretching our normal harmonic comprehension about as far as it can go without collapsing.

Because Mozart had the most subtle and superb ear in the history of music, he could manipulate these chromatic changes with relative ease. He had an uncanny sense of knowing exactly how to get back to home base using the most economical means. Time and again in his music, Mozart will seem to get himself trapped in harmonies that are completely foreign to his home key, then simply escape and head back home like some musical Houdini.

Mozart also knew exactly how far to push any effect. In the Serenade, he balances off this "modern" minuet and trio with two considerably more conventional ones. The minuet and trio which makes up the fifth movement of the piece is self-consciously old-fashioned. It is marked "Menuetto galante" and stands as one of the best representatives of a style that was passing out of existence in 1776 when Mozart wrote the Serenade. Listen to the stiff, formal elegance of the opening minuet, with its dotted rhythms and courtly pace. It is strangely restrained and non-communicative, cold and almost too perfect. Even in comparison with the rest of the piece, let alone the rest of his output, we can hear why the *style galant* would never have been enough for Mozart. His spontaneity and humanity would have chafed terribly at these formal bounds.

Mozart has written this minuet almost as a tribute to a disappearing world, and just so we know that he knows the style is dead, he follows his brittle minuet with a poignant trio, perhaps the most moving section in this otherwise joyous work. The trio is in a minor key, thus lending it an air of resignation and sorrow. But the moment passes, and the minuet returns to finish off this fifth movement.

There are other wonderful moments in the *Haffner* Serenade, and they all belong in the same category; they reflect a master musician aiming to please, playing with texture and sound for the pleasure of his audience. We can still enjoy the *Haffner* today — in fact, it is regularly included in symphony concerts. There is so much boisterous joy in the piece, it is hard not to be charmed by it. However, it is not intellectually connected, the way Mozart's works would be only a few short years later. Mozart the sensualist would soon give way to Mozart the complete artist. His youth would soon give way to his maturity.

However, it was becoming increasingly obvious to Mozart in 1776 that he could never find the creative climate he needed to foster that maturity in his home town. Salzburg was becoming increasingly unbearable for the maturing genius, and strained relations with the Archbishop were adding to his difficulties. Something had to be done.

In desperation, Leopold decided to try one last tour to find a good job for his son. Having sparred with the Archbishop about leaves of absences before, Leopold tried a new tactic and had Wolfgang resign from the Archbishop's staff so he would be free to travel. The Archbishop, in a show of pique, accepted both Wolfgang's and Leopold's resignations, even though Leopold's had not been submitted. A friend of the family made the following entry in his diary for September 6, 1777:

> In the afternoon I visited the Mozarts, where I found the father ill, because he and his son are dismissed the service because of the request which the latter made to His Grace for permission to travel.

One can imagine the illness that might have befallen Leopold Mozart that day. He, who had worked all his life to improve his family's fortunes and who was more than a little worried about money, had suddenly found both himself and his son without a source of income. Eventually, Leopold had to humble himself and was accepted back into the Archbishop's employ. But there could be no thought of Leopold accompanying Wolfgang on the trip they had planned to take to Munich, Mannheim and Paris. Instead,

Mozart's mother was pressed into service, and on September 23, 1777, the two of them set out on the trip that was to make or break Wolfgang's fortune.

The trip was a disaster, professionally and personally. In both Munich and Mannheim, Wolfgang was led to believe that he might be successful in his petitions to become a court composer and teacher. He waited in both centers for months before realizing that he was just being strung along. In Paris, he never even entertained serious hopes. Mozart hated Paris, its people and its music. He performed rarely, made few influential contacts, composed very little.

To add to his growing disappointment, he received increasingly hysterical urgings from his father, in letter after passionate letter, to get on with it, to make this contact, to talk to that person, to compose this sonata. Mozart clearly resented this constant hectoring from back home, but it was probably necessary. For the first time in his life, his complete inability to deal with the "real" world was having serious consequences. Mozart was not made for pressing his own suit; his was an elusive personality, made up of equal measures of reticence and pride. Half the time, Mozart hated having to ask for favors because he feared rejection. The other half of the time he was too proud to ask, and when some advantage came his way, he was often likely to refuse it. He might also have been just too innocent about the need to do these things, believing that all would work out in the end. He might also have been just a bit lazy.

Leopold's urgings were fueled by the reports he was getting from Paris about his son from Baron Melchior von Grimm, the same Grimm who had first seen Mozart in 1763, when he was a child. Grimm described Wolfgang to Leopold in what has become a famous portrayal of the composer's character:

> He is too trusting, too inactive, too easy to catch, too little intent on the means that may lead to fortune. To make an impression, one has to be artful, enterprising, daring. To make his fortune I wish he had but half his talent and twice as much shrewdness,

and then I should not worry about him. . . . You see, my dear maître, that in a country where so many mediocre and even detestable musicians have made immense fortunes, I very much fear that your son will not so much as make ends meet.

Mozart's professional disappointments in Paris were matched by personal frustration and tragedy. His mother, very much in the shadows during this trip, fell ill in the summer of 1778. She was bed-ridden for three weeks, and then suddenly died, in July. Mozart sat with her as she slipped into a coma, not knowing what to do to have her treated, not sure whether he had acted in the best way to save her life, terrified that his father would somehow blame him for her death. The day she died, a frightened Mozart sent off two letters to Salzburg: one to his father telling him that his mother was ill and another to a family friend begging him to prepare Leopold for the eventual news of his wife's death.

After Maria Anna's death and Wolfgang's continuing lack of success in Paris, Leopold decided that it was time for his son to come home. The young Mozart dreaded the trip, and tried every means at his disposal to delay his homecoming. In the end, he made the return journey as long as possible, partly because he had a compelling reason to revisit the cities of Augsburg and Mannheim: he had fallen in love with two women in these towns on his way to Paris.

The first of these women was his cousin, Maria Anna Thekla Mozart, daughter of Leopold's bookbinding brother. Wolfgang met her in the fall of 1777 as he was traveling from Munich to Mannheim. It was to Maria Anna (his Bäsle, German for "little cousin") that Mozart wrote a series of slightly pornographic, very scatological letters later that fall and during the next spring and summer.

Like many of his contemporaries and most Salzburgers, Mozart was fascinated with bodily functions, as was his entire family. "Shit in your bed until it bursts" seems to have been as common a salutation in the Mozart household as "I kiss your hands a thousand times." When this infantile love of "muck," as Mozart called it, was

joined with a developing erotic passion and Mozart's own unique
blend of fantasy and enthusiasm, the result was:

5 Nov 1777

Dearest Coz Fuzz:
I have received reprieved your dear letter, telling selling me that
my uncle carbuncle, my aunt can't and you too are very well
hell. . . .

 Well, I wish you good night, but first shit into your bed and
make it burst. Sleep soundly, my love, into your mouth your
arse you'll shove. Now I'm off to fool about and then I'll sleep a
bit, no doubt. . . . Oh, my arse is burning like fire! What on earth
does it mean? — Perhaps some muck wants to come out? Why,
yes, muck, I know. See and smell you . . . and . . . What is
that? — Is it possible . . . Ye Gods! — Can I believe those ears of
mine? Yes, indeed, it is so — what a long melancholy note! Today
letter the writing am 5th this I. Yesterday I had to talk with the
formidable Electress and tomorrow, the 6th, I am playing at the
great gala concert; and afterwards I am to play again to her in
private, as she herself told me. Now for some real sense . . .

How these Bäsle letters, as they're called, have confounded
musicologists and critics over the centuries. They were suppressed
for years, and even now have not been published in German in their
entirety. What can we make of a young man of twenty-two writing
in this mode and mood? Especially when that young man is Mozart,
the "genius of light and love," as Robert Schumann called him in
the nineteenth century (without having read the letters). Make of
him what we might, we cannot deny nor should we deny this part
of his complex reality. The Bäsle letters are as much a part of Mozart
as the slow movement to the Clarinet Concerto (one of his most
exquisite) or the *Requiem*.
 Maria Anna Thekla was not the only young woman to turn
Wolfgang's head in the fall of 1777. While in Mannheim, Mozart
fell desperately in love with a beautiful sixteen-year-old singer

named Aloysia Weber. Thus began a lifelong connection with this questionable family. Eventually, Mozart would marry Aloysia's younger sister, Constanze, and inherit a whole family of troubles. However, in the fall of 1777, Mozart had eyes only for Aloysia. He was enchanted by her, by her voice, by her beauty, by her musical taste and intelligence. He was immediately captivated and immediately forgot the purpose of the trip to Mannheim and Paris. Mozart decided that he would travel with the Weber family to Italy, accompanying Aloysia and teaching her at the same time. With unbelievable innocence, he wrote to Leopold asking his opinion of the plan. You can imagine Leopold's response. While Mozart's mother was watching this infatuation at close quarters with amusement, his father regarded it from afar with horror.

Mozart did not travel to Italy with Aloysia. As far as we can tell, she was relatively insensible to the impression she made on the young composer. She kept only one of the letters Mozart wrote her after he left Mannheim, and when he looked her up again on his return there in the fall of 1778, she rebuffed his advances curtly and definitively. Mozart was devastated: "Up to now it has been impossible for me to write to you," he told his father in December, "for today I can only weep. I have too sensitive a heart."

There can be little doubt that Mozart remained in love with Aloysia for many years, if not for his entire life, even after he married her sister. The great things he had predicted for her career all came to pass; she became one of the leading prima donnas of Vienna, performing in many an opera written by her brother-in-law. She sang Donna Anna in the first Viennese performance of *Don Giovanni* and premiered the role of Constanze in *The Abduction from the Seraglio*. Mozart wrote half a dozen of his concert arias exclusively for her, as late as the 1780s. She married an actor, Joseph Lange, but eventually divorced him, and her rejection of Mozart haunted her all her life. In 1824, thirty years after the composer's death, she was still trying to explain why she had rejected him. At the very end of her life, sixty years after her first meeting with Mozart, she went to live with her sister, Mozart's widow, in Salzburg. She died in the town in which he had been born.

Salzburg represented nothing but gall for Mozart at the beginning of 1779, when he finally arrived back home. Leopold had managed to secure a small post for him as court organist, a depressing comedown for the former prodigy. He was a few weeks shy of his twenty-third birthday, with nothing but Salzburg in his immediate future.

Mozart continued to hate Salzburg. Fresh from the latest of his many international forays, he found the little Austrian town horribly provincial, lacking in any real culture and populated by people who disgusted and embarrassed him. (Mozart could be proud and even vain when the spirit moved him, and in Salzburg he was moved with consistent regularity.) He also dreaded re-entering the service of Archbishop Colloredo, who was still suspicious of Mozart and either did not believe or did not care that Europe's greatest composer was churning out church music for him and the occasional piece for the inhabitants of the town.

Mozart spent three more years in Salzburg, but his artistic future lay elsewhere. A new city was beckoning him, inviting him to new artistic challenges, as well as new dangers for his personal life. Most of what we know of Mozart today, most of the music we listen to, was composed in that city in ten short years, the last ten years of his life. It was in Vienna, the center of the Austro-Hungarian empire, that Mozart's true destiny emerged.

CHAPTER FIVE

Declaration of Independence

I N THE SUMMER of 1780, Mozart received what was up to then his most important commission. The Elector of Bavaria asked him to write an opera based on the story of King Idomeneus of Crete, who promises Neptune to sacrifice the next person he sees in return for safe passage through a storm, only to find that that next person is his son. It was a serious story, and a serious opera. When *Idomeneo* was finally performed at the end of January 1781, Mozart experienced his first major operatic triumph.

In March of that year, Mozart was summoned from Munich to attend his Archbishop in Vienna. It was a fateful summons. Mozart never returned to Salzburg and lived in Vienna for the rest of his life. It is interesting to speculate what might have been the course of Mozart's life and Western musical history if Archbishop Colloredo's father had not taken ill in the Austrian capital, and Colloredo had not chosen to look after him there. Mozart might have remained bitterly obscure in Salzburg; more likely he would have found his way to Vienna eventually in the late 1700s, as it was the musical capital of Europe, and just down the road.

When he arrived in Vienna, Mozart was lodged with the Archbishop's entourage. At table he was placed between the valets and the cooks, the usual station of musicians at the time. Fresh from his triumphs in Munich, such treatment infuriated him. Worse, Mozart discovered in Vienna that he could make a fair bit of money by performing at concerts sponsored by members of the Viennese nobility. To do so, however, he had to obtain the Archbishop's permission; it was routinely denied. When Mozart was finally allowed to play a benefit concert for the widows of musicians living in Vienna, it was a roaring success. But no further permission was granted. Mozart was furious. He wrote to his father in the code the two of them employed for just such communication: "Well, how much do you suppose I should make if I were to give a concert of my own, now that the public has got to know me? Only this arch-booby of ours will not allow it."

On one occasion Mozart was forced to play at the Archbishop's rather than at a musical soiree at a Countess Thun's, which the Emperor was attending. Mozart estimated that he could have made more than half his annual salary of 450 guilden in that single evening. As Mozart fumed over the treatment being meted out to him during March and April of 1781, it began to dawn on him that he might be able to make a living as a freelance musician — a composer, teacher and performer — in Vienna. He began to think out loud in letters to his father. Perhaps not for the first time, he toyed with the idea of remaining in the Austrian capital and not returning to the dreaded Salzburg. As usual, Mozart exaggerated his prospects in Vienna for the audience back home (he was constantly exaggerating his prospects) and Leopold seems to have understood this, for he wasted no time in telling Mozart to return home as soon as the Archbishop decided when that return was to be. (We can infer this from a reply Mozart sent to Leopold, since all of Leopold's letters from 1781 on have disappeared.)

What Mozart truly felt about his father's summons we'll never know. Once Leopold had spoken, Mozart never mentioned his schemes again, and meekly made plans to return to his hated birthplace. But fate was to intervene. In early May, the Archbishop suddenly ordered the retinue back home and arrangements were made for traveling. Mozart had decided to delay his departure for a day or two when he was informed that the Archbishop had an important parcel for him to take back to Salzburg immediately. Mozart refused, preferring to keep to his original plans. This parcel, whatever it may have contained, led to a confrontation between the two men that reverberates to this day. Mozart's latest act of obstinacy was clearly the last straw for the Archbishop. The two met for a stormy last time on the ninth of May 1781. Mozart wrote to his father that evening:

Vienna 9 May 1781

Mon très cher père

I am still seething with rage! And you, my dearest and most beloved father, are doubtless in the same condition. My patience has been so long tried that at last it has given out. I am no longer so unfortunate as to be in Salzburg service. Today is a happy day for me. Just listen . . . [Mozart takes the story up to the point where he and the Archbishop meet.]

When I entered the Archbishop's room his first words were: — Archbishop: "Well, young fellow, when are you going off?" I: "I intended to go tonight, but all the seats were already engaged." Then he rushed full steam ahead, without pausing for breath — I was the most dissolute fellow he knew — no one served him as badly as I did — I had better leave today or else he would write home and have my salary stopped [that is, have the payment stopped]. I couldn't get a word in edgeways, for he blazed away like a fire. I listened to it all very calmly. He lied to my face that my salary was five hundred guilden, called me a scoundrel, a rascal, a vagabond. Oh, I really cannot tell you all he said. At last my blood began to boil, I could no longer contain myself and I said, "So Your Grace is not satisfied with me?" "What, you dare to threaten me — you scoundrel? There is the door! Look out, for I will have nothing more to do with such a miserable wretch." At last I said: "Nor I with you!" "Well, be off!" When leaving the room, I said, "This is final. You shall have it tomorrow in writing."

However, it wasn't quite final. The next day Mozart did appear before the Archbishop's Chamberlain, one Count Arco, with his resignation in hand. But there was a complication; Arco informed Mozart that he could not accept his resignation without Leopold's consent, and that consequently he would not pass on the petition to the Archbishop. Five times over the next month, Mozart tried to present his document, and five times Arco refused to accept it. Leopold had written to Arco, begging him to make Wolfgang change his mind, so if Leopold's consent was legitimately needed (Mozart was twenty-five at the time), it was certainly not forthcoming. Finally, in early June, Mozart insisted on seeing the Archbishop himself; he would be put off no longer. Now it was Arco's turn to lose his temper. He grabbed the petition out of Mozart's hands and threw him out of the antechamber in which they had been meeting, giving him a kick on the backside for good measure as he left the room. Poor Count Arco. Fairly or unfairly, he has gone down as one of the most ignominious figures in musical history for that well-aimed boot.

In one of their earlier meetings, Arco had delivered a warning to Mozart about his attempt at a new life in Vienna. In hindsight, it almost reads as a curse. "Believe me, you allow yourself to be far too easily dazzled in Vienna," the Count said. "A man's reputation here lasts a very short time. At first, it is true, you are overwhelmed with praises and make a great deal of money into the bargain — but how long does that last? After a few months the Viennese want something new."

Count Arco may have spoken truthfully, and he may legitimately have had Mozart's interests in mind, but the composer was not at all interested in such negative sentiments. He was exhilarated. The break with the Archbishop and with Salzburg was the decisive event in Mozart's life. It may have seemed sudden in the spring of 1781, but it had an inevitability about it that was not to be denied. With this declaration of musical independence, Mozart was in effect turning his back on the century in which he had been born, and throwing his lot in with a revolutionary century that had not yet come into being. He was blazing the trail for the freelance musicians who were to follow him in the years and decades to come. There were other independent musicians in Vienna in 1781, but most, if not all, had some appointment as a base for their activity. Mozart gambled on being able to make a living for himself on his talent alone.

There was one final impediment to be overcome for Mozart's independence to be complete — his father. Leopold was beside himself when he heard that Mozart was intending to resign his post. It struck at the heart of everything Leopold believed in and lived for. To him, it was a reckless decision, financially, personally and politically. He sent thundering letters to his son, ordering him to change his mind, to apologize to the Archbishop, to return to Salzburg. Mozart was hurt and confused, but for once he resisted the psychological pressure his father was forcing on him. He instinctively knew that Vienna was his destiny, that the growing confidence he had in himself as a musician and an artist could only find expression in that sophisticated capital. He was not going to let anyone, even his beloved father, stand in his way. Nonetheless, he desperately wanted his father to approve of his decision.

Leopold did everything he could to make Wolfgang change his mind. He wrote to Count Arco, pleading with him to help Wolfgang see reason. For a month, he sent Wolfgang letter after letter complaining about his behavior and insisting that he return to Salzburg. Although these letters have been lost, we can guess their contents from Wolfgang's replies:

Vienna 16 May 1781

Mon très cher père
I could hardly have supposed otherwise than that in the heat of the moment you would have written just such a letter as I have been obliged to read, for the event must have taken you by surprise (especially as you were actually expecting my arrival). But by this time you must have considered the matter more

carefully and, as a man of honour, you must feel the insult more strongly, and must know and realize that what you have thought likely to happen, has happened already. . . . I implore you, I adjure you, by all you hold dear in this world, to strengthen me in this resolution instead of trying to dissuade me from it, for if you do, you will only make me unproductive. My desire and my hope is to gain honour, fame and money. . . . Cheer up your son, for it is only the thought of displeasing you that can make him unhappy in his very promising circumstances. Adieu. A thousand farewells. I am ever, and I kiss your hands a thousand times as, your most obedient son

W:A: MZT

The approval never really came. The two continued to correspond regularly until Leopold's death in 1787, but the breach between them widened and widened. As the Vienna years rolled on, fewer and fewer of Mozart's letters are addressed to his father; by the end of his life, Leopold could hardly bring himself to mention Wolfgang by name. In his last letters to Nannerl, Wolfgang is always referred to as "your brother." One of the closest father-son relationships in the history of Western music sputtered to a tragic end.

Mozart's move to Vienna inaugurated the most important and creative period of his life. It was in Vienna that he finally matured as an artist and wrote his most profound, moving and joyous works. The Mozart we know and revere today is the Vienna Mozart. All but nine of his twenty-seven piano concertos were written there, works which are still staples of the standard repertoire; all the mature symphonies were written during this period, starting with the *Linz* symphony in 1785. His important chamber works — string quartets and quintets, serenades and divertissements — were all composed in Vienna. And the four great operatic master-pieces — *The Marriage of Figaro, Don Giovanni, Così fan tutte* and *The Magic Flute* — were all written in the last decade of Mozart's life. Despite his father's objections and the financial difficulties that Mozart was to face in the Austrian capital, his instincts were right when it came to his own artistic development, as they had been about Aloysia Weber's potential as an artist. Vienna was the right place for Mozart to be in the 1780s; the financial security that he left in Salzburg would have been no compensation for living in the artistic desert that it was. Vienna provided exactly the kind of intellectual, artistic and emotional stimulation Mozart's genius needed to fulfill its true potential.

Things started well for the young composer and performer. Mozart had made some contacts in Vienna during the time he had been there as part of the Archbishop's retinue, and they paid off for him in the summer and fall of 1781. He was engaged to teach several sons and daughters of the nobility and was often asked to perform at musical soirees and actual concerts organized by aristocratic patrons.

In the summer of 1781, Mozart received the libretto for a new opera called *The Abduction from the Seraglio*, an exotic piece with a Turkish theme. In less than a year, the opera would open to the most enthusiastic reception Mozart was to get for an opera until *The Magic Flute* was performed, ten years later. At the same time, Mozart began composing piano concertos for his own use as a soloist. The first set was composed in the fall of 1782. Although Mozart still remained on a somewhat precarious financial footing, lacking any permanent appointment, he was more than making ends meet. By the spring of 1784, he was very much in demand as a performer and composer; during the month of March in that year, the most successful of his life, he performed nineteen times in thirty-one days.

His personal life underwent sweeping changes in Vienna as well. When Mozart left the Archbishop's retinue in May of 1781, he had found lodgings with a part of his past. In the wake of Aloysia (Weber) Lange's success as a virtuoso, the Weber family had moved to the capital, and Mozart moved in with them, intending to stay for only a week. But he was still there in September, four months later, when scandalous rumors began to fly about him and Aloysia's younger sister, Constanze, then twenty. Mozart moved out of the Webers' house and moved several times over the next few months, but the rumors did not cease, primarily because they were being spread by Constanze's mother, who was intent on securing a husband for her second-youngest daughter.

The rumors eventually became true. By December, Mozart had declared his love for Constanze in a letter to his father, precipitating, it seems, yet another bout of parental fury. Leopold was certain (and he was right) that Madame Weber had manipulated Wolfgang into marrying her daughter with the help of Constanze's guardian, one Herr von Thorwart. The two had forced Wolfgang to sign a document obligating him to marry Constanze within three years or pay her the sum of three hundred guilden a year. (This to save Constanze's honor, they claimed.) Leopold's response is quoted in a letter Mozart wrote home in January 1782.

> I quite agree with you in thinking that Madame Weber and Herr von Thorwart have been to blame in showing too much regard for their own interests, though the Madame is no longer her own mistress and has to leave everything . . . to the guardian. . . . However, it is all over now; and love must be my excuse. Herr von Thorwart did not behave well, but not so badly that he and Madame Weber "should be put in chains, made to sweep streets and have boards hung round their necks with the words 'seducers of youth'." That is an exaggeration.

Constanze Mozart is yet another person in the Mozart biography elevated to world fame because of her connection with one of the world's greatest artists. In her case, the fame has been more negative than positive. Over the years, she has been accused of ruining Mozart's life, of conducting herself in a frivolous and extravagant manner, of bankrupting her husband and of contributing to his childish and irresponsible lifestyle. Certainly, after Mozart's death, Nannerl published far and wide the opinion that Constanze lay at the heart of Mozart's eventual ruin, and musical historians have traditionally accepted Nannerl's analysis.

Whether or not this view is accurate is a matter for debate. Constanze Mozart was twenty when she and Wolfgang eventually got married in the summer of 1782. She seems to have been as

Wolfgang described her to his father: not a great intellect, but warm-hearted, and a good companion for her husband's playful personality. If the household was extravagant, it is hard not to suppose that both partners were to blame; if the Mozarts were known to be light-hearted and somewhat irresponsible, Constanze was perhaps doing no more than following Wolfgang's lead. For his part, Mozart seems to have been devoted to his wife. And Constanze was a loyal companion, though for the last year and a half of his life, she was often away taking the baths at Baden to cure a variety of illnesses, whether real or manufactured. Did she understand her husband? Likely not, but then neither did anyone else. Did she love him? In her way, probably yes.

Constanze is another supporting player in the Mozart drama whose story does not end with Mozart's death. If she was frivolous and empty-headed during Mozart's lifetime, she turned into an expert businesswoman after his death, carefully selling the five-hundred-odd manuscripts he left at his death for the best price and competently organizing a series of benefit concerts for herself and her two sons. All the debts left at Mozart's death were repaid, with some money left over. Eventually, Constanze was remarried, to a Danish diplomat, and ended her life as something of a grande dame in the mid-nineteenth century.

The Mozarts seem to have had a good time in the early 1780s in Vienna, despite their sometimes precarious financial position and Wolfgang's persistent lack of a permanent court appointment. They were obviously happy, fun-loving and undoubtedly a bit silly. Mozart clearly found in Constanze someone who constantly tickled his active erotic imagination, as well as a companion who would share his love of jokes and fun. Mozart wrote home about parties in his house that lasted all night. He attended costume balls and created musical plays for entertainment. Vienna probably looked askance at the young couple; they seemed immature and irresponsible. Nonetheless, Mozart needed this release in play to balance off the concentrated artistic work he was constantly doing. Although he was not yet poor, he could never stop working.

Mozart's most celebrated exploits as a musician in his early days in Vienna were as a clavier performer, rather than as a composer.

Vienna was clavier mad, and Mozart was one of the greatest keyboard players who ever lived. The accounts of his playing are universally astounding. It seems he created a uniquely liquid sound at the keyboard, and his ability to improvise was unmatched by anyone. He had been at it since he was seven, but now, in his late twenties, his skill was even more captivating. He could spin out a simple theme for half an hour or more, without ever repeating himself. He would play other composers' works by memory, or do improvisations on them as he went along.

In the beginning, he played by invitation at concerts given in a noble house; eventually, he gave subscription concerts of his own. A famous one in March of 1783 was attended by the Emperor; another the next year attracted over three hundred patrons. Mozart had caught the Emperor's attention early on in Vienna, and on Christmas Eve in 1781, he had participated in a musical event that was still talked about in the capital a year and a half later. On that night, Joseph II invited Mozart and Muzio Clementi, the reigning Viennese virtuoso, to a musical duel. Each pianist played a prepared composition and then traded improvisations and extemporaneous playing. According to all accounts, Mozart was the clear winner, mainly due to the quality of his improvised work. Mozart's reputation as a major clavier talent was firmly established.

Today, of course, we are more interested in Mozart the composer than in Mozart the performer, and Vienna was working wonders on his compositional skill as well. It was in Vienna that Mozart caught up with the newest developments in instrumental music and finally broke through to the kind of sophisticated writing we saw in *Eine Kleine Nachtmusik*. Part of the reason for this change in Mozart's musical language is that, having mimicked the music of second-rate composers for the better part of a decade, Mozart was now modeling his work after another genius, Franz Joseph Haydn. The two met in Vienna, probably in 1782 or 1783, and it was not long before Mozart and the older composer, who was twenty-four years his senior, became something of a mutual admiration society. Mozart looked to Haydn as a guide and teacher in many musical matters; Haydn was unstinting in his praise of Mozart's music. It seems it was Mozart who thought up the nickname "Papa Haydn," which has stuck to this day. Haydn himself could not hear Mozart's name mentioned without tears coming to his eyes. But Mozart paid Haydn the ultimate compliment: he studied Haydn's music carefully and learned the most important lessons he ever received in composition by poring over those scores.

Mozart went so far as to dedicate one important group of pieces to his mentor, when a dedication to some member of the nobility could be worth a few guilden. His six string quartets, beginning with K. 387, had been modeled on a set of Haydn's, his Opus 33, and it was by studying these scores thoroughly that he familiarized himself with the sonata form that Haydn had been refining in the late 1770s and early 1780s.

Haydn was actually present one evening in 1785 when these quartets were performed, as was Leopold Mozart, on his one and only trip to see his son during the Viennese years. Haydn leaned over to Leopold and uttered what was the most profound appreciation any living musician ever gave Mozart: "Before God, and as an honest man, I tell you that your son is the greatest composer known to me in person or by name. He has taste, and what is more, the greatest knowledge of composition."

One of the classic pieces that Mozart composed during this period of his life, which showed both Mozart's taste and his knowledge of composition, was the Piano Concerto in C major, K. 467, a work he would have performed for a glittering Viennese audience. We turn now to this piece, one of the most successful works Mozart composed in a decade of unmatched successes.

CHAPTER SIX

A Master
Work

Between the time he composed the *Haffner* Serenade in the mid-1770s, and his move to Vienna five years later, Mozart continued to intensify his musical language. We saw that Mozart filled the Serenade with shimmering musical moments, but spent less time creating musical meaning by connecting these moments. As he matured as a composer, the connections between musical ideas occupied more and more of his attention. Led on by the examples he studied in the music of Haydn, Mozart created more pieces where the formal balance and interrelationship of idea to idea and movement to movement became essential to the emotional effect he was trying to create. The next step in learning to fully appreciate Mozart is to come to grips with complete pieces, and the manner in which those pieces are constructed. To investigate Mozart's complete works, we might have chosen to look at some of the quartets Mozart created in response to Haydn or one of the piano sonatas that he wrote in Paris on his ill-fated trip there in the late 1770s. However, we've decided to look at another category of piece to give us the clearest idea of how skilful Mozart could be in creating large-scale work. When we can appreciate all that these larger works have to offer, we can understand Mozart as he wished to be understood. We're using a piano concerto as our sample of a complete Mozart work because it was with his piano concertos that he made his most original contributions to the music of his time. That is not to demean his achievements in the symphony, quartet or sonata. Mozart was probably the most accomplished overall musician who ever lived; there was not a single genre of musical composition in which he did not excel. However, his concertos are a breed slightly apart. Perhaps because of his career as a piano soloist, perhaps because of the inherent drama in this kind of piece, which pits soloist against orchestra, Mozart was at his most brilliant in his concertos (and in his operas, which we will investigate in the next chapter).

Mozart wrote his mature concertos (seventeen in all) to give himself something to play at his own concerts. In Mozart's day, no one would have been caught dead playing the music of someone else, or even repeating one of his own works. So he wrote these incredible concertos, each one fresher than the one before — and knocked them off at a dizzying pace. Concertos 14, 15, 16 and 17 were written within two months for the spring season of 1784. Four more were written that fall for the fall season. K. 467, the one we will be looking at, was completed (from first sketch to completed manuscript) in less than a month in 1785. It takes almost that much time now to copy the parts.

How astonished Mozart would be to realize that these concertos, written for himself, most played a single time while he was alive, have become the standard repertoire for generations of concert pianists. Not a week has gone by during the last hundred years when one of them has not been performed somewhere in the world. They remain one of Mozart's greatest artistic legacies.

But that doesn't necessarily mean that everything that goes on in the concertos is immediately obvious if you don't know exactly how to approach them. So let's take the K. 467 in C major and see if we can find out what makes it tick, and in so doing, get a few hints on how to approach any big work by Mozart — another concerto, a symphony or a quartet. You will need a few guideposts and a little practice, but it's not that hard to figure out what's happening in a concerto. And once you feel less intimidated by a big three- or four-movement, forty-minute Classical work and learn how to listen, you will find that you will never be able to listen to a Classical work without discovering some musical treasure. There are great statements of extreme beauty in the large Mozart works; they are just waiting for you to come and unlock them.

The Piano Concerto in C major, K. 467, was finished on March 9, 1785, and performed the next day. It is sometimes referred to as the *Elvira Madigan* Concerto because its exquisite slow second movement was used to great effect in a Swedish film of that name in the late sixties.

Before we start our journey through the piece, there are a couple of things to keep in mind. On the one hand, Mozart's basic musical language and techniques stayed essentially the same for the last ten years of his life. The last dozen or so piano concertos, the last half-dozen symphonies, the last ten quartets and final piano sonatas all used the same techniques we'll see in K. 467. On the other hand, every one of these works is different; Mozart repeated himself far less than almost any other composer. Although his basic language is always the same, he uses it in a wide variety of ways from piece to piece. There are no hard and fast rules in Mozart. Every piece is an exception. A technique used in one piano concerto will be abandoned in the next, although they may have been composed less than two weeks apart. Eventually, with experience, we can learn to appreciate these differences from work to work. But for the time being, we'll concentrate on the similarities.

Don't be frightened by a large work like a concerto. You already have all the knowledge you need to understand and appreciate the whole thing. It is made up of the same four-bar packages of melody, rhythm and harmony that we investigated in *Eine Kleine Nachtmusik*, and its first movement follows the same sonata-allegro form we saw in the *Nachtmusik* as well. The only difference is in scale. A concerto or a symphony is a long work; its first movement can be thirteen or fourteen minutes long, which can be an eternity in music. What composers learned to do in their larger works was to build coherent, beautiful structures out of small, four-bar elements that were quite limited in and of themselves.

The first movement of the *Elvira Madigan* is a case in point. It is close to fourteen minutes in length; the opening movement of *Eine Kleine Nachtmusik* is often played in six minutes. There are 137 bars in the first movement of *Eine Kleine*, 417 in the concerto. Obviously, there is more music in the larger work, and there are more musical ideas. Where Mozart gives us four ideas before he begins his move to the dominant in *Eine Kleine Nachtmusik*, all of them played once, he uses about eleven ideas in the *Elvira Madigan*, repeated a number of times, to make up a section of about 34 separate four-bar phrases, before he hits the dominant.

There are many different ways to skin a musical cat, and many different ways to write a first movement, even to the same format. In K. 467, Mozart decided to see how many different musical ideas he could integrate into his movement; more so than in most of his concertos, there is a wealth of melodic material here.

The first time you listen to the work, or the first several times, you may just want to listen for those different ideas and not worry too much about how they're connected. You're sure to note that some are repeated and that others aren't, but don't worry why that happens. In effect, you can approach the *Elvira Madigan* Concerto in the same way you approached the *Haffner* Serenade. Relax, listen to the melodies and enjoy the beauties the piece has to offer. Then, the next time through, you can start listening for things like form and organization, which will reveal the true musical wonders the piece contains.

There is a definite organization to the first movement of the *Elvira Madigan*, and the organization is sonata-allegro form. Flip back to the diagram of sonata-allegro form on page 62 and keep it handy as you're listening to the first movement of K. 467; it's the game plan Mozart followed as he was writing the work. And remember that sonata-allegro form is really about drama in music, especially the drama inherent in the opposition of tonic and dominant tonalities.

We'll break our listening down into sections, starting with the exposition — in fact, just the first section of the exposition.

The most important musical idea in any Classical work, by far, is the opening idea of the piece. There are generally no introductions in Classical works; the piece opens up right in the middle of the action. Fix that first idea well in your mind — it is the key to hearing the structure. It begins the exposition; it often announces the start of the development; it almost always triumphantly returns to herald the recapitulation. That little four-bar phrase, as innocent as it may seem, is a vital part of a Mozart concerto, as it is of any large-scale work. It also sets the emotional tone of the entire piece. The opening idea of K. 467 appears in the first four bars:

As we have come to expect from Mozart, the phrase is beautifully balanced: the first bar and the second bar have two quite distinct rhythms; bars 3 and 4 are exact rhythmic replicas of bars 1 and 2. And take another look at those first four notes; the clipped notes in the strings. They will be the key to the entire piece. There is a hint of humor in this short, martial theme. It sounds like an old military man proudly walking to the club. Now notice the clear rhythmic character of the entire first theme; we will never have any difficulty recognizing it when it reappears.

Now it's on to the tonic section of the exposition. Mozart is going to write this section in a very specific way; he is going to pepper it with lots of musical ideas, almost a dozen, of quite different character and style. In so doing, he is playing a little trick on us. When you get used to listening to music in sonata-allegro form, you unconsciously start listening for musical clues that alert you that the piece is about to move into another section. Here, at the beginning of the work, you're always waiting for the move to the dominant, and Mozart knows it. So what does he do? Several times in this section he fools us into thinking we are moving into the dominant section of the piece without ever getting there.

The first instance of this occurs very near the beginning of the piece. Mozart follows his opening theme with another contrasting four-bar idea, and then the opening comes back again. This, in itself, is not that much of a surprise. Remember that we are into broader proportions here where we would expect a certain amount of repetition. But this repeat of the opening idea seems to be going somewhere; the little melody gets developed, is played in several keys and then leads to what sounds just like the kind of transition section we heard in *Eine Kleine Nachtmusik*, which, in turn, leads to a new theme that is quite different in character. This is the little melody in the woodwinds and brass that sounds like a sigh. (See bar 28 of the score in Appendix 2.)

This all fits the standard definition of a "second theme" — except for one small problem. We're still in C major, not the dominant, and we're nowhere near the true second theme of the work. Mozart is playing around with our expectations here, but he is also making a musical point. Despite the number of different themes, Mozart is alerting us to the fact that the form of this movement is going to be very broad. It will be a long time before he gives up his home key; the pace of change is going to be slow. It is almost as though Mozart has let the broad, military character of his opening theme set the mood for the form of the work — it will be reasoned, slow, majestic.

That little theme with its sighing phrase is lovely, but Mozart makes it clear that it is not to be given any special prominence. He does this by bringing his first theme back yet again (the third time so far), and developing it in yet another way (bar 36). Now Mozart has this theme in counterpoint with itself — that is, the different instruments start playing it one after the other, each one beginning before the previous one has finished, like an eighteenth-century version of "Row, Row, Row Your Boat."

The counterpointed theme is interrupted by yet another musical idea, this one moving by step, which sounds as if it is announcing the coda, or end of the exposition (bar 44). However, Mozart is playing the same trick he played a couple of bars earlier. Although the music sounds as if it is changing character and moving to another section, we are still in the tonic section of the exposition; structurally, we have yet to go anywhere. Then another theme pops up in bar 52 — a chromatic ascending theme — and it also goes nowhere. (We will see later in this movement just how unplanned these themes are.) Think of this opening to the piece as if it were the opening to a TV mini-series. Before we can get started, we must be introduced to all the characters. Because the piece is more an epic than a simple domestic drama, there are quite a few characters to get to know. So the opening four-note theme makes yet another appearance (its fourth), still in C major (beginning in bar 65), and finally gives way to the music that serves to introduce the piano.

The piano; we've forgotten about the star of the show. We're eighty bars into the piece, and the piano has yet to be heard. Actually, the introduction of the piano is the key point in any piano concerto. In some ways, we hear the entire orchestral exposition as one long introduction, leading up to the entrance of the star performer. While the orchestra plays, the soloist sits there, absorbing the music, and we almost ask ourselves, What does the piano think of this music? How will it respond? Anticipating the entrance of the solo instrument is one of the delicious moments in a concerto.

Mozart loved the drama of the concerto because he loved the notion of a single instrument taking on an entire orchestra, and having enough musical significance to balance off the music that sixty people could make. For his formal organization, however, the solo instrument posed something of a problem. Somehow, composers had to decide when the solo instrument should enter and what kind of music it should play when it did enter, without completely disturbing the formal plan of the piece. Eventually, they hit upon this solution: the exposition section in sonata-allegro form is generally repeated; why not have the piano enter the second time around? That would give the orchestra time to establish the main themes and character of the work, and provide that kind of anticipation about the soloist's musical role which was part of the fun of a concerto. But there was a problem with this solution. If all the soloist was going to do was repeat the exposition, where was the drama? Where was the special role for the solo instrument?

Mozart solved this second dilemma in a clever way in K. 467. As in many of his concertos, the orchestra here plays through only the tonic section of the exposition; the piano leads the piece to the dominant. This is yet another reason why Mozart refuses to modulate to the dominant at the beginning of the music, even though he pretends to more than once.

Giving the piano the lead role in the exploration of the dominant section of the exposition was clever on two counts. By having piano and orchestra introduced in different keys, Mozart strengthens the opposition between soloist and orchestra, an opposition on which the success of any concerto depends. By holding back the dominant key until the piano's entrance, he also gives the soloist something new to play, rather than just blindly repeating parts of the exposition.

I might add, as mentioned before, that there are no hard and fast rules in works by Mozart. Although many of the concertos follow this plan, and have the dominant held until the piano enters, many others follow a more normal organization and have the orchestra expose both first and "second" themes, tonic and dominant, before the piano arrives on the scene. You have to be alert to the peculiarities of any Mozart work you may be listening to.

You may want to stop your listening here for a moment and review what you've heard so far, and maybe listen to the opening again. From the opening to the introduction of the piano we are still in the beginning of the exposition, its tonic section. It is important to fix this in your mind; it has a key structural role to play in the piece. When you're ready, move on to the piano entry.

The piano seems to enter a few bars early in K. 467, as if to help the orchestra finish off its part of the exposition. Then, just after this modest entrance, a repeat of the exposition seems to begin. The opening phrase returns again, this time exactly as it appeared at the beginning of the piece, but then the piano takes up the answering phrase to the opening military four notes, wresting the musical spotlight from the orchestra.

Generally, the piano never repeats music from the orchestral exposition note for note, but embellishes it, making it the piano's own. It is as if the soloist has said: I've heard what you can do; now make way for a real virtuoso. This quoting of material from the opening of the piece can go on for some time, just to drive the point home. In K. 467, however, it is abruptly ended as the piano introduces a brand-new bit of music, which has no connection with anything that's gone before. And after playing this theme only once, the piano then begins a long passage made up of no theme at all, but a series of scales and broken chords (called arpeggios). This is the beginning of the second section of the exposition, the section leading to the dominant key.

These passages of "figuration" (being made up of figures rather than themes or melodies) are very common in the music of Mozart, and they are important on more than one level. Certainly, they gave the soloist an opportunity to show off some technique, a not inconsiderable benefit in a musical composition that was designed to spotlight a performer as much as a composer. But for the composition itself, these passages had two major benefits. For one thing, they allowed the audience to relax its concentration a little bit and not strain to hear innumerable small themes and four-bar ideas. Up to this point in K. 467, we have heard nothing but a succession of ideas hardly related to one another. We need a break where our ears basically register a series of slower-moving harmonies instead of fast-moving melodies. These figurative passages also allowed Classical composers to create vast sections which served the purpose of establishing a key and a harmony more than anything else. A long figurative passage could balance off in one key a highly melodic section that had been stated in another.

So don't attempt to follow melodies in these figurative passages; there aren't any there. The composer's main purpose in writing these sections is to create large-scale harmonic continuity.

This first figurative section in K. 467 plays one more important role — it leads us to the dominant. The piano runs through a number of scales, the orchestra joins in playing the G major scale (G is the dominant key of the work), and all of this prepares us for the introduction of the "second theme" (though it's actually about the eighth musical idea in the work), and Mozart goes and tricks us again.

The theme that should be in the dominant key of G major is replaced by one in G minor instead. See if you can hear the different character of the minor key; it is much too unstable to be held up in opposition to the tonic section. Mozart plays with this section for a brief time, and finally, in bar 128, heads to the true "second theme" in G major. This is the theme, played by the piano, that is made up of three descending figures. It does have a softer feel than the major opening theme, and serves as a true contrast to much that has gone before:

There are a number of ways to see this theme as an important structural component, as opposed to thinking of it as just another musical idea. It's definitely in G major, although sometimes you can see that better than you can hear it. But Mozart makes quite a bit of this theme; it is repeated several times, alternating between orchestra and soloist. Generally, hearing the true "second theme" isn't that difficult. In this work, however, there are so many musical ideas that it is hard at first to know which one is more important than the others.

Mozart has yet another surprise for us after he introduces this second theme. He brings back his opening four-note theme one more time — the sixth time. Here's why. Mozart has created a movement of immense proportion and many, many melodic ideas. He needs some unifying feature that will remind us of home and balance off the excessive variety of the exposition section. That little four-note theme does the trick. Every time it returns, we feel that we know where we are, that we can move with the piece to yet another section of the work.

This last quotation of the opening theme (in the dominant, this time) leads to a very long section, where the soloist gets a chance to move through a number of different chords, though still staying within the basic framework of G major. This is a prime example of one of those figurative passages we mentioned a page or so ago. The point here is to establish a tonality and rest our concentration, as well as to provide a good chance for the timbre of the piano to be established. Eventually, this section leads right to the development.

It's worthwhile to take a break right here, and look back at where you've come from. If you're listening to the work as you read, go back to the beginning and listen to the entire exposition again. It is enormously long in this work — over 190 bars in length. There are whole movements in Mozart that aren't this long, and we haven't even begun the development yet. However, that's how Mozart chose to write K. 467.

As you listen to the exposition again, remind yourself of a few things. Listen for each time the opening four-note theme reappears; it always marks some transition point in the music. See if you can hear all six entries, and hear the differences between them. Can you hear the significance of the exact replica of this theme where the exposition begins its repeat? This is a key point in the form; it helps if you can spot it. Listen, too, for the difference the piano makes when it finally enters, and for the way Mozart has balanced off the orchestra with its many themes, and the piano, with its long figurative passages and the one main "second theme." Finally, listen again for those "throw-away" themes in the orchestral exposition. You might just hear them again later in the piece.

The beginning of the development section in a large work always carries an air of anticipation. What will happen here, we wonder. The development section in this movement is somewhat on the short side, mainly because the exposition has been so long, but emotionally, it is quite dramatic. The development begins with a restatement of the main theme in the dominant, G major. Notice, however, that it is not the four-note theme as it first appeared in the work, but an analogy of the four-note theme in its second appearance. It is as though Mozart is beginning the development in the middle, putting aside the nice, even restrained version of the four-note theme that opens the work and opting for a slightly more intense version.

After repeating the theme twice in its normal formation, Mozart slows it down and repeats the first note of the second bar of the theme again and again, for dramatic power, in the new key of E flat major. Then he reaches into his bag of tricks with a technique we actually saw him use in *Eine Kleine Nachtmusik*. All of a sudden, we hear in the development, in a prominent position, those "throw-away" musical ideas from the exposition. Two of these ideas show up here: the little chromatic figure we identified way back in bar 52, and the musical idea that originally came right after it.

This surprise isn't enough for Mozart, though. He can't resist giving us another one. The little musical figure from the exposition gets extended over and over again, and Mozart moves us toward the remote key of E minor. Then, in B minor, right at the heart of the development, Mozart gives us a brand-new theme, which is unlike anything that has gone before, played by the piano. This is an extraordinary moment. In a movement with so many potential ideas to develop, Mozart has chosen to use none of them for the heart of his development. This is a brilliant stroke. He has used his opening idea so often already in this work that we're getting tired of it. But no other idea has really claimed our attention; how would you decide which one to feature here? So Mozart continues the melodic fecundity of the movement, and gives us yet another idea.

There's another exciting musical technique to notice in this part of the development. Rather than increasing the volume and the tension at this stage in the work, which is common for development sections, Mozart moves in the other direction. The texture is spare, the music quiet. By getting softer instead of louder, Mozart can actually be more dramatic.

What an expressive stroke of genius this new melody represents. Here, in the middle of the development, Mozart provides an emotional contrast to the almost aggressive jollity of the first movement. This minor section shows the underside of the martial masculinity of the opening theme. All of a sudden, the piece takes on a new emotional coloring.

The new theme in B minor is played once and followed by a return to some of the patterns the piano played in the long figuration section of the exposition. Now they are thrown from one harmony to another and, magically, begin to take on real musical significance. So little in Mozart happens by accident. Marvelously, in a movement with so many themes, Mozart has chosen to use his piano accompaniment figure to create the emotional tension of the development, and it works. Listen for this section to hear the growing tension that comes entirely from the harmonies. And listen as well for the inexorably ascending passage in both piano and flute that comes just before the end of the development. In its modest way, it provides real tension.

The development is short in K. 467, but you may want to stop here and listen to it again. It is worth listening for that B minor melody at the heart of the section to hear it for the brand-new idea that it is. When you've finished that, it will be time to move on to the third large section of the movement, the recapitulation.

Listening to recap sections in Classical compositions is different than listening to either expositions or developments. In the recap, you have something to compare your listening to. You expect the exposition to be repeated either exactly or with slight variation, and part of the fun here is to feel that the surprises are, by and large, over, that you can relax in the relative familiarity of the music from the opening of the piece. Admittedly, the first time you hear the movement, the music is not that familiar, but as you get used to a piece, that sense of being home in the recapitulation can be quite satisfying.

The recapitulation of the first movement of K. 467 starts out note for note exactly the same as the beginning of the piece. That first theme made so many appearances in the exposition that its return in the recap could have been tedious. But Mozart has foreseen this — that is why he added new material in the development. He needed some contrast before that ubiquitous four-note theme made yet another entrance.

After that re-presentation of the first theme, we move on to the section that originally took the piece from tonic to dominant. Of course, the transition will have to be changed in the recapitulation somehow, as the second theme is not in the dominant in the recap, but the tonic. What Mozart is going to do in this work is a real mystery, since he had so many themes in the exposition and so many fake transition passages. A lesser composer might have been confounded by this puzzle, but Mozart, as usual, cuts right through the Gordian knot. He repeats the exposition, virtually note for note, for twenty bars, and then heads to a new key, F major, where we get the four-note motif again, in both orchestra and piano. This little detour leads us directly to the "second theme," as we identified it, the descending figure that was first performed in the dominant and now appears in the tonic. The complexity of the exposition evaporates as Mozart presents his two main themes in the recapitulation, one directly after the other. The opposition between tonic and dominant, orchestra and soloist, has been reconciled.

So far, Mozart has broken the rules in both his extremely long exposition, and his short, newly composed development. And he's not finished yet. By presenting both main themes so early in the recap, this last section could end up being very short. But that wouldn't work; Mozart needs a good solid balance to the massive exposition he began with. So he doesn't shorten the dominant section of the exposition in the recapitulation, which would be normal after such a short re-presentation of the first and second themes. Instead, after the second theme has been heard in the tonic, away we go with a section very similar to the analogous section in the exposition, except that everything is in C major this time. The four-note phrase that originally followed the second theme is reprised, and the piano figuration that followed that is repeated, all in the name of structural balance.

Then, with just a slight turn in the harmony, what do we get but the little theme like a sigh that we last heard 330 bars ago. Remember that little idea that Mozart led us to believe was our second theme? Well, here it is again, in the recap, juxtaposed with material that was originally presented eighty bars away from it. Tricks like these are why it pays to listen carefully to the themes in a Mozart work. You just never know where an idea introduced in one spot will pop up again.

Mozart is not through reprising his material, though. After the little sigh-like theme, he jumps back to music that was first heard in the dominant section of the exposition. It is as though he were replaying his greatest hits from the beginning of the movement — phrases taken out of context, set beside neighbors they have never seen before. It is a masterful performance by a compositional professional. Finally, the main theme is stated one more time, introducing a special feature that you find only in concertos: the cadenza.

In Mozart's day, the cadenza was the section where the soloist got to show off his or her technique and ability to improvise. The soloist would comment on the music of the piece, putting in lots of technical flourishes. Structurally, the cadenza doesn't really exist — it is, strictly speaking, outside the pattern of sonata-allegro form, an interpolation that made soloists happy because they could show off their technique. During the cadenza, time was suspended, and soloists were free to roam wherever they wished. Today, most classical players have lost the ability to improvise, so the cadenzas are written out and memorized.

At the end of the cadenza, Mozart retrieves a few more ideas from his early exposition, ideas that we haven't heard for three hundred bars, including that little chromatic theme once again. (Mozart clearly was fond of that theme.) Then there's a final little coda, and the movement comes to a graceful close.

The first movement to K. 467 is one of Mozart's most massive, substantial movements. Breaking it into sections may help a lot in coming to assimilate it all. There's a lot of music in it, a lot of different things for you to listen to, literally enough for a lifetime. Don't worry if you only pick up a little bit of the complicated form or only a few of the many different musical ideas the first few times you listen. It's not as though the movement is unattractive just as a purely sensual experience. But listen again and again, reading this chapter, perhaps reading the score if you can, but concentrating on one detail or another. Maybe one time through you will do nothing but count the number of times that four-note idea at the beginning reappears in the movement. Another time, you might really listen for the piano part only; a third time, perhaps you will just concentrate on the development, to see if you can anticipate that new melody in B minor. Eventually, you'll hear more and more, and your appreciation of the movement will increase with each new detail. Finally, stop. Listen to as much of the detail as you like, but don't forget to just enjoy the piece as well.

The first movement of K. 467 is by far the most substantial part of the work, but there are two other movements in it as well. Among other things, they give the piece emotional balance — something that became extremely important for Mozart in his mature works. Not only did he use material from one movement in the next; he also considered the emotional effect of the whole three-movement structure as he was writing each one.

A major work like a concerto or symphony needs to have an emotional and musical logic behind its pacing, or flow, and, as we listen to a work, we must be aware of that flow. Any individual moment in the music has had a past and is prelude to a future. Our success as listeners consists in our increasing ability to hear each moment in a wider context.

But for now, we've done enough work on the *Elvira Madigan* Concerto. Treat yourself to the exquisite beauty of the slow movement and the light-hearted texture of the final one. If you happen to notice that the melody in the second movement is entirely made up not of four-bar, but of three-bar phrases, or if it dawns on you that the final movement is also written in sonata-allegro form, so much the better.

The piano concertos of Mozart will repay repeated listening every time. There is so much first-rate music contained in their pages, that you can live in them forever. Mozart displayed the full force of his imagination in his concertos because he was inspired by the dramatic possibilities of the form. This is music in its purest manifestation; not expressing a story or a series of planned emotions. It is beauty of form, proportion and perfect aesthetic logic. There was only one other kind of music that Mozart adored more: the pure musical drama of opera. It is to Mozart the composer of some of the world's great music-dramas that we will next turn.

CHAPTER SEVEN

The Shakespeare of Opera

LEOPOLD MOZART was in the audience on the 10th of March in 1785 when Mozart first performed the *Elvira Madigan* Concerto. Since the previous January, he had been in Vienna visiting his son and his daughter-in-law. Perhaps it was for Leopold that Mozart composed some of the little jokes we saw in the first movement of the concerto: no matter what their other disagreements were, Mozart never stopped trusting his father's musical judgment. How might Leopold have reacted to the compositional surprises contained in that first movement, or to the intense beauty of the second movement?

We will never know, although we do know that Leopold was amazed at the amount of activity in the Mozart household during his visit. A dozen times during his stay, he watched Mozart's heavy piano being carted out of his son's apartment to some noble house or other in preparation for a concert. Wolfgang and Constanze were constantly on the go, either performing, composing or entertaining. It was one of the busiest periods in their lives.

Mozart must have been proud of the successes he was having both as a composer and as a performer. His compositions — like the one we just finished investigating — were taking on a new confidence, and he was beginning to achieve widespread recognition as a musician.

Only one thing was missing. Since 1782, he had not received a single opera commission. *The Abduction from the Seraglio*, written soon after his arrival in Vienna, was the last opera he had written. Mozart loved opera; there was no other form of composition that fired his imagination in such a powerful way. He loved setting stories to music, working with the singers to perfect their arias, finding musical equivalents for literary emotions.

Then, in 1785, Mozart began working on another operatic project. Even as he was writing and performing the *Elvira Madigan* Concerto, an idea was forming in his mind for a musical drama. He had read Beaumarchais's play, *The Marriage of Figaro*, and began to contemplate turning it into an opera.

The Marriage of Figaro became a turning point in Mozart's fortunes, both personally and artistically. It was also a major event in the cultural life of his adopted city. Opera was perhaps the most significant art form in Mozart's Vienna. It was through opera that composers made their reputations, and audiences flocked to the theaters to see and hear whatever was the latest operatic rage.

It may be hard for us today to understand the enthusiasm with which opera was greeted. Classical music in general may seem inaccessible, but opera is often seen as the most inaccessible of the inaccessible. Little in our day-to-day experience prepares us for its conventions. We might not normally listen to classical music, but we do listen to music, and we have some idea of how we might approach a new kind of music. But opera is different. Somehow we are expected to take seriously the notion of a dramatic spectacle, often presented in naturalistic settings and scenery, where everyone nonetheless sings to each other, rather than speaking, where men and women are impaled by swords only to spend the next several minutes belting out their death scene in accents and tones that shake the third balcony, where we are expected to believe in love scenes where the two principals never touch each other except to sing past each other's ears to the audience, where wooden acting and staged set pieces are often the order of the dramatic day, and where we are expected to spend an evening in the theater without understanding a single word of the dialogue.

Opera is ridiculous, or so it seems, yet, mysteriously, there are fanatical devotees of the form who claim for it a primary place in the pantheon of Western art, who view opera as the greatest achievement of Western musical culture. Can we reconcile the two views? Is opera the most formalized and irrelevant of all elite art forms or is it a living means of artistic communication?

Eventually, of course, as with all other art forms, the meaning that any of us chooses to derive from opera is a matter of personal taste. However, many reject opera for the wrong reasons — because they misunderstand its conventions. Opera does take a little bit of effort. But once you have crossed that barrier into the operatic world, many delights await you. Certainly, it is impossible to fully appreciate Mozart's musical genius without understanding his skill as a musical dramatist. For many, even those who marvel at his incredible achievements in instrumental music, Mozart's brilliance as an artist as well as a musician is most fully realized in the operas.

Before we look into the charm and excitement of Mozart's mature operas, a few words about opera in general. There are some fairly simple rules about how to approach the art form so as to overcome those problems with operatic conventions that we spoke about earlier. Get used to the fact: people in operas sing to each other, instead of speaking to each other. It may seem a little difficult at first to accept the juxtaposition of naturalistic sets, costumes, acting styles and plots with sung dialogue, but it's obviously what opera is all about. Those who have celebrated opera throughout the ages love the extra dimension that music brings to drama: they feel that its subtlety and beauty deepen the dramatic experience in a way that straight theater can never do. To open yourself up to the power that opera can undoubtedly have, you must let the music speak to you as you would if it were a piece of orchestral music, and forget the inflated theatrical trappings that sometimes accompany that music.

We in the modern age have a wonderful advantage over previous generations when it comes to appreciating opera — the recording. Ironically, it is almost better to approach opera via recordings than through the theater. There are so many distractions in the theater: the believability of the story may be destroyed if the singers do not look the part. The acting may not be up to scratch; the musical performances themselves may disappoint. One of Mozart's great idolators, Søren Kierkegaard, the Danish philosopher, a passionate devotee of Mozartean opera, and of *Don Giovanni* in particular, would always listen to the opera from the lobby. He never entered the theater. In the lobby, his imagination could take hold, he could listen to the music undistracted by any of the problems he often encountered inside. What bliss Kierkegaard would have derived from the compact disc. Now we can recreate his lobby listening in the privacy of our own homes, with the greatest casts in the world performing for us. These are ideal conditions for beginning to appreciate opera.

If you are going to begin your listening to opera at home, there are a few hints that will greatly increase your potential pleasure. The first time you listen to an opera, listen just for the story. You cannot really judge the success of the music without understanding the plot and the motivations of the characters in the play. Since very few operas have been written in English, you will have to follow along with the translated libretto (the Italian word for script) that will have been enclosed with your recording. Here is the first advantage over your listening colleague in the theater.

For years, operas were generally performed in the language in which they were written, even if few in the audience actually understood that language. Opera audiences regularly sat for hours watching a musical play without understanding a word of the dialogue. Things have changed in some opera houses since then, however. Translated lyrics are projected above the stage so that audiences can follow the story. These "surtitles," as they are called, are extremely controversial in the world of opera. More than one opera director has threatened to resign if surtitles were introduced into his theater. However, where they have been introduced, they have proven immensely popular. People want to know what the words in opera mean, even if the translations are a bit rocky.

At home, however, you have none of these problems. As you listen to the Italian or German original, you can follow the English translation at the same time. Your reading may bring you some pleasant surprises. We have come to value the music for operas so highly we tend to forget that they are musical plays, and that some of them have been quite well written. This is especially true of the three operas that Mozart wrote with his collaborator, Lorenzo da Ponte — *The Marriage of Figaro, Don Giovanni* and *Così fan tutte*. All three libretti are beautifully crafted, full of dramatic twists and turns, providing Mozart with dozens of situations to express depths of character or to comment on the action of the stories through his music.

Mozart claimed to have read and discarded hundreds of opera librettos in his career. He was extremely particular about the librettos he eventually set to music and regularly suggested changes to the author to heighten the dramatic possibilities of the work.

As you begin your listening, you will probably notice two kinds of music in most operas, each of which has a completely different dramatic role. Every so often, one of the principal characters will sing an aria, either to express their feelings about the dramatic situation in which they find themselves or, occasionally, to further the action of the plot. It is on the arias that composers lavish the most attention. These are the famous tunes from the opera; the tunes the composer hoped would be sung by the audience as they left the theater.

Arias are often sung by more than one character; they can be in the form of duets, trios and quartets where several characters express their feelings or react to one another simultaneously. Mozart excelled at writing ensemble pieces like this. We will see a number of examples where Mozart has several characters commenting simultaneously on the same dramatic situation, from quite different points of view.

The other kind of musical passage most common in opera is the recitative — longish sections that sound almost like spoken dialogue, most often accompanied by a solo keyboard instrument, where the musical interest is quite weak. Recitatives are sections whose point is to further the plot. Musically, they are spare and unengaging so that full attention can be paid to the dialogue. They are there to provide breathing space between arias.

As opera developed over the centuries, the recitatives gradually became absorbed in the musical drama of the opera, losing their distinctive character as low-key musical sections. In Mozart's day, however, recitatives were still very much part of the operatic convention. On your first listen to a Mozart opera, you may want to concentrate on these sections carefully. Although they are not usually of great musical interest, it is often through the recitatives that you can best understand the story.

After you have a general idea of the story of the opera, you are ready to listen to the work a second time, concentrating this time on the music. You may wish to ignore the translated libretto altogether and just focus your attention on the musical beauties in the piece. Listen carefully to the arias, duets, trios and other "set" musical pieces. These gorgeous songs and dramatic scenes deepen the emotional impact of the drama, allowing composers to express subtle meaning that unvarnished speech could never convey. The very beauty of many arias gives them a power pure speech will always lack. Either in the melody itself, or in its accompaniment, composers can make references back to other parts of the opera, to remind the audience that this part of the opera is linked to another. The structure of the song or the accompaniment can also add a purely musical meaning to the aria, which corresponds to the meaning expressed by the words themselves. Composers can also indulge in a sort of tone painting, where ideas in the text are given musical expression.

Mozart was especially fond of this kind of musical painting; lovers' arias are often accompanied by regular pizzicato strings that sound like the beating of a heart; when characters are in a hurry, there is often a string accompaniment that sounds like someone gasping for breath. Never forget in opera to listen to the orchestra as well as the singers.

Using devices like this, the operatic composer becomes more than a musician. He or she becomes a dramatist as well, an artist who creates a story, provides a musical expression of the emotions contained in that story and comments on the entire work at the same time, in this third role almost acting as a member of a celestial audience watching the entire musical drama unfold from on high.

To fully appreciate the musical and dramatic aspects of opera as a form, it is worthwhile to listen to your opera recording once more, this time focusing on the dramatic and the musical together. As with so many older forms of art, there is more to opera than immediately meets the eye or ear. Those who consider opera the greatest of all musical forms love its ability to speak to us on a variety of levels at the same time: they revel in the purely sensual beauties of the music itself, the dramatic ambiguities the music is able to express and the combination of music and the traditional characteristics of the theater — suspense, surprise and reconciliation. Not everyone who learns to actually listen to opera becomes a true devotee, but there is undoubtedly a host of artistic wonders to be enjoyed when you learn a few of the tricks opera composers use to create their art.

So far we've been talking about opera as though all opera composers through the ages had used the form in exactly the same way. This is certainly not the case. Opera as a form was invented around the year 1600 in Venice, where it started as the addition of a few musical numbers to a dramatic piece. By the end of that century, opera had become extremely formalized. A hundred years later, the creators and consumers of opera had become obsessed with spectacle. Plots were now almost all drawn from Greek and Roman mythology, the characters were all one-dimensional and wooden and the emphasis was on a florid, highly ornamented singing style, where the vocal pyrotechnics of famous singers overwhelmed any sense of plot or character. The form of the opera usually had nothing to do with its plot or with the emotions of the characters. This type of work, known as opera seria, or *opéra héroïque*, became less and less an artistic event and more and more an excuse for a social occasion for the nobility of the late eighteenth century.

In the late Baroque era, which was coming to an end in the decades just before Mozart's birth, opera seria was the dominant form all over Europe. Aristocrats throughout the continent vied with one another to create elaborate opera houses (many are still standing), with equally extensive companies and stage decorations, to present these stilted, cold, formal works. Before long, opera seria was widely understood as a symbol of the aristocracy of the *ancien régime* in all its glory — aloof, fabulously wealthy, living in a fantastically constructed world of mythological heroes and heroines.

The first challenge to this world came from Italy. Opera buffa, or comic opera, was the antithesis of opera seria. In opere buffe, the plots were lively, the characters more realistic, the music charming and accessible. The new operatic form was seen as a revolutionary phenomenon, giving a nascent middle class the opportunity to see and hear itself in accents and phrases that belonged to them.

When Mozart started writing operas in his early teens, opera seria were still extremely popular. They were even still around at the end of Mozart's life; *La Clemenza di Tito*, an opera he completed only weeks before his death, was very much in the seria style. But it was opera buffa that truly liberated Mozart as an opera composer. Mozart found in the buffa style a perfect balance of opposing forces, of humor and seriousness, of simplicity in music and complexity in emotion, of the naturalness of real life blended with the artificiality of dramatic art.

Yet Mozart's two initial operatic triumphs were in quite different genres. *Idomeneo* was the opera seria he had composed for Munich just before the Archbishop of Salzburg summoned him to Vienna in the spring of 1781. It was an extremely serious piece, full of tragic and noble emotion. A year and a half later, Mozart wrote *The Abduction from the Seraglio*, an exotic opera with a Turkish theme that became all the rage in Vienna.

However, if *Idomeneo* and the *Abduction* gained Mozart popularity, it was not until he composed three opere buffe in Vienna in collaboration with his best-known librettist, Lorenzo da Ponte, that his genius as a composer of operas blazed into prominence. The three operas are still at the heart of the operatic repertoire — one of the three almost always tops every new list of the world's greatest operas. In 1786, Mozart and da Ponte wrote *The Marriage of Figaro*; a year later, they created *Don Giovanni*; in 1790, they ended their partnership with *Così fan tutte*.

These three operas, along with Mozart's last, *The Magic Flute*, are among the greatest achievements in the history of Western opera. Musicians, other composers and critics have fallen all over each other trying to outdo superlative with superlative in describing these works. Here is Johannes Brahms, a composer not given to extravagance, on *Figaro*: "In my opinion, each number in *Figaro* is a miracle; it is totally beyond me how anyone could create anything so perfect; nothing like it was ever done again, not even by Beethoven." And now to Søren Kierkegaard on *Don Giovanni*: "I am in love with Mozart like a young girl. Immortal Mozart! I owe you everything; It is thanks to you that I lost my reason, that my soul was awestruck in the very depths of my being . . . I have you to thank that I did not die without having loved." So what is it about these works that occasioned such extravagant praise and devotion?

In many ways, *Figaro, Giovanni* and *Così* are very different operas. The first is a social comedy, an opera buffa par excellence, the second a dark look at the deserts of evildoing, the third an artificial but polished comedy of manners. What links them all is a superb sense of characterization and musical dramatization. In these three operas, perhaps more than in any other, the characters are presented as real people — natural, many-sided and ambiguous. The artificial characterization of opera seria couldn't be further from Mozart's achievement in these three pieces. With a vividness that has often been compared to Shakespeare's writing, Mozart created (with da Ponte's help) eternal characters that have interested and intrigued opera goers for two hundred years. A lifetime of observation of people — clear-eyed, yet sympathetic — has been poured into these operas. The operas remind us that Mozart was watching his world and the people in it with great interest and acuity all his life.

Mozart proves himself in his operas the truest of true artists; we now see a loving and intelligent understanding of humanity and human nature allied with his spectacular musical gifts. He showers us with a profound sympathy for human frailty, without denying us the irony and bitter humor that was part of his life and his art. Irony and deception are recurring themes in all three operas. Figaro sets about to fool his master, Count Almaviva, by deceiving the Count into allowing Figaro to marry. Giovanni is a hero in his opera because he is a deceiver with a certain amount of integrity. *Così fan tutte* is all about deception. Two men adopt disguises to test the fidelity of their lovers. The opera's plot rests on this deception; by opera's end, it becomes difficult to determine who is being deceived and how. Generations of opera goers have argued about the questions and contradictions posed by all three operas as they have argued about the greatest plays of Shakespeare.

Let's start off with *Figaro*, in some ways still the most popular of the three. *Figaro* is Mozart's first mature opera buffa written at the end of his most prolific period as a composer. It just bursts with life and the pure enjoyment of creativity.

Figaro has significance on several levels, not the least of which is political. Pierre Augustin de Beaumarchais wrote the original play on which the opera is based — *The Marriage of Figaro* —in Paris in 1784. It was an immediate *succès de scandale*. The play, which was explicitly political, was seen as a direct attack on the aristocracy — on its privilege, its intelligence, its right to govern — in a country that was five years away from the storming of the Bastille. If *The Marriage of Figaro* was seen as a provocative act in France, it was seen as positively revolutionary in the rest of Europe. It was immediately banned in many European countries, including Austria. Under no circumstances was Joseph II prepared to see *Figaro* on the stage. Enter Lorenzo da Ponte — adventurer, poet, ex-priest, librettist. It was Mozart who asked da Ponte if he could turn *Figaro* into an opera. Da Ponte did so (in six weeks, if one can believe his memoirs), and then personally convinced the Emperor that he had eliminated the offending scenes from Beaumarchais's *Figaro*, and turned the piece into a harmless, farcical comedy. Under those conditions, the Emperor relented, and *Figaro* went ahead.

It is no surprise that Mozart was attracted to *Figaro*. He knew that the story of the valet who outsmarts his master was no mere bedroom farce; he understood the implications of this plot for his time. He most likely played an active role in shaping and revising the not-so-innocent libretto as well. Although we have no record of changes he might have made, his letters requesting changes to *Idomeneo* and *The Abduction from the Seraglio* suggest that he was intimately concerned with the details of his operas' librettos and their dramatic structure. The writing of *Figaro* was Mozart's most overtly revolutionary act in an era of impending revolution. At the same time, the opera must have had personal as well as political meaning for Mozart. Remember that only a few years earlier, Mozart had himself rebelled against his master, the Archbishop of Salzburg.

Figaro can be appreciated on several levels, but the first and most immediate is that of the music itself. There are probably more charming and wonderful melodies in this work than in any other Mozart opera. When Mozart went to Prague for the premiere of *Don Giovanni*, a year and a half after *Figaro* was staged there, he discovered to his delight and astonishment that people were singing numbers from *Figaro* in the streets. To today's opera lovers, however, this is not as surprising. At least half a dozen of the thirty or so numbers from *Figaro* would make anybody's greatest operatic hits list: Figaro's "Non più andrai" and "Se vuol ballare," Cherubino's two early arias "Non so più, cosa son" and "Voi che sapete," the Countess's plaintive "Dove sono" and several others. In this his first comprehensive attempt at modern opera buffa, Mozart poured into the score the same generosity of melodic invention that he had lavished on the *Haffner* Serenade, years before.

The opera is more than just lovely music, however. Mozart and Da Ponte created a dramatic piece that subtly mixes madcap bedroom farce with a serious political and dramatic message. The genius of *Figaro* is that the frivolous and the serious coexist in perfect harmony. Figaro's first-act challenge to his master, Count Almaviva, "Se vuol ballare" (If you would dance, my pretty Count, I'll play the tune . . .) is perfectly consistent with the conventions of opera buffa. In Mozart's hands, however, this comedic challenge is fraught with political overtones. A society is being challenged in *Figaro*; the Viennese nobility listening to Figaro's challenge to his fictional master would not have missed the subtle undercurrents of bitterness and anger that mark the music Mozart composed for Figaro to sing. They would have heard it as it was meant to be heard — as a challenge to their supremacy.

But perhaps the most lasting legacy of *Figaro* and its most permanent feature is its cast of characters. Long after the political content of *Figaro* has ceased to be controversial or even noticeable, the characters in the opera still seem alive and palpably real to us. Somehow, within the mysteries of the music, Mozart has fashioned a series of superb portraits: the Countess, Count Almaviva's wronged wife who, in most other hands, would have been a stock character but is here portrayed as a contradictory, pathetic, honest person; Susanna, the cool-headed chamber maid who often controls the proceedings of the opera; Cherubino, the page just entering the confusing and delicious world of adolescence; the Count himself, the perfect portrait of a man used to power and its exercise, who is constantly frustrated by the circumstances around him. The music in *Figaro* is stirring and gorgeous, but it is the lasting portraits of its characters that make the opera a masterpiece.

The plot of *Figaro* is simple. Count Almaviva, an "enlightened" nobleman of the seventeenth century, has just abolished the feudal "*droit de seigneur*" which allowed him the wedding night pleasures of any of his female servants. However, having abolished his legal entitlement to these pleasures, he has decided he wishes to enjoy them anyway, with his wife's chamber maid, Susanna, who is to be married to his valet, Figaro. The opera is concerned with his attempts to get Susanna into bed with him and Figaro's eventually successful attempts to prevent him from doing so. As in most Mozart operas, sexual tension is never very far from the surface. In this case, the relationship of sex and power runs through the opera like a leitmotif. No wonder Figaro's original audiences could not simply be charmed by its musical beauties; beneath the charm, they were being confronted with a disturbing spectacle.

The opera opens on a scene of pure domesticity: the Count has given Figaro and Susanna a bed as a wedding present, and Figaro is measuring the spot in their new apartment where it will be set up. Susanna is admiring a hat which she has just made for herself. As is often the case in this opera, characters are revealed not in stand-alone solos, but in combination with others. The opera is full of duets, trios, quartets and quintets. In essence, this opening scene is a trio, with the orchestra taking the third part. Figaro's measuring and Susanna's primping are held together by a cheery, melodic and graceful accompaniment. Susanna asks Figaro what he is measuring, and he tells her that this room, right outside the Count's apartments, is to be theirs. In a charming duet, Susanna suggests that this is something less than a fine idea, reminding Figaro that the proximity of the Count to him as his valet has a reverse side: the proximity of the Count to her when Figaro is away.

These two opening numbers, both less than three minutes long, are a perfect introduction to the characters of Figaro and Susanna. When you listen to them, notice how carefully Mozart has chosen the music he has written for each character. It is Susanna who understands most clearly the currents and undercurrents in the castle; Figaro is a little naïve about them. However, once he understands what is going on, Figaro is the one who is moved to action. When Susanna tells him that Don Basilio, her singing teacher, presses the Count's suit to her every afternoon, Figaro throws down the gauntlet to the Count in his famous cavatina, or "little song" "Se vuol ballare": "Bravo, signor padrone!" Figaro exclaims. "Now I begin to understand the mystery, to see plainly your entire project." But, "non sara, non sara (it shall not be, it shall not be)," he says. "Figaro il dice! (Figaro speaks)." Thus is launched one of the most defiant arias in opera. "If you would dance, my pretty Count, I'll play the tune on my little guitar. If you will come to my dancing school, I'll gladly teach you the capriole."

Listen to the music Mozart has created to set these words. He gives Figaro a deliberate speaking style; it is almost as though he were spitting out the words. But just to keep things balanced between light and dark, Mozart introduces pizzicato strings in the orchestra to impersonate Figaro's "guitar." Listen also for Figaro's defiant "si"s. By displacing the "si" note an octave higher every other time it is sung, Mozart forces the singer performing the role to expend a burst of extra energy, which is perfectly consistent with Figaro's state of mind as he sings his challenge.

Mozart also changes the tempo of this aria three times within the course of the two minutes or so in which it is sung. These changes correspond exactly to the mental state we imagine to be Figaro's as he sings. Soft passages alternate with loud, defiant shouts; as Figaro's mind races, so does the music, eventually to settle down in the cold-blooded accents of the opening. These are the techniques that make Mozart the dramatic master that he is; he has joined musical expertise to a psychological acuteness that makes his characters intensely real. "Se vuol ballare" was one of the first completely successful arias that the mature Mozart was to write. In one fell musical swoop, Figaro's character is unmistakably drawn, the basic mood of the opera has been set, the audience has heard a good tune they can remember and an immediate dramatic conflict has been established which will take the rest of the opera to play out.

"Se vuol ballare" can give us some hints as to how we might want to approach all of Mozart's operas. When you listen to a Mozart aria, first listen for the overall mood, for the abrupt changes in tempo or key that might correspond to a change of mood in the text. Listen, as well, for the overall melodic line. Even when there are no abrupt changes in the melody, its shape corresponds to the overall effect that Mozart is trying to create. Finally, don't forget to listen to the orchestral accompaniment. Mozart always has his orchestra performing a sort of running commentary on the opera or playing musical tricks that are worth listening for.

Shortly after Figaro issues his challenge to the Count, Mozart introduces one of his most celestial characters, the youth Cherubino. He sings only two solo arias in the entire opera, both early, both obsessed with his growing awareness of his own and others' sexuality. "Non so più, cosa son" (I no longer know what I am, what I do; now I'm all fire, now all ice, every woman changes my temperature, every woman makes my heart beat faster) is one of Mozart's greatest psychological/musical portraits. You can hear the frantic, rushing, excitable youth in the short, panting phrases Mozart has given him to sing (actually her, the role is always sung by a woman). Even if you had no idea what the words to this aria were, you would probably understand its point through the music alone. Again, Mozart has managed to draw a musical portrait of this character which is detailed and vivid.

Cherubino is an enchanting character musically and an extremely important one dramatically. In the end, it is Cherubino more than Figaro who is set off in opposition to the Count. Cherubino is the youth full of love in its first, most innocent, but often most dangerous manifestations. He is a temptation to every woman in the opera: to Susanna, to Barbarina, the gardener's daughter, and especially to the Countess, with whom he is completely infatuated. The Countess, caught in a loveless marriage, longs for the affection she once received from her husband. Cherubino, for all his innocence and childishness, provides the Countess with the affection she desperately needs; he is thus a delight, a temptation and a bit of a plaything for her all at the same time.

If Cherubino is love and desire in its first, open, almost comical aspects, the Count represents an older, more cynical, more desperate desire. The Count is never desired in this opera (except by the wife he rejects); it is his power, his position that is the source of whatever sexual conquests he makes. In this, he is the direct antithesis of Cherubino, whose charm simply pours out of him. Da Ponte and Mozart understood this antithesis and made the most of it. The Count banishes Cherubino three times during the play — a great deal of the dramatic action is tied up with Cherubino's being discovered in places he is not supposed to be. The Count is constantly alternating between annoyance at this pesky page and outright jealousy of him.

Cherubino and Almaviva have their first encounter in Act 1. Cherubino has come to seek Susanna's aid in convincing the Count to rescind his first banishment orders. In the middle of his pleas, the Count enters; Cherubino hides and overhears the Count pressing his attentions on Susanna. Eventually, in true buffa fashion,

Don Basilio interrupts the Count and Susanna, and the Count also finds a hiding place in Susanna's chamber. A trio of Susanna, Almaviva and Don Basilio shows Mozart using his music here not to illuminate character, but to create dramatic action, an operatic technique Mozart virtually invented. The Count's discovery of Cherubino, his anger and his subsequent consternation when he realizes that Cherubino has overheard his conversation with Susanna are all played out in the music. In this and other action episodes, Mozart uses the Classical techniques of composition that he had perfected in his instrumental music. Just as his concertos and symphonies are full of dozens of contrasting ideas, so too are these action pieces full of a wealth of musical ideas. As the action progresses, the music changes to match a new twist in the plot, or a new combination of characters. Mozart learned in instrumental music how to set up these juxtapositions without seriously disturbing the musical flow of his work; he uses this same technique to advantage in the operas. Listen during these action scenes for the number of changes the music can go through in a very short period. Each change either marks or comments on a change in the drama.

Once the Count discovers Cherubino, he realizes that he cannot simply discipline the young page because of his knowledge of the Count's intentions towards Susanna. On the spur of the moment, he makes Cherubino an officer in his regiment and assigns him to a foreign posting. Act 1 ends with Figaro bidding farewell to Cherubino in the most famous aria from the opera, "Non più andrai" (No more will you, amorous butterfly, flit around the castle night and day). This is simply a great tune, a great comic piece. It is Mozart at his most playful and entertaining. *Figaro* is a comedy, after all, and Mozart wrote a great Act 1 closer to remind us of that. He has matched musical statement to text perfectly, providing an ironic statement on the pleasures and pitfalls of the military life for a thirteen-year-old boy.

"Non più andrai" was the opera's immediate hit and it was so popular that a year later, Mozart used it in *Don Giovanni* to play a musical joke on himself. As Don Giovanni dines, a wind ensemble plays "Non più andrai" as the Don's servant, Leporello, comments, "Now that tune I know only too well."

Even before the opera was staged, "Non più andrai" was recognized as a masterpiece. Here is an account of how the aria was received at the first full rehearsal of *Figaro*, when most of the cast and musicians would have heard the piece for the first time. An Irish singer, Michael O'Kelly, who played Don Basilio in the first production of the opera, provides the account.

I remember at the first rehearsal of the full band, Mozart was on stage with his crimson pelisse and gold-laced cocked hat, giving the time of the music to the orchestra. Figaro's song "Non più andrai, farfallone amoroso," Benucci gave, with the greatest animation and power of voice. I was standing close to Mozart who, sotto voce, was repeating, Bravo! Bravo! Benucci, and when Benucci came to the fine passage, "Cherubino, alla vittoria, alla gloria militar" [the passage that ends the aria] which he gave out with Stentorian lungs, the effect was electricity itself, for the whole of the performers on the stage, and those in the orchestra, as if actuated by one feeling of delight vociferated Bravo! Bravo! Maestro. Viva, viva, grande Mozart. Those in the orchestra I thought would have never ceased applauding, by beating the bows of their violins against the music desks. The little man acknowledged, by repeated obeisances, his thanks for the distinguished mark of enthusiastic applause bestowed upon him.

The first act of *Figaro* sets out the major themes of the opera, establishes its light-hearted character and introduces all its major characters, save one. We know from his correspondence that it was Mozart's idea to wait until Act 2 to introduce the Countess — a stroke of dramatic genius. Throughout the piece, the Countess provides a sort of counterpoint to the sometimes farcical goings-on of the rest of the characters. By delaying her entry until well into the opera, Mozart and da Ponte point up her distinctiveness. Only Figaro seems untouched by the Countess's presence in the end. Susanna is her servant, her loyal confidante, Cherubino is hopelessly in love with her and even the Count cannot escape her stately and majestic presence.

Act 2 begins with Susanna, at the Countess's insistence, recounting the details of her attempted seduction. The Countess then sings the first of two poignant arias which capture perfectly her continuing love for her philandering husband — "Porgi, amor" (Grant, love, that relief to my sorrow, to my sighing. Give me back my treasure). Mozart has captured the complexity of the Countess's emotional state by combining two musical techniques. The aria is full of chromatic turns, especially in the orchestra, often the accompaniment to songs full of tragic emotion. However, the aria is not, as might be expected, in a minor key. Mozart uses the major here to remind us that the Countess has not completely given up hope. In her heart of hearts, she believes her husband will return to her.

Mozart has created for the Countess perhaps his most sympathetic female role and he has given her arias full of divine smoothness and perfection. She always sings slowly, deliberately, in long, full phrases designed to give full rein to her profound emotions. Listen, for example, to the variety of ways in which Mozart sets the line "O mi lascia almen morir" (or at least let me die). In one setting, the melodic line swoops up, as if ascending towards the heavens; in another, it speeds up; in another, the line finishes off a phrase.

Learning to listen to opera means learning to listen for these kinds of musical effects. You don't listen to opera as you do instrumental music, by trying to pick out the form of a piece or by listening for subtle connections in the music. In opera, especially in the arias, you need to be alert to the melodic line, listening for the various clues the composer gives you, so you can figure out the emotional state of the characters.

As the opera proceeds, the characters are developed in two different ways. Susanna and Figaro are developed almost entirely through the action, rather than through the arias they sing. In fact, the only aria that reveals Figaro's state of mind before the fourth act is "Se vuol ballare." Then in the fourth act, he is given another single aria when he suspects Susanna of being unfaithful to him. For the most part, Figaro's character is revealed either in the recitatives, when he explains his various schemes, or in duets, trios and larger ensembles where he interacts with other characters in the opera. The same is true for Susanna. Her only real aria is in Act

4, when she taunts a hidden Figaro with her supposed love for the Count. Otherwise she only acts as a foil to other characters in the opera.

Whether they emerge triumphant in the end or not, Mozart still reserved his most powerful musical portraits for the nobility — the Countess and the Count. We have mentioned the abiding interest audiences have had for Countess Almaviva. Along with "Porgi, amor," a second aria in Act 3 perfectly reveals her troubled emotional state. "Dove sono" (Where are the golden moments of tranquillity and pleasure?) may be the greatest aria in the opera and has become a favorite soprano showpiece. Like "Porgi, amor," Mozart wrote "Dove sono" in a major key, rather than a minor, creating a perfect musical realization of the resignation, sadness, suffering and hope that make up the character of the Countess. It is through her music that the Countess is most fully revealed, not through her words.

After singing this aria, which begins in despair and ends in hope, the Countess sits down, and in an extraordinary scene, dictates to Susanna the letter which Susanna will send to the Count asking for a romantic meeting. This "echo aria," in which Susanna repeats the phrases back to the Countess, adds to the poignancy of "Dove sono" in a manner that only an opera could achieve. Through *Figaro*, Mozart never ceases to find new and amazing musical techniques to delineate character without ever abandoning his basic musical style of elegance and grace.

Though the Count is the "villain" of the piece, he is not a cardboard character. For all his buffoonery, he is realistic and frightening. In his scenes with his wife and with Susanna and Figaro, his power and anger lie just beneath the surface, and sometimes explode. In the third act, after the Count overhears Susanna and Figaro plotting against him, he expresses his outrage in a recitative and aria, "Vedro, mentr'io sospiro" (Shall I live to see a servant of mine happy and enjoying pleasure?). By using a technique not dissimilar to the techniques we saw in the opening of *Eine Kleine Nachtmusik* (combining small phrases, which are different from each other but still linked), Mozart shows the Count going through a variety of emotions, culminating in a desire for revenge. Listen for the tympani with which Mozart announces the Count's resolution — a perfect sonic analogue to the determination of a powerful man.

These characterizations provide *Figaro* with its abiding interest, occasioning heated debates even today among opera lovers about the Countess, or Cherubino. But we must not forget another significant feature of the opera — its dramatic ensembles. In three or four places in the work, Mozart creates a series of scenes, all set to music, which run into each other, providing a whirlwind of dramatic action. Acts 2 and 4 end with such a series of scenes, and there is a partly frightening, partly hilarious scene in Act 2 in the Countess's bedroom involving the Countess, the Count, Cherubino and Susanna. Listen carefully to these scenes; each moment succeeds the next according to a meticulous plan of keys and melodic relationships which Mozart worked out in advance. The overall effect of a series of quite disparate moments is still one of musical unity, thanks to the skill of the composer. *Figaro* is almost as interesting for these scenes as it is for its lifelike character portraits.

In the end, *Figaro* still captures our attention and love because of the sheer ongoing excitement and passion of the work. It teems with beautiful music, complication upon complication in the plot, and one fascinating character after another. It combines comedy and farce, seriousness and frivolity, all presented with an energy — Mozart's musical energy — that is infectious and attractive. Here is Mozart at the peak of his powers as a composer and musical dramatist. Brahms was right; there is a perfection about *Figaro* that has never been surpassed.

The world Mozart and da Ponte chose for their next opera was far removed from the sunny, noonday world of *Figaro*. If that politically charged opera buffa was a surprise to Viennese audiences, *Don Giovanni* was a shock. In fact, *Don Giovanni* was premiered in Prague, not Vienna, and did not have a performance in the Austro-Hungarian capital until months later. *Figaro* had been a greater success in Prague than in Vienna, and it was for the Bohemian city that da Ponte and Mozart prepared their second collaboration.

The story of *Don Giovanni*, or Don Juan, had been around for a hundred and fifty years when da Ponte made his adaptation of it. The dissolute nobleman, seducer, murderer, who is hurled to his fate by supernatural intervention, had been considered a pot-boiler for the theatrical rabble for a century. In Mozart's hands, however, *Don Giovanni* became a dark tale of amorality and revenge, told, unbelievably in a buffa style. In no other opera is the combination of comedy and tragedy more complete or more breathtaking. Fierce emotion and comic buffoonery not only exist side by side, but are often played out simultaneously. Characters whose majesty is more typical of opera seria — like Donna Anna or Donna Elvira — rub shoulders with characters right out of a buffa comedy — like Giovanni's servant, Leporello. We are tossed about a fair bit emotionally in the opera, moving from laughter to pity to disgust quickly and often. On the strictly emotional level, *Don Giovanni* is probably Mozart's greatest achievement.

But in the end, *Don Giovanni* succeeds not primarily because of its plot or the emotional depth of its characters, although, like *Figaro*, both plot and characters have been skilfully outlined. *Don Giovanni* represents an advance on *Figaro*, if such a thing is possible, in that it is the whole atmosphere of the opera that communicates to us, the whole that is greater than the sum of its parts. The opera begins and ends in the key of D minor, and the key of the opera is significant. During his life, Mozart wrote a whole series of works in minor keys which seem to have a special place in his output. There are two symphonies in G minor, one early and one late, that breathe a special sense of sadness and tragedy. There is a quartet in D minor, a quintet in G minor and a piano concerto in D minor, all of which evoke the same somber, reflective atmosphere. *Don Giovanni* stands at the pinnacle of these minor-key creations.

You can hear that minor-key character of the opera right from the beginning of the overture, which begins with two enormous chords: one in D minor, the second in A major, the dominant of D minor. This is followed by a slow introduction to the overture, which is identical to the music of the final major scene of the opera, when Don Giovanni is hurled into hell. This conscious linking of the beginning and end of the opera represented a new technique for Mozart, a desire for unity that was more often found in symphonies or concertos. *Don Giovanni* succeeds partly because of these massive linking devices, which play just at the edge of our consciousness and give the opera an extra dimension of coherence.

Listen in this slow introduction for the atmospheric effects Mozart creates in his minor key. It is two minutes of very eerie music, perfectly setting the scene for the dramatic action to come. Notice especially the scale passages up and down in the strings about halfway through the introduction. These are the most famous scales in classical music. By minutely modifying the notes of the scales as they ascend and descend, Mozart manages to create the most exquisite harmonic tension out of the single most mundane musical effect we have — the unadorned scale. *Don Giovanni* is full of these kinds of atmospheric effects, where the orchestra, more so than in *Figaro*, takes a sizable role in the overall musical scheme.

We saw in *Figaro* the attention Mozart lavished on characterization and the importance of following the development of the characters to fully appreciate the artistry of the opera. There are important characters in *Don Giovanni* as well, but they are fewer, and there are a number of characters who are developed rather lightly in the piece. Giovanni himself is the most imposing character in the opera, a contradictory combination of courage, nobility and depravity. The character of the Don was given its most complete realization by Mozart and da Ponte; it remains titillating and tantalizing to this day.

Don Giovanni dominates the work. The other characters are not as well drawn, with the possible exception of the two female characters who act as protagonists to the Don — the heroic and somewhat cool Donna Anna and the more emotional and tragic Donna Elvira. Giovanni either attempts to seduce or actually seduces Donna Anna as the opera opens (da Ponte leaves the answer purposely ambiguous), then kills her father, who has come to her aid. She pledges revenge on her unknown seducer and follows through on that revenge throughout the opera. Donna Elvira has been loved and abandoned by Giovanni. She has returned to Seville (where the opera is set) to find him, make him repent of his wrongdoing and warn others of the fate that may befall them, as it befell her. Donna Elvira is by far the most interesting of the two women, torn between the love she still feels for Giovanni and her implacable hatred of him.

The other characters in the opera are considerably less interesting. Leporello, the Don's servant, remains something of a stock buffa character for the whole piece, although an important one. Don Ottavio, Donna Anna's betrothed, is something of a stick, perhaps the least interesting character da Ponte and Mozart ever created. The peasant couple, Zerlina and Masetto, are a little better; she because of the attentions Giovanni forces on her, and he, because of his reaction to these attentions. However, the true excitement of *Don Giovanni* as an opera comes less from the delineation of individual characters than from the extraordinary way in which Mozart has combined them all in dramatic scenes. There are certainly many fine arias in *Don Giovanni* — some extremely famous — but the key to the opera, and where you might first direct your attention, lies in the great dramatic scenes. We will look at three to give you an idea of how carefully Mozart composed these ensemble pieces; the very opening of the opera, the finale to Act 1 (there are only two acts in this opera) and the penultimate scene. In all three, Mozart's genius for combination and his ability to create more than one emotional response at the same time are fully exposed.

The first scene of *Don Giovanni* is set at night in the garden of the Commendatore's (the Commandant's) palace — one of many nocturnal scenes in this opera. Although we cannot escape the sensation of doom and foreboding engendered by the introduction to the overture, the overture itself is pretty lively, and Mozart opens the opera proper with comedy. Without ever exactly ending, the overture modulates from D major to a rollicking F major and Leporello's opening aria, "Notte e giorno faticar" (Slaving night and day for one whom nothing pleases). Leporello comically bewails his fate: he gets to pace up and down in the cold while his master enjoys the heat and pleasures inside. The wide leaps of the melody lend a tone of fun and exaggeration to the aria; Leporello is exhibiting the traditional buffa characteristics of the abused servant. For the first, but not the only time in the opera, Mozart has us approach the terrifying from the comic side, letting us feel the macabre humor of a situation before we feel, or as we begin to feel, its more terrible aspects.

Suddenly Leporello hears voices, and the humor of the opening scene gives way instantly to a hysterical and violent confrontation between Donna Anna - the daughter of the Commandant, and her masked assailant (Giovanni, of course). The music quickly modulates to B flat major as Donna Anna screams her curses at Giovanni and he threatens her to be quiet. The atmosphere has become supercharged in seconds, but Mozart is not through. In the midst of this scene, Leporello comments to himself on it: he's seen these scenes before, and he knows he'll see them again. Listen to Leporello's bass line as he provides an ironic counterpoint to the scene being played out before him. Two emotions, two responses are magically combined.

The curses Donna Anna spits out at Giovanni ("Like an avenging Fury I'll pursue you forever") will prove truer than either of them know, but once again, after about only a minute of music, the scene changes character completely as Donna Anna's father, the Commendatore, comes to her aid. You can be sure when Mozart changes character in a scene, he will change key, and the B flat major of the Donna Anna confrontation moves into the minor (G minor at first) with the entrance of the Commendatore. The outbursts of the previous part of the scene give way now to longer notes as the two men prepare to fight. Leporello is still commenting on the action from his hiding place, but his patter has given way to a more fearful line ("If I could only get away somehow").

Giovanni at first refuses to draw his sword against such an aged opponent. But eventually, he is goaded into doing so, and in a chilling threat, confronts the Commendatore: "Misero, attendi, se vuoi morir" (Poor fool! Stay then, if you really wish to die). The threat, of course, is uttered in D minor. Mozart, in the space of three and a half minutes has taken us through three mini-scenes and three keys to return us to D minor for the fight between Don Giovanni

and the Commendatore. Although most listeners will not consciously look for these key changes as they follow the action, they
will subconsciously begin to associate certain keys with certain
moods and characters. The key changes are not accidental. Mozart
is using the principles he employed in his symphonies — creating
large-scale unity through keys and tonalities.

Giovanni and the Commendatore fight (in D minor), and the
Commendatore falls, mortally wounded. The music then magically
transforms itself into C minor and an andante tempo as the Commendatore dies and Giovanni and Leporello comment on his death.
One is tempted to make fun of opera scenes where people in their
death throes manage to sing out an aria or two, but I defy anyone
to make fun of this tender, affecting moment in *Don Giovanni*.
Leporello, still commenting on the action from behind the scenes,
has turned his patter song into prayer; Giovanni stops a moment
to think about death, a death that might have been his own. The
scene ends as Mozart has the orchestra sound a musical version of
the Commendatore's life ebbing away. In five minutes of music, the
plot, mood and character of the opera have been completely set.

Giovanni's remorse at the killing of the Commendatore is not
quite enough to prevent him from attempting a second seduction
a few minutes later. He sees Donna Elvira, does not know immediately who she is and attempts to console her in her obvious
distress. Only then does he realize that he is the cause of her distress,
and he beats a hasty retreat, leaving Leporello to "console" Donna
Elvira with the famous catalogue aria, in which he reads the list he
keeps of the Don's conquests. But Elvira is not so easily dealt with.
She vows to pursue Giovanni until she has been avenged, as Donna
Anna has similarly sworn earlier in the opera and as the Commendatore has sworn to do from beyond the grave.

The third scene of the opera introduces the third potential
partner for Don Giovanni in the peasant girl, Zerlina. Mozart and
da Ponte will play off these three women and the different worlds
they represent throughout the opera — the high-toned seriousness
of Donna Anna, the emotional vengefulness of Donna Elvira and
the innocence of Zerlina and her groom-to-be, Masetto. Giovanni
actually comes upon Zerlina as she and Masetto are preparing to

celebrate their wedding. In no time, he has sent Masetto off to his castle with Leporello and is preparing to make love to Zerlina. His "Là, ci darem la mano" is one of the smoothest seduction arias in opera — mild, insistent, captivating. It is probably the best-known aria from the opera. At one and the same time, it provides a beautiful tune and a faithful portrait of the practiced seducer.

Eventually, the Don's schemes start to come apart. Donna Elvira intervenes to save Zerlina's honor; Donna Anna and Don Ottavio come to realize that Don Giovanni is the man they are looking for, Masetto is determined to win back his bride, and Donna Elvira, Donna Anna and Don Ottavio close ranks to get their revenge.

The action of the opera fits a pattern established halfway through Act 1. On the one hand, the forces opposing Don Giovanni circle closer and closer around him. As the tension mounts, Giovanni himself becomes bolder and bolder, cooler and cooler. His innate courage, even in the midst of his depravity, is compelling. Never does he renounce his ways; never does he repent. He is what he is and will remain that until the opera's end. In this he is heroic in an odd way, staking out a path and holding to it, no matter what befalls him. The enduring fascination with Giovanni as a character is this contradiction between his baseness and his heroism.

The first real clash of all these forces comes in the finale to Act 1, at a ball that Giovanni is giving, with characteristic boldness and extravagance, at his castle. This finale is one of the greatest operatic scenes Mozart ever wrote and one of his most famous. We saw in the opening scene how Mozart combined different characters and their differing perceptions in a single scene; he takes this technique to extremes in his Act 1 finale.

Finales in Mozart's operas begin and end in the same key, and the key here is C major, a long way from the world of D minor which we associate with the Don in this opera. Somehow, though, the Don's C major cheerfulness is more unsettling than his normal D minor diabolical nature.

The finale begins with a scene between Zerlina and Masetto, plotting to catch the Don in his attempted seductions. Giovanni enters with a chorus of villagers and tells them to prepare the feast he has planned for them. Offstage, we hear a minuet start up, the first of three dances Mozart composed for this scene: three dances which will eventually play simultaneously, but in different keys and different time signatures, to represent the three levels of society that will be present at the party. This minuet, the first we hear, is for the bourgeoisie. Suddenly, the music modulates to D minor with the arrival of three masked figures — Donna Elvira, Donna Anna and Don Ottavio — adding yet another complication to this scene, and introducing a completely different musical element. The three pledge their continued resolve in a passage full of chromatic changes and finish their brief moment just as the music shifts again — this time to F major — and the second minuet of the party begins. To the strains of this famous minuet, Leporello invites the three masked figures to join the festivities. They accept, and in another wonderful trio — introduced by yet another change of key — invoke Heaven's protection in their task of revenge. Each moment of this drama is built on the last by abrupt changes of mood and key. We hear, as much as we see or understand from the dialogue, the dramatic complexity of the scene.

Mozart then moves the musical action to E flat major as Giovanni and Leporello invite their guests to go in and enjoy themselves. Giovanni is everywhere in this finale; if he cannot have his pleasure with Zerlina, he quickly moves on to other potential conquests. His energy in pursuing his own pleasure is boundless and exhausting. Nothing must stop the fulfilment of his carnal desires.

The minuet we heard before begins again, introducing a section where all the characters comment on what they see and hear. On stage, two other orchestras first tune up, then play their own dances — a country dance and a waltz — an incredible moment. Here is Mozart at his most complex, playful and dramatic all at the same time. He has three different dances going, one in the orchestra proper and two on stage, as well as interweaving the thoughts of six characters as they comment on the action unfolding before them. The scene builds to an almost unbearable level of tension and complexity.

Suddenly, Zerlina is heard offstage, screaming for help. All go to break down the door of the adjoining room, only to find Giovanni, sword drawn, accusing Leporello of having attacked the peasant girl. Donna Elvira, Donna Anna and Don Ottavio drop their masks, and in a trio in F major tell Giovanni he can escape them no longer, they have come to avenge themselves on him. In the finale's finale, back in C major as it began, Giovanni just manages to escape the gathering storm.

This finale has lasted about eighteen minutes and we've gone through half a dozen scene changes, but the whole thing hangs together with a kind of symphonic unity, thanks to Mozart's use of keys and tonalities as linking devices. When you listen to it, notice how often the music changes character without losing touch with the whole. This is Mozart at his most skilful.

The finale of Act 1 is one of Mozart's most famous operatic scenes. None, however, are better known than the opera's last scene but one. All the horror, excitement and power of *Don Giovanni* are wrapped up in this extraordinary scene. Its prelude is this: during one of his adventures, Giovanni has taken refuge in a cemetery, where he has seen the statue erected in memory of the Commendatore, the general he killed in the first scene of the opera. Much to Leporello's horror and Giovanni's cool amusement, the statue speaks to them; in a moment of bravado, Giovanni tells Leporello to invite the statue to dinner. By a nod of the head, the statue accepts.

Giovanni, having forgotten about his invitation, sits down for dinner. Wine is poured, the music plays. Distractedly, Donna Elvira enters, begging Giovanni one last time to have pity on her and restore to her the love he once gave her. He is contemptuous of her; she goes to leave and utters a piercing scream. Giovanni sends Leporello to the door; he too screams. The statue is at the door; Leporello begs the Don not to let him in. But the statue makes his way in and the orchestra begins to play the eerie D minor passage we first heard in the overture.

The Commendatore tells Giovanni to repent; his time on this earth is at an end. Giovanni refuses, and is sent to hell when he shakes the statue's hand. Leporello watches the action trembling under the dinner table. This is a scene to listen to several times. Through it all the orchestra never leaves its repeated Ds, establishing its foreboding tonality with insistence. Listen once for the orchestra alone; Mozart uses colors here that are often absent from his other operas. Listen a second time for the chromatic harmony Mozart uses to create tension in both orchestra and voices. Finally, try to follow the actual words and plot of the scene. Its incredible power must have made an enormous impression on its original audiences; the scene still has the ability to move us today. Mozart never attempted musical tone painting of such expressive force again in his life.

Nineteenth-century audiences adored *Don Giovanni*. It was virtually the only Mozart composition that managed to speak to the new Romantic aesthetic. While most of Mozart's other pieces were seen as mere light-hearted elegance, *Don Giovanni* was considered something of an operatic shocker. It was and is intoxicating in its use of music to express horror, revenge and even macabre humor. Its combination of seriousness and frivolity is breathtaking, it is so bold. And the story itself, the heroism of the lonely individual, whether heroism of virtue or of vice, made a powerful impression on a century discovering the primacy of the individual in artistic and political life.

If the nineteenth century adored *Don Giovanni*, it detested *Così fan tutte*, the last opera that da Ponte and Mozart worked on together. *Così* is as light as *Giovanni* is dark. Written a year and a half after *Don Giovanni*, it premiered in the first few weeks of 1790. Soon after its premiere, and for many years afterwards, it was reviled and abused. Da Ponte, it was said, had saddled Mozart with an inferior libretto. Although Mozart had tried his best with the material, the story was too slight, too frivolous, too unbelievable to hold its own. It had none of the exuberance of *Figaro*, none of the power of *Don Giovanni*. In the nineteenth century, completely different libretti were written to match Mozart's music, and the original story was lost. For much of that century, *Così* was performed that way, when it was performed at all. Only in our century were the original libretto and music restored.

The plot of *Così fan tutte* is certainly cast in a different mold than those of *Figaro* and *Don Giovanni*. Supposedly based on a true incident, *Così* concerns the attempts of two soldiers, Guglielmo and

Ferrando, to test the fidelity of their two sweethearts, the sisters Fiordiligi and Dorabella, by posing as two Albanians and pretending to make love to each other's betrothed. In this test, they are egged on by their old friend Don Alfonso, who sets them the wager in the first place, and by the ladies' servant, Despina.

The people who hate Così think the plot absurd and beneath Mozart's notice. The characters seem one-dimensional, their motivations unlikely, the capitulation of the two women too quick and unbelievable, the final resolution contrived. Yet Mozart loved this opera and was proud of it. He invited the one musician whose opinion he most valued, Joseph Haydn, to the dress rehearsal of the work. Can we find a way to approach this piece so we can reconcile the seeming difficulties in the libretto with Mozart's pleasure in the work?

Those who choose to neglect Così do so because they judge it harshly against the standards of naturalistic operas and plots. But Così is clearly a fantasy: the soldiers, Albanians and women are not so much real characters as archetypes for a variety of emotions. Così is a fantasy like Shakespeare's A Midsummer Night's Dream and Ingmar Bergman's Smiles of a Summer Night. Taken out of the "real" world, it becomes a powerful statement on the one theme that engaged Mozart and da Ponte for their entire operatic career: the difference between appearance and reality.

In Così, this theme animates every scene. The two couples in Così seem interchangeable as the opera begins. I defy anyone to remember whether Ferrando is Dorabella's or Fiordiligi's sweetheart. How true their affection can be for each other is left to question. However, as the two soldiers, in ludicrous disguise, woo each other's sweethearts, a strange thing happens. All four of the characters begin to take on real shading and real emotions. Fiordiligi especially leaps out of the shadows and develops into a real personality. The love which the two new couples profess for each other also seems real, even though for the men, it is supposed to be feigned. All of a sudden, the game the men are playing stops being a game.

But just as quickly as the cut-out figures start to turn real, they return to their original shallowness. The ruse is revealed, the couples reunite and everything ends happily. Or does it? We are left with the sinking feeling at the end of the work that both happy couples will be miserable, each looking longingly at the other's partner as their true love.

Seen in this light, as a parable about what is true emotion, *Così* can no longer be called simple-minded, and the libretto that da Ponte gave Mozart, far from being flawed, may be the most sophisticated he ever wrote. Certainly, the care with which the characters pass into this middle area of dawning self-realization is superbly crafted.

As always, it is Mozart's music that expresses the true subtleties of the plot. Look at how he treats his two soldiers. In the opening numbers of the opera, they are carbon copies of each other, finishing each other's sentences, often singing in thirds — that is, singing exactly the same music, but three notes apart. Don Alfonso, with his ironic, challenging bass arias, is a constant musical reminder of their naïveté.

The two women are given the same treatment in their first few scenes. The two of them compare their lovers in a self-satisfied way as they are introduced to us for the first time: "Ah guarda, sorella" (Ah, look, sister). Within a few minutes, their self-satisfied world is shattered as Don Alfonso brings "bad news" to them, based on the plan the three men have concocted with the help of Despina. The two soldiers have been suddenly called away to battle; they must leave immediately. The two men enter on cue, and cry their crocodile tears at leaving.

But then a magical musical moment happens — one of Mozart's most heartbreaking ensembles. As the men leave, the four principals and Don Alfonso sing a quintet ("Di scrivermi ogni giorno"), in which they pledge to write every day and to stay faithful. The two men, of course, know that this departure is a ruse; the women assume it is serious. Don Alfonso can hardly speak for laughing. Yet the music is of unearthly beauty, without a hint of the irony the scene actually contains.

Mozart is telling us something here, perhaps that he finds the women's emotions, even if they are misplaced, more real than those of the men. He reinforces this in a trio immediately following this quintet, sung by the two women and Don Alfonso. They wish the soldiers fair winds as they sail for their destination. Again, the music is superb and graceful, without a hint of irony or mischief. Mozart never wrote two more affecting numbers than this trio and the preceding quintet. They alone make the opera worthwhile. They should also hint to us that *Così* is not quite the silly farce it seems to be on first glance.

The soldiers departed, the plan of deception is ready to be put into action. At first, the two sisters are unmoved, but they quickly find themselves more susceptible to the charms of the two Albanians than they might have wished. We can follow the progress of the change, and of Mozart's skill in suggesting the unintended consequence of this change in three successive arias given to Fiordiligi, by far the opera's most fascinating character. First, there is the aria that she sings at the first attempt at contact, in which she claims to be completely unmoved. "Come scoglio," she sings. "As the rock remains unmoved against the winds and the storm, so this spirit is still strong in its faith and in its love." Mozart has crafted a wonderful combination of a heartfelt statement and parody of just such a statement for this aria. Fiordiligi makes almost absurd vocal leaps in her protestations, which can only suggest the theatrical character of her emotions. At this point, Mozart is saying (strictly through the music) that Fiordiligi is pretending to resist more than she is truly resisting. See if you can hear this element of parody in the aria.

Compare this parody of emotion with Fiordiligi's truly heartfelt aria "Per pietà, ben mio" (Have pity, my love, forgive the error of a loving spirit) in Act 2. Fiordiligi knows she is succumbing to the attentions of Ferrando in disguise. Unlike Dorabella, who is only too happy to lend an ear to the blandishments of her attractive stranger, Fiordiligi suffers for this knowledge. In this extraordinary aria, accompanied by four horns, she begs forgiveness in advance for whatever infidelity she might commit.

Unlike so many of Mozart's numbers in *Così*, this aria is almost eight minutes long, full of the most heartfelt sentiment. Now the leaps that Fiordiligi makes in the music are not theatrical parodies of real emotion, but emotion truly and simply expressed. Those who would consign *Così fan tutte* to a secondary place in Mozart's output cannot have listened too carefully to numbers like this one, or understood the subtle play of emotions that both he and da Ponte crafted in this domestic and somewhat fantastic opera. *Così* is more than meets the eye, but not, one is tempted to say, the ear. Mozart has created some of his most beautiful music for this work. No wonder he was proud of his accomplishments.

Fiordiligi finally loses all resistance to the disguised Ferrando in a remarkable duet, "Fra gli amplessi" in Act 2. She decides to join her Guglielmo in the field to escape the temptation back home, but Ferrando intercepts her and threatens to kill himself if she leaves. She weakens and weakens throughout the scene, and finally gives in, on a sorrowful high A: "Cruel man, you've won." No seduction scene in opera is sadder. From this emotional high point, where true emotion seems to have broken through the fantastic and formalized bounds placed upon it, the opera quickly returns to the cartoon character of the opening. The ruse is uncovered, and the women are "forgiven" by the men. The men themselves don't bother to ask forgiveness for their own behavior. All returns to the placid state of the opening.

But it is difficult to believe that the experiences of the opera will not have left their mark upon the participants, that the introduction of the truer emotions that were forced upon all of them in the seduction scenes will not have a lasting effect. *Così fan tutte* may be one of Mozart's less successful operas, but it is the most subtle and ambiguous work he ever created, speaking to his own lifelong personal struggle with appearance and reality, with understanding the relationship between men and women and with dealing with the ambiguity and cruelty of the world.

It is tempting, and has been tempting for two centuries, to assume that Mozart expressed his true feelings and ideas about life and art in his operas, that it is in these works that his true character is revealed. Frustratingly, this is not the case. As always, we are reduced to the realm of speculation. *Così*, like *Figaro* and *Don Giovanni*, wait for you to experience them, to divine their secrets for yourself. In the end, no one interpretation of any of the works is definitive. The works themselves are so subtle and ambiguous —

like the composer — that everybody hears different things in them. This is their great joy; they are complex and intriguing, as works of art are meant to be. Opera does take a little more time to appreciate than pure instrumental music. In the end, however, its very complexity allows the musician to make an exceedingly profound and complete artistic statement.

For the Europe of the nineteenth and early twentieth centuries, it was the Mozart of the operas who was the best known. The characters that Mozart and da Ponte created in *Figaro, Don Giovanni* and *Così* have become part of the general spirit of the Western world. In a manner that can be compared only to the reaction to Shakespeare's characters, two centuries of critics, audiences, writers, poets and the general public have been fascinated with the Countess and Susanna in *Figaro*, with Don Giovanni, with Fiordiligi in *Così fan tutte*. Mozart's ability to create living, breathing, contradictory characters in his music has won him a revered position in the pantheon of Western dramatic artists.

Yet, the period of Mozart's great operas was a period of increasing personal isolation and poverty in his adopted Vienna. Perhaps, as Count Arco had prophesized, Mozart was no longer popular because he was no longer a novelty. Perhaps *Figaro* had offended the nobility on which Mozart still depended to make a living. Perhaps his strange character began to prey on people's nerves and sensibilities. Perhaps he was the victim of intrigue and gossip against which he was incapable of defending himself. For whatever reason, the great success of the early years in Vienna dwindled rapidly as the 1780s progressed, and by the end of the decade Mozart and his music had begun to change. A new man and a new artist were beginning to emerge.

CHAPTER EIGHT

◆

Decline and Fall

IN THE SUMMER of 1788, Mozart wrote, in one phenomenal creative burst, his last three Symphonies. The E flat major symphony, no. 39, was completed on June 26th; the 40th in G minor, one of his most famous, on July 25th; the 41st, the *Jupiter*, on August 10th. We will never know what mysterious force compelled Mozart to write these three masterpieces in almost demonic haste. His last symphony had been composed a full eighteen months earlier, and altogether, he had written only four symphonies in the six years he had been in Vienna. Then he composed three in six weeks. As far as we can tell, these three works were written for no occasion, on no commission. Almost unique among Mozart's output, they seem to have been written strictly from the heart. History records not a single performance of any of the three symphonies in Mozart's lifetime.

Mozart's situation was increasingly desperate during this summer. The excitement and relative good fortune he had experienced in his first few years in Vienna had long disappeared. Two years earlier, Mozart had reached the peak of his success as a performer and composer. In the spring of 1786, when Mozart was thirty, one of his concerts had 120 subscribers. In the spring of 1788, a planned subscription was canceled; only one subscriber had put his name forward. For seven years, even though he had no imperial position, Mozart had managed to more than make ends meet through his teaching, performing and composing. He moved to larger and larger quarters during this time, he had a child, circumstances were somewhat under control. He had joined the Masonic order in 1784, testament to his growing disillusion with traditional religion, but also a sign of his acceptance into conventional Viennese society. All that was changing now, for good.

The path on which he had set himself was becoming a dark and tortuous one. As a freelance musician, Mozart was about a generation ahead of his time. His quest for greater artistic and personal freedom may have puzzled and offended potential patrons. Perhaps *Figaro* was the last straw for a noble class that had always been suspicious of Mozart's personal declaration of independence from the Archbishop of Salzburg. *Figaro* was not a great hit in Vienna; it is possible that Mozart's decline dated back to the appearance of this work.

Undoubtedly, a combination of factors led to Mozart's increasing isolation and alienation in Vienna. He had never been very interested in looking after the mundane business of making a secure living for himself. When the Viennese public started to tire of him, as Count Arco had prophesied they would, Mozart was as incapable of securing himself a steady position in the Imperial capital as he had been throughout his life. Despite the fact that he had a wife and a series of children (all but two of whom died), he depended solely on the odd commission and occasional pupil. And in his later years, he seemed to be less and less interested in currying favor with the nobility who were still the main source of musical employment in Vienna.

Although Mozart never achieved the full independence of the Romantic artist, using his art to pursue an intensely personal vision, neither could he content himself with merely accommodating the desire of those who commissioned works from him, or whose pleasure and acceptance he needed to cultivate. His artistic impulse led him into new realms. He was constantly strengthening and deepening his musical expression, in the process leaving much of his public behind, a little baffled, a little confused.

It may be hard for us to believe today that Mozart's music became increasingly unpopular in the last years of his life. But his audiences had become accustomed to listening to the vapid musical charms of true society composers, and they heard in him only the complex, the confusing and the difficult. His music was criticized for being too "highly spiced," too difficult to perform, too hard to understand. The tone of the following review, published in 1789, when Mozart's powers were at their height, is typical of the reaction his later work received:

The works of Kozeluch [a contemporary of Mozart completely forgotten today] maintain themselves and find access everywhere, whereas Mozart's works do not in general please quite so much. It is true, too, and his six quartets dedicated to Haydn confirm it once again, that he has a decided leaning towards the difficult and the unusual. But, then, what great and elevated ideas he has too, testifying to a bold spirit.

But there was more to the Mozart decline. Mozart's own personality must have contributed to his fall from grace. When he was performing regularly and successfully, his high spirits and eccentricity probably added to his charm, but as he began to fade from the scene, these same eccentricities would likely have been viewed with some distaste, even disgust. Indeed, by the end of his life, the most extraordinary rumors about the composer had spread throughout Vienna. The three thousand guilden that he owed at his death became thirty thousand guilden; story after story circulated about his sexual depravity, none of which has ever been substantiated. Undoubtedly beset by enemies and rivals, as he had been all his life, Mozart would have been too naïve and trusting to protect himself from their barbs and slanders.

Whatever the factors that came together in the late 1780s, their combination meant one thing: the great promise of Mozart's youth, the superhuman musical skill he possessed and his magnificent artistic achievements were not enough to protect him from a life of poverty and desperation. The greatest musical artist of his generation, perhaps of any generation, sank lower and lower into the depths of oblivion in his adopted city. Pupils became more difficult to find, fewer and fewer people subscribed to his concerts and compositions, appointments were not to be had. In 1788, when the famous Gluck died, Mozart was finally given a court appointment in Gluck's place, but at a paltry 800 guilden annually, a third of what Gluck had received in the same position.

During that summer, the incredible summer of the three last symphonies, Mozart was writing pitiful letters to a friend and fellow Mason, Michael Puchberg, who was a music lover and a wealthy Viennese merchant.

Vienna, 27 June 1788

Most Honourable Brother of the Order, Dearest, Most Beloved Friend!
    I have been expecting to go to town myself one of these days and to be able to thank you in person for the kindness you have shown me. But now I should not even have the courage to appear before you, as I am obliged to tell you frankly that it is impossible for me to pay back so soon the money you have lent me and that I must beg you to be patient with me! I am very much distressed that your circumstances at the moment prevent you from assisting me as much as I could wish, for my position is so serious that I am unavoidably obliged to raise money somehow. But, good God, in whom can I confide? In no one but you, my best friend! If you would only be so kind as to get the money for me through some other channel! I shall willingly pay the interest

and whoever lends it to me will, I believe, have sufficient security in my character and my income. If you, my most worthy brother, do not help me in this predicament, I shall lose my honour and my credit, which of all things I wish to preserve. I rely entirely on your genuine friendship and brotherly love and confidently expect that you will stand by me in word and deed. If my wish is fulfilled, I can breathe freely again, because I shall then be able to put my affairs in order and keep them so. Do come and see me. I am always at home. During the ten days since I came to live here [Mozart had just moved to cheaper quarters in the Vienna suburbs] I have done more work than in two months in my former quarters, and if such black thoughts did not come to me so often, thoughts which I banish by a tremendous effort, things would be even better, for my rooms are pleasant — comfortable — and — cheap. I shall not detain you any longer with my drivel but shall stop talking — and hope.

Ever your grateful servant, true friend and B.O.
W.A. Mozart

Two days after Mozart wrote that letter, his young daughter, Theresia, suddenly died of intestinal cramps. She was six months old. Three days after Theresia's death, Mozart wrote to Puchberg again in haste and desperation:

Vienna, beginning of July, 1788

Dearest friend and B.O.

Owing to great difficulties and complications my affairs have become so involved that it is of the utmost importance to raise some money on these two pawnbroker's tickets. In the name of our friendship, I implore you to do me this favour; but you must do it immediately. Forgive my importunity, but you know my situation. Ah! If you only had done what I asked you! Do it even now — then everything will be as I desire.

Ever your   MOZART

Two hundred years later, it is still acutely painful to read these pathetic letters. It is hard to imagine how one so talented and blessed could have been brought to such a low estate. These begging letters to Puchberg which began in the summer of 1788 continue until Mozart's death, three and a half years later. Tragically, Mozart found himself playing out the dark prophecy his father had held up to his imagination almost ten years earlier in a letter Leopold wrote to Wolfgang as he made his way home from his abortive trip to Paris:

> It now depends solely on your good sense and your way of life whether you die as an ordinary musician, utterly forgotten by the world, or as a famous Kapellmeister, of whom posterity will read, — whether, captured by some woman, you die bedded on straw in an attic full of starving children, or whether, after a Christian life spent in contentment, honour and renown, you leave this world with your family well provided for and your name respected by all.

Mozart's response to his straitened circumstances was as complex and mysterious as we might expect from this complicated man. Nowhere in his music is the increasing tragedy of his life reflected; this period sees the composition of some of his most positive works. And in his day-to-day life, Mozart had not lost his *joie de vivre* and his propensity for a practical joke. This is the period when Mozart was leaping over chairs and miaowing like a cat, performing a mock funeral on the death of his pet starling and writing mock Hindu aphorisms for a costume ball.

His contemporaries became increasingly fed up with his behavior as they became more and more befuddled by it. Only one friend seems to have tried to understand him. His brother-in-law Joseph Lange, Aloysia's husband, remembered this about Mozart in his memoirs of 1808:

> Never was Mozart less recognizably a great man in his conversation and actions, than when he was busied with an important

work. At such times he not only spoke confusedly and discon-nectedly, but occasionally made jests of a nature which one did not expect of him, indeed he even deliberately forgot himself in his behaviour. But he did not appear to be brooding and thinking about anything. Either he intentionally concealed his inner tension behind superficial frivolity, for reasons which could not be fathomed, or he took delight in throwing into sharp contrast the divine ideas of his music and these sudden outbursts of vulgar platitudes, and in giving himself pleasure by seeming to make fun of himself. I can understand that so exalted an artist can, out of a deep veneration for his Art, belittle and as it were expose to ridicule his own personality.

Joseph Lange might have been able to make allowances for Mozart's behavior, but he was in a small minority. As much as Wolfgang deserved and desperately needed emotional and material support during the years following 1786, he received none, and seemed doomed to exasperate those who might have helped him. His relations with his father and sister dried up to a cold shell of their former warmth and passion. Leopold, clearly disgusted with his son's marriage and way of life, could barely speak his name after 1785, when he made his first and last visit to Mozart's household in Vienna. By the time of Leopold's death in 1787, father and son were living in separate worlds. Even his sister Nannerl herself communicated with Wolfgang less and less frequently in Vienna; it was during this period that she seems to have developed the theory that her brother was some sort of *idiot savant*, a musical genius who was incapable of acting other than as a child in all other aspects of his life.

The Mozart character, and the many contradictions inherent in it, will remain an object of speculation for as long as we have a Western musical culture curious about the great talents that have illuminated our artistic and aesthetic landscape. We can never "know" why Wolfgang acted the way he did; almost assuredly, he did not know himself. Mozart's statements about himself are so rare in the letters that we tend to doubt the authenticity of the few that break the pattern. What moved him, what he truly cared about, what he thought important, will forever remain as mysterious to us as to his contemporaries. Mozart gave us only his music; not himself.

Certainly his works give us no clue about their creator. Every single emotion is eventually played out in Mozart's compositions, but not in relation to his own personality. Perhaps he poured into his music all the thoughts he had about life in general, interpreted somehow through the perspective of his experience and individual genius, and spent very little time thinking about himself at all. Nonetheless, in those desperate, difficult years, a new maturity, a new depth of feeling does creep into his music. The Mozart of those years is as powerful as any musician before or since. Although he never strayed from the musical language we have been investigating throughout this book, with its inherent grace and charm, the works of those hard last years took on a new intensity and power. Nowhere is this more evident than in the three symphonies that he composed in that intense summer of 1788.

Of the three symphonies, the first, in E flat major, is perhaps the simplest to understand and appreciate. Stately and majestic, it is composed in a key that Mozart often used for works to be played at Masonic ceremonies. Different keys took on different psychological meanings for composers in the Classical era. Where C major was often used for positive affirmation and D minor for somber reflection, E flat evoked stateliness and an almost religious character.

The remarkable Symphony in G minor, no. 40, the second in this set of three, may be Mozart's most poignant, anxious and nervous work. Using techniques that looked ahead to the nineteenth century, the G minor Symphony may also be Mozart's most "modern" work. Although the lack of connection between his life and his work is generally a constant in Mozart's output, it just may be that this work is an exception, creating in its minor-key sadness a portrait of the personal tragedies, financial woes and "black thoughts" that Mozart mentions in his letter to Puchberg. Emotionally as well as technically, this work looks the nineteenth century right in the eye; even today, it has a unique position in the Mozart canon.

The last symphony in the trilogy, the *Jupiter*, Mozart's last symphony, has yet a different character. Composed in C major, the *Jupiter* inhabits a realm that is clearer and simpler than earlier works in that key, but also infinitely more intense and emotionally riveting. Although the *Jupiter* was written a mere three years after the *Elvira Madigan* Piano Concerto, the depth of the symphony is far beyond anything in the earlier work. The contrast between the two, the one written during one of Mozart's happier periods, the other a product of an increasingly difficult time in his life, gives us the most compelling portrait of the emotional and musical maturity that came to Mozart in his last years in Vienna.

So let us complete our examination of Mozart's instrumental music by taking a look at his 41st Symphony, K. 551, the *Jupiter*. This powerful work is in four movements, with the standard symphonic minuet and trio movement added between the slow second movement and the lively finale. The form of the first movement is basically the same as that of the *Elvira Madigan* Concerto and of most first movements that Mozart composed during the last decade of his life — sonata-allegro form.

Don't be alarmed that we will be investigating all four movements of this symphony. As we shall see, as Mozart matured as a composer, the unity of the movements in his pieces became more and more important to him. If we want to be true to the *Jupiter*, we must look at it all. You have all the equipment you need to do so; and once you have listened to a complete work, there is no musical height you cannot scale.

We shall see and hear in a moment what distinguishes this piece emotionally from just about everything that Mozart composed before it — but musically, the major innovation is the use of counterpoint.

One of the few noblemen who stood by Mozart throughout his difficult years in Vienna was one Baron van Swieten (who would also become a good friend of Beethoven in a later decade). Van Swieten was a true connoisseur of music, who regularly sponsored musical evenings in his home, and Mozart was his most honored guest night after night. Van Swieten was a great lover of the music of Johann Sebastian Bach, an affection which was exceedingly rare in the Vienna of the late 1780s. Bach the elder was virtually unknown at this time — another forty years would pass before his music became universally known and loved — but Van Swieten introduced Mozart to Bach's *Art of the Fugue* and the *Well-Tempered Clavichord*, with its forty-eight preludes and fugues. Mozart was entranced; he played the Bach fugues over and over again (Constanze was especially fond of them) and attempted to compose a few of his own. Although Mozart never really composed an academic fugue according to the very strict rules laid down in the Baroque era, counterpoint began to show up in more and more of his pieces after his discovery of Bach, and towards the end of his life, this form of composition became a major feature of his music.

Basically, counterpoint is the musical procedure whereby two or more different lines of music play simultaneously in a piece, bouncing off each other point against point, point "counter" point. As we saw in Chapter 6, a round like "Row, Row, Row Your Boat" is the simplest form of counterpoint, where a single line plays against itself over and over again. We saw a rudimentary form of this kind of counterpoint near the beginning of the *Elvira Madigan* Concerto.

Counterpoint is a very sophisticated form of musical expression because it forces an audience to listen to two, three or even four separate musical ideas at the same time. It is therefore an intense, complex form of music. But what it gains in intensity, it often loses in comprehensibility; in the wrong hands, it can be a dry, academic kind of music making.

Since counterpoint had been one of the mainstays of the Baroque era and the Baroque style, when musicians left that world behind, counterpoint was virtually abandoned as a compositional technique. The complex nature of this style of writing took a back seat to simple, direct melodies and clear, articulated phrases. For most of his career, Mozart used contrapuntal procedures sparingly. But near the end of his life, perhaps as part of an unconscious search to express greater meaning and intensity in his work, Mozart was drawn back to counterpoint, on both the small scale and the large scale. Perhaps nowhere is this more apparent than in the *Jupiter* Symphony. In all four movements, but especially in the first and last, musical lines are tripping over each other all the time. The symphony is wonderfully intense because of the perfect balance with which Mozart blends his usual musical language with this technique of a musical era long past. For when Mozart uses contrapuntal procedures, it is not in imitation of the Baroque. Rather, he blends the best of Classical style with the spirit of the more formal era. The most complete integration of the techniques of the two approaches is in the extraordinary finale to the *Jupiter*, the fourth movement; but the impact of the contrapuntal style is evident right at the beginning too.

Counterpoint is a formidable-sounding term, but it is nothing to be alarmed about as a beginning listener — especially when you're listening to the works of Mozart, who always took pains to make sure his pieces were clear and comprehensible. For Mozart, counterpoint allowed him to intensify his music, to make it more dramatic — in other words, to liberate in the music the dramatic possibilities it always had. This increasing intensity is a major feature of Mozart's late style, and one you should be listening for. As he matured as a composer, he used fewer and fewer ideas in his pieces, but used each in a more complex and heartfelt manner. Many consider the *Jupiter* Symphony Mozart's single most powerful orchestral work; let's see if we can hear why it has earned its extraordinary reputation.

A new musical world opens out to us at the very beginning of the work. We've mentioned before how the very first phrase of a piece sets its entire emotional tone. The *Jupiter* is about intensity, terseness and power. Compare the brutal directness of its opening phrase to either the beginning of *Eine Kleine Nachtmusik* or the *Elvira Madigan* Concerto. (See the scores that start on the next page.) Where the emphasis had been on elegance and wit in those earlier works, here we are confronted with raw music.

In just eight bars, Mozart has set both the tonality and the emotional character of the work. We can also see, from the first eight bars of the piece, that balance and symmetry remained an

important part of Mozart's aesthetic approach, even as he entered new emotional realms.

Look carefully at the first four bars. Dynamically, the first two bars of this four-bar phrase are marked "forte" (loud), while the third and fourth bars are marked "piano" (soft). Texturally, a broad unison passage in the first two bars is balanced off by a sparser, lightly accompanied first violin line. Rhythmically, triplets in the first two bars give way to a syncopated figure in the last two. And melodically, whereas the melody is constantly dropping down from a C to the G below in the first two bars, it ascends from a C to the G above in the last two. The balancing act between bars 1 and 2 and bars 3 and 4 encompasses every musical element. And then, to balance off the entire phrase, the whole thing is repeated in bars

5 to 8, a fifth higher. Symmetry, always Mozart's aesthetic ideal, is here taken to a near-perfect level of realization.

Mozart follows this opening idea with an even simpler, more direct, masculine passage of brass and drums, which features a descending thirty-second note theme (in the second violins and violas) (see the score on the next page).

See if you can hear the difference between the Mozart of the *Elvira Madigan* Piano Concerto and this late Mozart. The music here is almost too simple; the harmonies alternate back and forth between tonic and dominant (C major and G major) like the work of a beginning composition student. There is almost no melodic interest at all. Notice, as well, that the music comes to a complete halt in just the twenty-third bar.

The earlier Mozart would never have permitted such an interruption of the melodic flow. But Mozart is in a different world now, a world of simple elements and more complex means of organizing them. Drama has entered his instrumental music in an extremely forceful way with both these new techniques.

After the dramatic pause, Mozart continues with the tonic section of his exposition. We are back to that first idea, for the second time, with a slight variation. While the strings are playing that majestic

opening, the winds have already added a counter-melody to it —
which provides a nice bit of ambiguity early in the work. Where is
our ear supposed to go? Is it to follow the flutes and clarinets or
stay with the strings?

For a brief moment, we are not exactly sure where to listen. Then
Mozart resolves the ambiguity for us — it is the strings that are still
carrying the main theme. This small technical trick is symbolic of
what Mozart will pursue for the entire movement — slight changes
in emphasis to allow him to concentrate a great deal of attention
on just a few musical ideas.

In effect, Mozart in the *Jupiter* Symphony has taken the compositional style of the *Elvira Madigan* Concerto and turned it on its
head. Remember all those little melodic ideas with which Mozart
built up his exposition in the piano concerto? There, the technique
was to create a movement by constantly adding new elements to
one another. In the *Jupiter*, Mozart does the opposite. Very few
musical ideas are used in the first movement — only two or three
in all — but each one is repeated and exploited for all its musical
worth. This constant repetition creates a new musical feeling for
Mozart. The elegance and balance of his earlier style now gives way
to power and intensity.

The tonic section of the exposition of the *Jupiter* is incredibly
short: 56 bars in length. (The comparable section in the *Elvira
Madigan* Concerto was almost twice as long.) It is short because it
has only two musical ideas in it. We begin with the main theme,
follow that theme with a second idea which features the steady
alternation of tonic and dominant harmony, return to the main
theme for a second time (as mentioned above) and then spend the
rest of the exposition playing around with one-half of one musical
idea — the second half of the first theme, the music first exposed
in bars 3 and 4. Listen to the exposition carefully to hear how many
times that little syncopated figure is repeated, each time with
increasing harmonic tension. Simplicity is the key here: not a riot
of different musical ideas cleverly strung together, but one or two
ideas, with every drop of musical meaning wrung out of them.

Listen to this section of the exposition again. It is simple and
direct, and seems to get from point A to point B with concentrated

intensity. That is the essence of the style that Mozart developed in his last years.

In keeping with that efficiency, the "second theme" and the dominant key are already in place by bar 56 of the first movement of the *Jupiter*. But it will be a "second theme" with something of a difference.

Contrasting with the martial character of the tonic section of the exposition, this theme begins with a smooth upward glide of three notes, balanced off by a typical Mozart light-hearted phrase:

Second theme

The roughness and intensity of the opening of the symphony seem to be behind us now as Mozart gently plays around with that "second theme." We seem to be back with the Mozart of a different era in this section, except for one small point that's worth noting. Even though Mozart clearly wanted us to hear this dominant section as a contrast to his opening tonic section, he goes to some pains to connect this second theme with the first one. If you listen carefully to the accompaniment that the lower strings add to the second theme, you will notice that at one point they play a little syncopated figure that may sound somehow familiar (see the score on the next page).

This little figure should sound like something you've heard before, because it is a direct quote from the second half of the first theme, the same bit of music Mozart repeated so insistently at the beginning of the piece. This is no mere trick, as we'll see in a moment, but a calculated compositional technique on Mozart's part.

Second half of First theme

Second half of First theme

The dominant section of the exposition is humming along quite nicely when Mozart does an extraordinary thing. Right in the middle of the section — in the middle of a phrase, actually — he stops the music dead in its tracks, and then begins again with a completely different musical idea which leads almost immediately back to the intensity of the opening of the movement, and a further development of that slim musical idea from bars 3 and 4 of the first theme, now elevated to a major musical idea. Listen for this incredible moment, unparalleled anywhere in Mozart's music. What can we make of this abrupt end to the second theme? It is Mozart at his most epigrammatic. It is as if he's saying to us: "I've given you the idea for the second theme, let's cut through the transition theme and get right to the coda."

Then a little Mozart surprise. (He hasn't entirely changed his artistic spots.) Where we were expecting a little tie-up bow of a coda to lead us to the end of the exposition and the beginning of the development, Mozart gives us instead a lovely, fresh new theme.

It is the most charming music we have heard so far in the movement and comes as a welcome relief from the anxiety and intensity of the music up to now:

Third theme

On the wings of this charming melody and a reprise of the 32nd-note figure from the very opening, Mozart leads us to the end of the exposition in a neat 120 bars.

Mozart never wrote a more tightly packed, economical exposition. Listen to it more than once and see if you can imagine a single note being changed or moved. Not a note has been wasted in this section; everything has a specific place.

The very tightness of the exposition section in the *Jupiter* now forces Mozart to conceive of his development section in an entirely new light. He has presented us with very few musical ideas in the exposition and has already begun to develop them. If he tries to further develop those same ideas without some contrast, his intense language will tip over into excessive repetition, and music that should be powerful will merely be boring. Although he has changed the proportions of the work, the twin gods of unity and variety must still be satisfied.

So how does he solve this artistic problem? To begin with, he balances off his "excessive" use of C major and G major in the exposition by immediately modulating to a new key in the development. Within three bars, we have moved to E flat major. And then a surprise. Rather than using his first or second theme in the development, Mozart starts to play around with that third theme that he introduced late in the exposition. The theme is replayed in its entirety in E flat major, and then a fragment of it is tossed around in true development fashion from E flat major to F minor to G minor, over a dozen times in all, with upper and lower strings in counterpoint with one another, increasing in intensity. Eventually this counterpoint leads to a soft, delicate passage in E major.

By using this third theme to begin his development, Mozart purposely makes it a bit difficult to tell where the exposition ends and the development begins. It is almost as if we were still in the exposition, going through a series of different keys. Perhaps Mozart is doing this to compensate for the shortness of the exposition proper.

But hold on a second; it looks as if the development is going to be as short as the exposition. Listen to what's happening a mere forty bars into the development, just after that delicate E major passage. It seems as if the recapitulation has begun already — at least the first theme is making a recap-type reappearance.

Now admittedly, this theme is in F major rather than C major, which you would expect in the opening bars of the recapitulation, but that is something more easily seen than heard, and even if you could tell it was not in C major, Mozart sometimes begins his recaps in a key other than the tonic. So it seems as though the recapitulation has begun after a short development section.

As you might have guessed, though, this is just another of Mozart's tricks. He is about to pull a little musical rabbit out of a hat. What we have, in effect, is a second development section, one of the most intense Mozart ever composed.

He has been holding back one idea all the way through the piece so far. He has not even attempted to develop the strong, majestic triplet motif that began the piece, which is strange, because the first theme is always the single most important musical idea in the work. Throughout the exposition, it was the second half of the first idea that he played with — never the first half or the whole thing. Now, at the very heart of the movement, he turns his attention to that opening and magically joins it with the 32nd-note idea which first showed up in bar 9 (see the score on the next page).

Listen to this section carefully. It is as though these ideas were meant to be played with each other, but had somehow got separated, and it has taken them the whole length of the piece to be reunited. The few bars in which Mozart combines these ideas are among the most powerful he ever wrote.

Melodically, they are very rich, and harmonically, full of surprises. But the greatest difference between this development section and others that Mozart wrote is its attention to musical drama. Mozart uses the element of surprise in a way that is new for him. He combines ideas and juxtaposes different ideas with a new freedom and boldness. Although still graceful and balanced, elegance has given way to intensity in this movement. In his newfound desire to make every note count and not waste a single phrase, Mozart was pushing music towards its future, a century where power of expression, rather than formal balance, became the artistic ideal.

The true recapitulation of the first movement of the *Jupiter* begins in bar 191. (We were still in the exposition in bar 191 of the *Elvira Madigan* Concerto.) As with the other two sections of the first movement of this symphony, the recap is straightforward, terse and to the point. In many ways, it is a more exact replication of the exposition than many of the recaps Mozart wrote earlier in his career. The section does what it is supposed to do; it reconciles the distinction between tonic and dominant present in the exposition. All three major themes are in the recapitulation; the first in the tonic key of C major, as it was in the exposition, and the second and third in the tonic as well, rather than the dominant key in which they were first heard. Except for a couple of clever changes of harmony to allow these last two themes to be heard in the tonic, and a wonderful new woodwind texture for the beginning of the section, the recapitulation is almost note for note a repetition of the exposition.

Mozart is trying to do two things with this simple recap. First, he is maintaining his straightforward style. Second, he is saving some of the true power of his work for the last movement. We saw earlier that the main focus in many of Mozart's compositions was on the first movement. However, as the dramatic significance of the sonata style began to be felt more and more powerfully by composers like Mozart and Haydn, endings took on a greater significance. Drama is based on a one-way conception of time; everything moves forward, the key question is always, "What happens next?". Musically, this meant that final movements began to take on a greater and greater role in the late 1780s and beyond. Composers began to realize that they had to save some special material for their last movements.

Although the first movement of the *Jupiter* is relatively short, it is an intense musical experience. Mozart knew that, and was very conscious of the need to provide a balance to this intensity in his next two movements, before his remarkable finale. When you listen to any complete work by Mozart, try to conceive of all the movements of the piece as part of one long play. Listening to the proportions of the whole work is an important part of the overall musical experience.

The second movement of the *Jupiter*, marked "andante cantabile," which means "in a slow singing style," seems on first hearing to be yet another of Mozart's sublime slow movements where the soul of the world breathes in sound. This music seems to follow a logic known only to itself as theme and counter-theme, chromatic section after chromatic section guide the ear along paths of luxurious musical phrasing. But if we listen more closely, we will see that the movement is actually written in sonata-allegro form; Mozart has followed one first-movement form with another. Admittedly, the movement travels so far down so many winding paths harmonically that it is difficult to hear the form, and actually, you don't really need to do so, in the explicit way that it is important to hear the form in a true first movement.

Mozart uses sonata-allegro form here because he is after intensity, and this was the most concentrated musical structure he knew. He is not expecting his audience to follow each twist and turn in his formal plan, because the point of slow movements is to relax the ear and the musical intellect. If his listeners somehow sensed that there were connections in the music that increased its comprehensibility and power, Mozart would have been satisfied.

However, the combination of the concentrated form and the beautiful chromatic intensity of the melodies make this one of the most engaging slow movements ever to come from Mozart's imagination. The combination of the aggressive first movement and this seductive second give the *Jupiter* a depth of expression unheard of for Mozart up to this time.

After two movements of serious purpose and musical intensity, Mozart — always with the notion of balance at the back of his mind — gives us a little break in the third-movement minuet and trio. After the lengthy, spun-out phrases of the second movement, the squareness of the minuet is a welcome relief. It is made up of three balanced ideas, which makes for a very symmetrical sixteen-bar opening (see the score on the next page).

Having established the symmetry of that opening phrase, however, Mozart immediately begins to disturb it. Like the minuet in the *Haffner* Serenade, this one is highly chromatic. Whether played in the strings or the winds, it is constantly moving by half-step. As you listen to the opening of the movement, let your ear "wander" within the texture of the music to see if you can hear the numerous ways in which Mozart uses that simple chromatic idea. All of a sudden, Mozart starts to play around with his music as though we were in the middle of a development section. The simple minuet has been infected with the spirit of the symphony as a whole, which makes the expressive most out of the musical least. However, never

for a second does Mozart desert the stately elegance that lies at the heart of all minuets — quite an accomplishment.

Time for another Mozart joke. In a minuet and trio movement, the trio is supposed to provide a contrast to the minuet with music of a completely different character and mood. A different mood we have here — but contrast? Here's Mozart's joke. See if you can hear it:

He starts the trio with a cadence, the musical formulation that always ends a phrase. Because of this, the audience will interpret this little two-note phrase as the end of the minuet. Only when it continues do we realize the joke; this cadence is being used as a musical element in its own right. It is not to be interpreted as an end, but a beginning.

Listen for the moment. All of a sudden it seems as though the winds are closing off the first minuet, but they are actually beginning the trio. It is a little whimsy on Mozart's part; his audience (had there been an audience for the *Jupiter*) would have got the joke. He tells the same joke a second time in the trio when the little cadence returns after a louder contrasting section. This time everyone in the house is fooled; it seems so certain that the little cadence figure ends the previous bit of music rather than beginning the next.

Finally, the minuet returns, and this little movement is complete. Even here, however, Mozart has infused his music with touches of counterpoint and rhythmic and harmonic complexity. No movement in this work is free from the intensity introduced in the first.

We are three movements into this substantial work, and it's time to regroup. Unlike earlier works, Mozart has balanced his first three movements fairly evenly here. The first movement of the *Jupiter* does not overwhelm the others in the way the first movement of the **Elvira Madigan** pushes its fellow movements aside. The *Jupiter*'s second movement is substantial; even the minuet and trio demands musical attention.

However, after three movements of the work, you do wonder what surprises might be in store for you in the last. And Mozart is not going to let you down. The finale of the *Jupiter* Symphony is one of the most complex movements he ever composed. It is a fabulous movement, but not an easy one to completely grasp the first time, the second time or even the third time through. You need some special listening hints for this movement, so you can not only appreciate it on the surface (a level which was always important to Mozart), but also find a way of hearing the extraordinary things going on underneath that surface.

The complexity of the finale comes from its counterpoint: it is awash in contrapuntal effects. There is hardly a bar in which some instrument is not imitating another, either a bar later or in a different key, or providing contrast with a slightly different melody or rhythm. At the same time, the whole thing is in strict sonata-allegro form — the third movement in this symphony written in that form. You can listen to the movement on two quite separate levels — for all the manipulation of thematic material Mozart has going on in the background, or for the festive sonata-allegro patterns he puts in the foreground. The net effect of these two things going on simultaneously is a dizzying whirlwind of musical and emotional intensity.

Let's start with the counterpoint. The entire movement is made up of five musical ideas, so your first step in appreciating the movement is to isolate the five ideas and try to remember them. If you can play the piano, play them for yourself. If not, listen to them one at a time, as they appear in the music.

The first two ideas are easy; they show up right at the beginning of the movement. The first, and always the most important, is that four-note phrase that you hear in the first violins as the movement opens:

Four-note phrase (Idea 1)

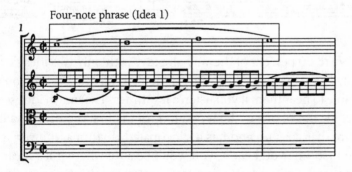

The second idea is the little answering phrase that immediately follows those four notes, also in the first violins. It's the one that begins with the repeated note on the next page.

Idea 3 also shows up very near the opening of the movement. It actually starts the first transition section after the first two ideas have been played twice. Think of it as a scale — that is really what

it is, a descending scale from doh-to-doh, with a characteristic syncopated rhythm right at the beginning.

We're 60 percent of the way already, with only two ideas left to spot. These two are a little more difficult to identify — but you will be able to hear them if you listen a few times. The fourth idea seems to come out of one of the repetitions of the first theme. It is a little figure that goes up and has a syncopated rhythm at the very end. The first time you hear it, you won't be sure whether it's meant to be a theme on its own. Only after it appears again and again do you realize that you are supposed to hear it as an individual element. Here is a clue to help you find it, though: it makes its appearance the fourth time the main theme appears in the movement. The fourth note of the theme is suppressed, and instead, the idea on the next page takes its place.

Finally, the fifth idea Mozart uses for this movement is not just any old idea. It also serves as the official "second theme." It is first heard in the dominant, and has quite a different character than the ideas that went before it. It begins with three longer notes, which go down and then up again. It looks like this:

Before you start listening to the movement, or before you start to listen in earnest, see if you can just pick out the five ideas. Don't worry about the form or about anything else. Just listen for the five bits of music. Now it's not always easy because they are almost always combined with something else — either one of the other ideas, or with some form of the same idea. Maybe you'll want to follow just one idea at a time. Listen through to see how often you can spot the original four-note opening, or the ascending scale figure. Don't be discouraged if you get a bit lost. With experience, everything will begin to become clear for you.

Once you can pick out the ideas, see if you can hear the various ways Mozart has combined them. There are basically only two real ways of writing counterpoint. One is to play two quite different melodies at exactly the same time, having constructed them in advance so that they fit perfectly when played together. Mozart does this a few times in the piece, most notably at the end when he has all five ideas playing simultaneously. The trick in listening to this kind of counterpoint is similar to aural juggling. Somehow, you have to keep both musical lines in your consciousness at the same time.

The other major contrapuntal technique, and the one Mozart uses most often in the *Jupiter* finale is to start a second version of an idea before the first is finished. This is the technique used in "Row, Row, Row Your Boat" and it appears over and over again in this movement.

Just in case I've terrified you into never wanting to listen to the rest of this piece, let me remind you that it is Mozart we're talking about, the composer who never lets the complexity of his music get in the way of its clear appreciation. The *Jupiter* finale is an extremely accessible piece of festive music making. You can appreciate the movement a good deal without having to follow the various techniques that Mozart employed in its composition. However, like any other composition, the more you understand, the greater your enjoyment.

Once you're comfortable with the finale's five musical ideas, you'll be ready to start listening for how Mozart weaves them all together. (Remember that the movement is also in sonata-allegro form.) Let's start with that opening four-note motif. Since this is the main theme of the movement, its various returns will mark the beginnings of new sections. This motif (the idea we've called idea 1) is followed by the little counter-idea we have called idea 2. The four-note theme is then repeated (in bar 9), and Mozart announces the contrapuntal nature of the movement by creating just a little counter-melody in the woodwinds to balance off the four-note motif. The little idea we called idea 3 is then introduced, as though it were a normal transition theme in a normal sonata-allegro movement, and that leads to the next repetition of idea 1. We can be sure we are still happily in the exposition of this movement as long as that first idea keeps coming back regularly.

However, with this third repetition of idea 1, Mozart creates a slightly more elaborate contrapuntal effect, and has that four-note idea treated almost like a Bach fugue. See if you can hear some of the entries of that four-note sequence: it's played by every voice of the strings, one after the other. Starting first in the second violins, it then goes to the first violins, then the violas, then the cellos, then the basses:

What makes this section so interesting is that the instruments don't stop once they've played that four-note theme. They keep going, creating a very complicated texture that can be hard to follow. Your ear just doesn't know what to listen to next. Remember that the most important thing is to listen first for the four-note motif. It is almost always present in one voice or another during this brief section of the work; it is your home base. As for the complexity of the other voices, that's part of the fun of this work.

To end this first contrapuntal section, Mozart has all the strings play the first theme, but this immediately becomes transformed into the bit of music we've identified as idea 4 — that quick ascending figure (see page 193). Mozart plays this bit of music against itself, like a round, alternating between the violins and the basses. He then reintroduces idea 3, the descending figure, and uses it like a round, beginning each entry of the idea before the previous entry is finished. The round-like use of both these motifs leads us quickly to the dominant key, and the introduction of the second theme of the movement.

This is the idea we labeled idea 5. It is in G major, the dominant of C, but Mozart gives it a little less prominence than is normal for a "second theme." Because he is trying to integrate several musical ideas in this movement, rather than having one or two stand out, the second theme is stated only once before it is joined with fragments of ideas 3 and 4, all spun out in a wild contrapuntal combination that increases in complexity as the dominant section of the exposition is played out.

By this point, you may be yearning for the clear simplicity of *Eine Kleine Nachtmusik*. But don't be discouraged; after all, Mozart was not considered one of the world's most sophisticated composers for nothing. This is a movement you should expect to listen to many times before its pattern and complicated elements become clear to you. If you're getting lost, take a break. Stop the music, and then start again, perhaps listening for that opening four-note theme once more. Or, if you like, forget about looking for anything, and just enjoy the music. As is always the case with Mozart, the music can speak to you beautifully and directly, whatever your degree of attention.

The four-note theme that began the piece reappears at the beginning of the development, now in the dominant. Listen for that motif; it is your clue that the development has begun. The theme may be familiar, but the harmonic and emotional ground has shifted since its first appearance at the beginning of the movement. Although this development section is only one minute long, it may be the most intense, expressionistic bit of music Mozart ever wrote. Two ideas — the four-note motif we've labeled idea 1 and the syncopated idea we've labeled idea 3 — literally fight it out for pre-eminence in this tight little section. First, we hear the four-note theme played quietly, matched by the syncopated idea, as though they had originally been created as a unit. But after the second repetition of the four-note theme, the syncopated idea explodes into contrapuntal fury, in a passage that combines four separate statements of the idea, all played by different instruments, all starting at slightly different times. The effect is electric.

This passage is repeated with differing harmonies five times before the initial four-note motif desperately tries to reassert its prominence. This time, Mozart has the syncopated figure brutally interrupt the first idea, not once, not twice, but three times. There is pain in this music, pain and anger; it comes as close to a real emotional outburst as can be found in Mozart's work. But the moment passes quickly, and Mozart reconciles the two ideas of the development, modulating rapidly back to C major (though the development has gone all over the harmonic map) to begin the recapitulation. We see in the development that Mozart does not dress up in this contrapuntal finery merely to show off. Using counterpoint, he can create highly emotional musical moments in ways he had never been able to do before.

The recapitulation of the *Jupiter* finale must serve two purposes. It has to close off this final movement, and it must close off the entire piece. To meet these requirements, Mozart increases the proportions of the recap and adds new combinations of his various motifs, including idea 2, which has been totally ignored until now.

The climax of the entire piece comes just before the end of the movement. Mozart announces his four-note motif one last time, but now slowly and majestically. The breezy little tune that began the movement has undergone an emotional catharsis; it began as a child, it is now an adult. One by one, Mozart piles his five ideas on top of each other, weaving them into a texture of incredible counterpoint. (See excerpt starting on page 200.) Mozart has gathered up all the creative forces he let loose in the movement and finally reconciled them all. In some ways, the entire piece has been building up to this moment.

The *Jupiter* finale — indeed, the whole symphony — is undoubtedly one of the most compelling pieces of music Mozart ever composed. Its emotional pattern is new for him, and directly foreshadows the musical experiments of the next generation of European composers, despite the fact that its texture and language were still those of the eighteenth century. It is not hard to imagine the reaction of Mozart's well-bred Viennese audiences to the *Jupiter* and particularly the finale, had they heard it. Slack-jawed astonishment wouldn't be a bad guess. The complexity of the music, the intensity with which the ideas are presented, the aggressive simplicity of the first movement compared with the overwhelming complexity of the last would likely have left his audience either gasping for air or apoplectic with rage. We have in this music a symbol of Mozart's growing alienation from and disenchantment with his time. There is pain in this symphony, not just in its immediate predecessor, the Symphony no. 40 in G minor, written only a few weeks earlier. The pain here is of an artist capable of great musical feats, capable of writing music that expresses deep emotion — in fact, becoming increasingly incapable of writing any other kind of music, but who is conscious of the futility of his effort, given the conventions of his time and his lowly position within the established orders. Mozart overreaches his intensity to make a point that his audience might understand, but in so doing, alienates them even further.

It is in this very alienation, however, that an artist is being nurtured, the kind of artist we have come to understand — the lonely individual communing with beauty, creating structures of perfect order and passion, unsure of their eventual destination, creating them for their own sake as much as to please any audience.

As always with Mozart, this artistic sensibility is more hinted at than ever made explicit, but the *Jupiter* Symphony is the closest Mozart came to declaring his true artistic colors.

Three years of life were left for this increasingly misunderstood composer, years in which he was content to compose much occasional music, make his living any way he could, and often suppress his growing artistic sensibility. That is, until the extraordinary last year of his life — 1791 — which saw the creation of some of his most important works, including perhaps the most perfect valedictory statement ever created.

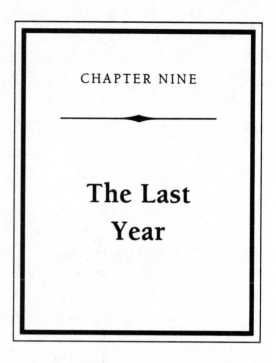

CHAPTER NINE

The Last
Year

IN JANUARY of 1791, Mozart turned thirty-five. Although everyone in Vienna and many throughout Europe knew his name, he
had become a forgotten man in his adopted city. He had no pupils,
hardly performed, and was forced to accept any odd commission
that came his way. He still held his position as court composer for
the Emperor, but the work was just as uninspiring as ever. All he
did was to compose dances and light entertainment music for the
court. This was the way Mozart occupied himself during the month
of his thirty-fifth birthday: six minuets for orchestra, K. 599, were
composed on January 23rd; they were followed during January and
February by a set of German dances, two contradances, two minuets, six Ländler and other dances and minuets. Mozart hated this
work; he dashed off the trifles with distaste and unhappiness.
Mozart loved to compose, but not music with which he could have
no connection.

He made one last attempt to win himself a more favorable position at court. Emperor Joseph II had died in late 1790, and his brother, Leopold, had succeeded him. At his own expense, Mozart had traveled to Frankfurt for the installation of Leopold, hoping to win a court appointment for his pains. Although the concerts Mozart gave in Frankfurt and on the way to and from the German city were a success musically, he returned to Vienna no further ahead than when he had left. His prospects seemed bleak, although he continued to be optimistic about them, or so he pretended to Constanze back home. From Frankfurt, he wrote her this letter in the fall of 1790:

.... I am longing for news of you, of your health, our affairs and so forth. I am firmly resolved to make as much money as I can here and then return to you with great joy. What a glorious life we shall have then! I will work — work so hard — that no unforeseen accidents shall ever reduce us to such desperate straits again.

Mozart's sentiments may have been positive, but his situation was not. Neither pupils nor a court engagement were to come Mozart's way in 1791. In March, however, he received a by now extremely rare commission: but it was not exactly what he had in mind. Some German manufacturer had invented a mechanical organ as a novelty, one of those noisy contraptions that plays a little tune automatically. In this case, the tune was to be by Wolfgang Amadeus Mozart. His *Fantasia for a Mechanical Organ* was written in April; the *Andante for a Small Mechanical Organ* was written in May. It is scarcely believable that the greatest composer of his day was reduced to composing works for an oversized music box, yet that is precisely what happened. In 1791 Mozart was not in a position to turn down commissions of any kind.

Personally, Mozart was very isolated in January of 1791. His father had died three and a half years earlier, relations with his sister had virtually ended, he seems to have had very few friends. The nobility that had subscribed to his concerts five years earlier, had invited him to their homes and had engaged him to teach their children had completely abandoned him. Joseph Haydn had gone to London to seek his fortune the previous December, thus depriving Mozart of his greatest musical colleague and supporter.

The one person to whom Mozart was devoted during this period was his wife, Constanze. There seems to have been genuine affection in the relationship between these two, and even if Constanze was a frivolous woman, she at least provided Mozart with some comfort and human contact, as well as opportunities for fun and merriment — opportunities he increasingly lacked elsewhere. Despite their extremely difficult circumstances, it seems they did not completely lose their love of fun. In the winter of 1790, a Viennese tavern keeper visited them and came upon this scene, which he described years later:

> Mozart and his wife were dancing merrily around the room. When I asked if Mozart was teaching his wife to dance, Mozart laughed and said, "We're only getting warm, it's freezing in here and we can't afford any wood." I hurried away and at once brought them some of my own firewood. Mozart accepted it and promised to pay generously for it when he had some money.

The letters of the last few years of Mozart's life are not nearly as numerous as in other periods, so it is difficult to say how deeply Mozart's financial circumstances affected him. Before 1791, at least, we see glimpses of the old Mozart all the time — the merry prankster, the practical joker, the sensual wit. But then, in the very last year of his life, a change seems to have come over Mozart. His mood seems to have alternated between his usual boisterousness and a profound melancholy. Our first evidence of this is in another letter Wolfgang wrote to Constanze from Frankfurt in the fall of 1790. A new sentiment appears that finds little resonance in anything Mozart had ever written before.

> If people could see into my heart, [he wrote] I should almost feel ashamed. To me everything is cold — cold as ice. Perhaps if you

were with me I might possibly take more pleasure in the kindness of those I meet here. But, as it is, everything seems so empty.

A month later, the same sentiment is revealed at the end of another note to Constanze:

PS While I was writing the last page, tear after tear fell on the page. But I must cheer up — catch! — An astonishing number of kisses are flying about — The deuce! — I see a whole crowd of them! Ha! Ha! . . . I have just caught three. They are delicious.

Although we will never know exactly what Mozart might have been feeling at any given time in his life, who would have blamed the man if he wasn't getting a bit tired and worn out by the fall of 1790 and the winter of 1791? His debts were mounting, his wife was often ill, he may well have understood that the change in his fortunes was not going to be temporary. It is possible that Mozart was finally looking at himself and his situation with a clear, objective eye.

Mozart corresponded with Constanze frequently in the early summer of 1791, as she was in Baden, taking the famed baths there to cure some unknown ailment. She was also pregnant with what was to be Mozart's second surviving child, Franz. Mozart seems to have been extremely troubled that summer. He refers in letter after letter to some financial business that he was trying to settle, but could not. He tells Constanze of his fits of depression, and his need to be with people during those times. Some nights he slept alone in their apartment; often he spent the night at friends'. The most complete expression of this unsettled feeling in Mozart's life comes in a letter he sent Constanze in July:

My one wish now is that my affairs should be settled, so that I can be with you again. You cannot imagine how I have been aching for you all this long while. I can't describe what I have been feeling — a kind of emptiness, which hurts me dreadfully — a kind of longing, which is never satisfied, which never ceases, and which persists, nay rather increases daily. When I think how merry we were together at Baden — like children — and what sad, weary hours I am spending here! Even my work gives me no pleasure, because I am accustomed to stop working now and then and exchange a few words with you. Alas! this pleasure is no longer possible. If I go to the piano and sing something out of my opera, I have to stop at once, for this stirs my emotions too deeply. Basta! The very hour after I finish this business I shall be off and away from here.

The pain in this letter is unlike any Mozart ever admitted to before, if he had ever experienced it before. Yet the opera that Mozart refers to in his letter to Constanze in July, the opera he wrote in the midst of perhaps the darkest period of his life, was *The Magic Flute*, the most perfect expression of all that is good and honest that Mozart was ever to conceive. Whether he intended it that way or not, *The Magic Flute* became Mozart's testament, his summing up of all that he believed important in life and in music.

In it, at the end of his life, he reminds us that simplicity, the childlike simplicity of fantasy and the profound adult simplicity of true morality, must be the goal to which we aspire. At a time when his mundane circumstances pressed on him insistently, he wrote the most timeless and universal work of his career.

Or so some see it. Actually, more controversy swirls around *The Magic Flute* than any of Mozart's operas. Not everyone sees in the *Flute* a perfect representation of the forces of good and evil, simplified and presented in the most appealing of forms. Many think the opera one of Mozart's least important works, complaining of the outright stupidity of the libretto, the improbability of the plot, the hackneyed exploitation of religious symbolism, the offensive treatment of women. Certainly this opera is quite unlike the three great operas he wrote with da Ponte. The subtlety of characterization that lay at the heart of *Figaro, Don Giovanni* and *Così* is absent here; the music is almost childish in its simplicity. The *Flute* is a world away from the sophisticated operas that Mozart had been composing for years.

In fact, according to the conventions of the time, *The Magic Flute* was not quite an opera at all, but a *singspiel*, a popular entertainment with music, that was often targeted to the lower economic classes. The major difference between a *singspiel* and an opera is that there are no recitatives in a *singspiel*. The dialogue between the arias is spoken, not sung. Consequently, the form is a lot easier to understand and accept. The *singspiel* is a forerunner of the contemporary Broadway show, the musical play with dialogue. It has the same feel as a Broadway production — accessible, fun, down to earth.

The Magic Flute had its origin with one Emanuel Schikaneder, actor, impresario, theater owner, Mason. Depending on which source you choose to believe, Schikaneder was either one of the most important men of German theater of the late 1700s, a leading Shakespearean actor and patron of an indigenous theater, or a sleazy charlatan of an impresario, loose in his morals and interested in pleasing none but the simplest of theatrical tastes. Whichever Schikaneder we choose to accept, there is no doubt that the idea of *The Magic Flute* was his, and that he approached Mozart to write the music for the work in the spring of 1791.

Schikaneder did have a company and a theater on what were then the outskirts of Vienna. His Theater auf der Wieden was given over to the production of popular theatrical fantasies, short on plot, but long on stage machines, elaborate costumes and fancy stagecraft. *The Magic Flute* seems to have started out as a normal Schikaneder production, full of dragons and princes, evil queens and sorcerers, as well as fantastical comic characters — in this case, a man dressed as a bird, Papageno the birdcatcher.

But somewhere along the line *The Magic Flute* changed course, or so it seems. Although the first act of the opera is a conventional *singspiel*, the second act takes on a completely different tone, and becomes an opera about enlightenment and truth, borrowing quite heavily from Masonic symbolism and doctrine. Since both Schikaneder and Mozart were Masons, they may have decided to use

The Magic Flute as a vehicle to communicate their Masonic beliefs and symbols.

The resulting script is consequently something of a mishmash, although it has its great defenders, who see in it a subtle blend of fantasy and deep religious significance. Basically, it is two operas rolled into one, with a very different tone and style in Act 2 than in Act 1 (the second act may well have been written by someone other than Schikaneder). However, it is a mistake to damn it for what it is not. Whatever one might think of its libretto, Mozart's musical response to that libretto has become one of the most cherished creations in the history of music.

The story of the opera is as follows: Tamino the prince is being chased by a dragon as the opera opens. He faints as the beast approaches and does not see the three women who appear out of nowhere to slay the beast. They are emissaries of the Queen of the Night, the ruler of the land into which Tamino has strayed. When the three leave to tell the Queen of their discovery of the handsome young prince, onto the scene comes Papageno, the birdcatcher who traps birds for the Queen (the role Schikaneder created for himself). Tamino is amazed by Papageno (he is covered with feathers) and leaps to the conclusion that Papageno has killed the dragon. Papageno takes credit for the demise of the beast until the Three Ladies return. They chide Papageno for lying, and put a padlock on his mouth to prevent him from doing so again. They then show Tamino a portrait of Pamina, the abducted daughter of the Queen of the Night. A wicked sorcerer, Sarastro, has stolen Pamina away to his castle, and the Queen has chosen Tamino to get her back. The Queen herself appears in a blaze of starry light, and tells the prince the whole sad story herself (in one of the most difficult soprano arias ever written). The Three Ladies arm Tamino with a magic flute and Papageno — unlocked — with a set of magic bells, and send them on their way: Tamino full of proud courage, Papageno frightened and complaining.

The scene then changes to Sarastro's fortress, where, true to the Queen's prophesy, Pamina is being cruelly pursued by one of Sarastro's slaves, Monostatos. She has just attempted to escape, and

Monostatos has recaptured her. Just then, Papageno enters: Monostatos runs away, and Papageno (in a nice switch) rescues Pamina.
The scene changes, and three young boys, sent by the Queen, lead
Tamino to Sarastro's castle, which Tamino seeks to enter, to rescue
the abducted Pamina.

Here is where the opera suddenly changes gears. Tamino is led
to a grove surrounded by three temples — the Temple of Wisdom,
the Temple of Reason and the Temple of Nature. In a long scene
with a character identified only as the Speaker, Tamino is informed
that he has got it all wrong. The Queen is the evil one and Sarastro
is the good and wise ruler of the Temples of Wisdom and Reason
who had to abduct Pamina to save her from the evil clutches of her
wicked mother. In one short scene, the entire first third of the opera
is turned on its head.

There has been much speculation for the last two hundred years
as to what occasioned this change. Some feel that the change was
premeditated, that Mozart and Schikaneder planned the sudden
reversal of characterization in the work for a calculated effect. Most,
however, think that the two creators of the *singspiel* decided
hurriedly to switch their plot around and turn the light-hearted
fantasy into a different kind of work — based on Masonic beliefs.
The Magic Flute is full of Masonic rhetoric, symbols and music. It
is also written in the key of E flat major, the one that Mozart often
used for his Masonic compositions. The Masonic number, three, is
heard in three large chords at the very opening of the work, and then
again several times in the body of the work. Sarastro, a corruption of
Zoroaster, an ancient Persian philosopher, is a Masonic-style spiritual
leader, and so on. The second act of *The Magic Flute*, while still
retaining something of the fantastic, childlike quality of the first is
taken up almost entirely with Tamino, Papageno and Pamina's
spiritual trials as they attempt to enter Sarastro's brotherhood. The
light-hearted touch of the first act disappears, true sentiment vies
with absurdly mundane homilies in the libretto, the dramatic action
of the beginning is dissipated. The libretto of *The Magic Flute* is a
problem; it is not even in the same realm as the superbly crafted
drama of *Figaro, Giovanni* or even *Così fan tutte.*

In the end, though, it really doesn't matter. The music that Mozart created for this last opera is so masterful — so simple and childlike, yet at the same time so moving and profound — that the weakness of the libretto only serves to highlight the perfection of the score. *The Magic Flute* was something new for Mozart; his operas before it had been ultrasophisticated forays into the new worlds of musical drama. Here, now, at the end of his life, was a form that seemed to work an intoxicating effect on his compositional powers. Somehow the unreality of the libretto liberated him from attempting to reflect more day-to-day concerns in his music. Whether silly or not, the *Flute* provided Mozart with a needed opportunity, at the end of his short but difficult life, to reflect on those things that meant the most to him. *The Magic Flute* gave him just the right blend of fantasy and significance to allow him to make these musical statements without overstepping the bounds of good taste and decorum which he observed all his musical life.

As well as allowing Mozart to reach back into his own fantasy life, the *Flute* also freed him of the responsibility of trying to amuse an aristocracy from which he had become almost totally alienated. Schikaneder's popular theater was the perfect forum for playing out his love of low humor and playful fun. For once in his career, the man who loved to play practical jokes and amused himself with vulgar humor could indulge his artistic populism without restraint. Whether Mozart came to the project because he was desperately in need of funds or because Schikaneder prevailed upon him, whether he deeply believed in the project or just saw it as another assignment, something in the story and world of *The Magic Flute* spoke to artistic and creative forces deep within him.

Many facets of *The Magic Flute* can be admired, but perhaps the greatest wonder of the music comes from its charming expression of the exaggerated emotions of fantasy — whether they be comic, tragic, heroic or vengeful. The Queen of the Night has but two major arias, yet in both of them Mozart tosses her into the stratospheric range of the soprano voice, thus guaranteeing that her character will be vividly etched in the imagination of the audience. When the Queen of the Night's arias are properly sung (no mean feat), the effect is hair-raising. The Three Ladies, attendant to the

Queen, are also charmingly drawn: three angels of salvation at the beginning of the opera, who turn into three furies by the end. And then there is Papageno, the birdcatcher, the character whose good-humored skepticism about all things around him provides the opera with one of its chief unifying devices. It is Mozart's ability to fashion human archetypes out of these cardboard characters that makes *The Magic Flute* as popular as it is, and as powerful.

What is there to listen for in the music of *The Magic Flute*? Actually, the special character of the opera is established right from the opening notes of the overture, with its three E-flat chords and its slow-moving, somber introduction, which tells us that we are in for something other than a night at the comic opera. However, the slow introduction gives way quickly to a playful little theme which immediately establishes the fantastic nature of the entertainment to follow. If you choose to listen carefully, you will realize that the overture is written in sonata form and uses many of the same contrapuntal techniques we saw in the *Jupiter* Symphony. It is a powerful little musical statement, albeit written in the cause of fun.

Cue Dragon and Tamino, and the opera begins. The Viennese audience would have been delighted with the mechanical beast that would have been the first thing they saw on stage, but this predator's musical accompaniment is equally arresting. The opening scene of *The Magic Flute* has a concentrated dramatic action similar to what we saw in the opening scene of *Don Giovanni*: in both operas a number of dramatic moments are each announced by a key change and a different texture and sound. In the *Flute*, rather than dealing with murder and mayhem, we have dragons and princes and magical ladies. But the technique is the same: Tamino is chased around the stage in C minor; the Three Ladies appear and slay the dragon in a glorious E flat major; then there is a silky passage in A flat major, an ode to the beauty of youth.

Listen for these transitions as you listen to the opera; they are Mozart's way of alerting you to a change in emotional character for a new mini-scene. Each moment in *The Magic Flute* is perfectly drawn in this way. We are not dealing here with the psychological realism we saw in the da Ponte operas. These characters are comic-book figures, but beautifully drawn nonetheless.

Unlike any other opera Mozart composed, *The Magic Flute* is made up of a number of differing musical styles. The opening scene, and others like it, hark back to the technique of musical dramatization that Mozart developed in his opera buffa. The arias of the major characters, especially Tamino, Pamina and the Queen of the Night, look back to opera seria for their motivation and language. But for the character of Papageno, Mozart dips into the repertoire of Viennese music hall comedy. Papageno was Schikaneder's character, and the two collaborators actually have Papageno involved in eight different numbers in the opera, over a third of the piece. In each case, Papageno is given beautiful folk-like melodies to sing, Mozart at his most simple and accessible. With his pipes around his neck, his feathers and his bird-cage, Papageno always provides a welcome contrast to the more serious goings-on in the opera. His first aria, "The bird catcher, that's me," sums up Papageno for us. In square, simple phrases, Mozart gives him a light, catchy melody to sing. Mozart never created a simpler or more directly appealing character.

The next two numbers of *The Magic Flute* provide yet another contrast in musical style. Tamino's major aria "This portrait is enchantingly beautiful" is a romantic piece that has its roots more in the music hall than the grand opera; it is full of changes and exaggerated emotion. More than one disapproving critic has pointed out that it is faintly absurd for Tamino to fall in love with Pamina solely on the basis of a miniature portrait but, then again, this is a fantasy.

Tamino's outpouring of love is matched by one of the most extraordinary arias Mozart ever composed, the first of two incredible arias for the Queen of the Night. As Tamino gazes on Pamina's portrait, the Queen appears out of the heavens and tells Tamino the sad story of Pamina's abduction. Then, in a transition from a tragic G minor to a fearful B flat major, the Queen tells Tamino that he must rescue Pamina. This aria was originally written for another of Constanze Mozart's sisters, Josepha, who must have had a phenomenal range. The piece hits a high F, well above the normal range for all but the most extraordinary soprano voices, and is full of figurative passages that come right out of opera seria. But this is no opera seria, and the Queen's use of this technique lends a faintly malevolent air to the piece. The Queen of the Night is not a carefully drawn psychological portrait in *The Magic Flute*; she is a cartoon figure of anger and revenge, but a wonderfully effective cartoon.

The Three Ladies return to arm Tamino with a magic flute and Papageno with a set of magic bells, and then the scene changes, and we are in Sarastro's castle. True to the Queen's prediction, Pamina is being terrorized by Sarastro's slave, Monostatos. Papageno comes on the scene, and in a nice twist, it is he rather than the prince who rescues the princess. Just as they are about to flee, they sing one of the most popular duets in the opera, "Bei Männern, welche Liebe" (In men who feel love). No other Mozart aria is as full of folk-like simplicity. Pamina and Papageno trade homilies about the proper relationship of men and women and the importance of love to every creature. Was Mozart pulling our leg here, or was he serious? He has placed these sentiments in almost a simple-minded form, suggesting that he was aware of the prosaic nature of the sentiments expressed in Schikaneder's libretto, but the very simplicity of the music invests it with great power. You decide for yourself: when Pamina and Papageno sing, "Man and woman, and woman and man, reach towards the Godhead," is Mozart serious or not?

By this point, as we approach the Act 1 finale, it seems that Mozart has sketched out most of the major characters and themes he will be using for the rest of the opera. However, things will change in the finale, which may be the spot where Schikaneder and Mozart decided to re-orient their plot.

It is worth looking at this finale in some detail, because it contains virtually everything we have come to love in *The Magic Flute*: fantasy, humor, seriousness and endearing music. The charm of *The Magic Flute*, and its enduring power, come from just this blend of the fantastical, the spiritual and the spectacular.

The finale begins with a trio of children: the three young boys the Queen of the Night has sent Tamino to lead him to Sarastro's fortress. The "drei Knaben," although children, are the guides to wisdom; they tell Tamino that he must conquer like a man, he must be "constant, patient and discreet." They begin this finale in C major (as it will end), but this time C major is used not to express the magisterial expansiveness that we saw in the *Jupiter* Symphony, but to represent simplicity itself.

Mozart uses all sorts of little musical tricks in this brief number. It is made up of two four-bar phrases that are first heard in the orchestra. At the end of the little aria, they are heard again, but the second phrase is played first, the first second. A small trick, not that important, but enough to remind the careful listener that, despite the folk-like character of this opera, it is still composed by a sophisticated musical mind.

The angelic simplicity of the music for the "drei Knaben" gives way to Tamino's long dialogue with Sarastro's representative, "the Speaker." Mozart offers us a number of subtle musical clues to help underscore the content of this long dialogue, which is that Sarastro is a beneficent ruler, and that it is the Queen of the Night who is the evil one. When Tamino knocks on the door of the Temple for entrance, a chorus of voices sings "Zurück" (Turn back). Mozart modulates at this moment from Tamino's D major to a more "spiritual" B flat major, thus giving us a subtle musical hint that Sarastro will not be exactly what we have so far been led to expect.

Eventually, in a long passage in A flat major, Tamino is led to understand the true story and to believe that Pamina is still alive. Back in C major (these key changes are carefully planned by Mozart for an overall sense of dramatic and musical unity), Tamino first plays on his flute, then sings an aria of thanks for Pamina's apparent safety. The seriousness of the dialogue with the Speaker is abandoned and pure fantasy returns. As Tamino plays the magic flute, the beasts of the forest appear, charmed by the music. And, as if by magic, Tamino hears Papageno's little panpipes; the magic flute has brought Papageno (and Pamina, although Tamino is unaware of this) to him.

The scene changes, and we see Papageno and Pamina fleeing from Sarastro's palace when they hear Tamino's flute. Now Tamino is offstage and Papageno on, as they trade phrases on their respective instruments. Their escape is abruptly stopped by Monostatos, who intercepts them and begins to take them back to Sarastro. Papageno pulls out the magic bells the Three Ladies have given him. "Nothing ventured, nothing gained," he says, and begins to play.

What follows is one of the most charming moments in Mozart's output. Papageno plays a simple melody on his bells; Monostatos and his cohorts, who had been ready to capture Pamina and Papageno, are entranced, and they dance around the stage happily. As the slaves cavort around the stage, Papageno and Pamina philosophize on what they have seen: "If every honest man could find bells like that, his enemies would then vanish without trouble. Only the harmony of friendship relieves hardships; Without this sympathy, There is no happiness on earth."

Here is the ambiguity of *The Magic Flute* in a nutshell. Every possible emotion has been captured by Mozart in this brief scene: we are as charmed by it as Monostatos and his cohorts. And the little homily at the end? Bourgeois philosophizing, or deeply felt emotion? Mozart leaves you guessing, as he does throughout the opera. Certainly, in his own life, he had every reason to wish that friendship and harmony would replace hatred and vengeance, whether it was the hatred of musical rivals or the "vengeance" of his father.

The scene changes again, and Sarastro is ushered on stage, attended by a large group of celebratory priests. He is the one character we have yet to meet, and the character on whom the entire interpretation of the opera hangs. If Sarastro turns out to be evil, the Queen is right; if he is good, the Queen is clearly manipulating Tamino. As Sarastro enters, we are back in C major again, this time the C major of majesty and ceremony. Pamina throws herself at his mercy; she was trying to escape because Monostatos was pressing his affections on her. Sarastro is understanding; he tells her to arise and explains why he has abducted her: to deprive her mother from working her evil influence on her daughter. Mozart very quickly paints the picture of Sarastro that will come to dominate the rest of the opera. He sings in slow-moving but deeply felt phrases; he is wise and understanding, a musical portrait of wisdom itself.

Monostatos enters with Tamino, whom he has captured. The two lovers see each other for the first time in a burst of joy. Monostatos is punished for his crimes, and Tamino and Pamina are led to the temple to await their induction into Sarastro's order. The transformation of the opera into a vehicle for Masonic declarations is complete; the fantasy and fun of the opening have been transformed into the spiritual world of Sarastro and his somber priesthood.

The finale of the first act of the opera takes about twenty-five minutes to perform. From the Knaben to the Speaker to the magic bells, to Sarastro's seriousness and the joy of the two lovers, Mozart has mixed an incredible palette of emotions. Listen for the succession as you follow the opera. The skill with which he has achieved all these effects, and the obvious care he took in creating this music, gives the lie to those who believe that Mozart tossed off *The Magic Flute* in a desperate attempt to pay some bills. Although the style is completely different from anything he had written before, even *The Abduction from the Seraglio*, which is the only work even to come close, this is still Mozart at work, the most delicate and painstaking composer in Western musical history.

The second act of *The Magic Flute* contains fewer complexities than Act 1. The entire act is concerned with three fairly straightforward themes: the trials of Papageno and Tamino as they anticipate entering Sarastro's brotherhood; the growing relationship between Pamina and Tamino; and Papageno's attempts to find his Papagena in Sarastro's castle. The mood is generally one of extreme seriousness, even of solemnity, as Mozart paints a musical picture of the purity and profundity of Sarastro's world.

The mood begins with the Act 2 overture, composed by Mozart the night before the first performance of *The Magic Flute*. The boisterousness of Act 1 is gone, replaced by the placid simplicity of Sarastro's court. This atmosphere is intensified with Sarastro's moving ode to his gods, "O Isis und Osiris," which opens the second act. Sarastro has convinced his associates that both Tamino and Pamina should be inducted into the order and should take over command of the order from himself.

The trials of Papageno and Tamino begin with the reappearance of the Three Ladies, now in a different role. They attempt to convince the two that Sarastro has laid a trap for them, and urge them to escape. The temptation fails, and the Three Ladies are consigned to the depths. The gentle charm of the Three Ladies in Act 1 has been replaced with a more insistent tone here. Now they are wheedling and aggravating, rather than calm and charming.

Then the Knaben make a reappearance. They deliver the two men the flute and bells that had been taken from them when they were captured by Monostatos in Act 1. This wonderful little trio, reminding us of the charms of Act 1, was also a big hit in the original production. It was one of only three numbers encored on opening night. Tamino plays his flute, which brings Pamina to his side. Unfortunately, he has been instructed not to speak to her, as part of his initiation into Sarastro's brotherhood, and although she pleads with him, he remains silent. This sets up one of the most spectacular arias in the opera, Pamina's "Ah, I sense it has vanished." This is an aria which has its antecedents in the Countess's "Dove sono" in *Figaro*, and in Donna Elvira's arias in *Don Giovanni*. But nowhere has Mozart captured the grief of unrequited love more powerfully and mysteriously as he has in this number, perhaps the most extraordinary of the opera. Listen for this aria, and expect to listen to it time and time again. The simple accompaniment of strings, the increasingly complex vocal line and harmonic meaning, even the four-bar instrumental denouement at the end of the aria, all make this perhaps the most perfect number in any Mozart opera. Pamina, with this aria, steps out of the fairy tale, and becomes an achingly real person.

The majesty of Pamina's unrequited love is matched by the low comedy of Papageno's unsuccessful search for his Papagena. Late in Act 2, Papageno decides to end it all and hang himself from the nearest tree. The Knaben (of course) intercede at just the right moment and remind Papageno of his magic bells. What follows is yet another magical moment in the opera. Papagena appears, and she and Papageno stammer out each other's names in one of the most charming duets in operatic history. Originally, if legend is to be believed, the duet proceeded quite differently, but at the first rehearsal, Schikaneder called out, "Hey, Mozart. That's no good, the music must express greater astonishment. They must both stare dumbly at each other, then Papageno must begin to stammer: Pa-papapa-pa-pa. . . ." If the story is true, Mozart certainly followed Schikaneder's advice, and the result is completely captivating.

Throughout *The Magic Flute*, the sublime and the ridiculous vie with one another, and it is only at the end of the second act that we see them both in harmony. Tamino and Pamina pass the tests imposed upon them by Sarastro and become the leaders of the priestly order. Purity and goodness are victorious, and a heaven on earth is on the verge of being established. At the same time, the simple and unpretentious Papageno has found his Papagena and they plan to create a whole brood of Papagenos and Papagenas. The lofty and the mundane are joined in the opera's finale, as they exist side by side throughout the opera.

The compulsively positive nature of *The Magic Flute* is one of its most astounding features. Mozart poured into this, his last opera, all his love of fantasy, his concern for people, his good humor and his most profound thoughts on life and music. *The Magic Flute* lies at the heart of all that Mozart believed, as an artist and as a man. That he would clothe some of his most profound musical thoughts in the garb of fantasy and play, mixing the profound and the profane, is consistent with all we know about him: his aloofness mixed with boisterousness, his vulgarity mixed with extreme sensitivity, his love of music that communicates sensual pleasure matched with his need for formal perfection and order.

The Magic Flute has become one of Mozart's most successful compositions, one of his most ambiguous, yet most endearing. Somehow, in the combinations of simple melody, foolish plot and heartfelt sentiment, Mozart struck a chord which resonates powerfully today. In listening to the *Flute*, it is worthwhile to suspend your judgment, at least temporarily, on the potential weaknesses of the dramatic structure. Allow yourself the opportunity to become familiar with the music before you attempt to make sense of the plot and the Masonic-style sentiments. It is very likely that Mozart deeply believed in the philosophy he set to music; this was his attempt to set down for posterity his musical thoughts on what he believed to be the most important questions facing humankind, questions of love and harmony, of justice and wisdom, of peace and contentment. That he needed something like *The Magic Flute* in the summer of 1791 is undeniable, as he was groping for some understanding of his life. The opera may have provided a welcome vehicle, virtually his last, for Mozart's life was drawing to an untimely and tragic end.

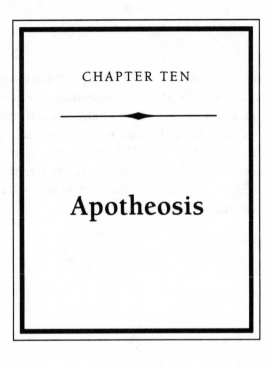

CHAPTER TEN

Apotheosis

T HE MAGIC FLUTE opened at the Theater auf der Wieden on September 30, 1791. It was an immediate hit. Mozart conducted the orchestra on opening night and attended performances several times during the first two weeks of the run. He clearly loved the reception the opera was getting. His excited letters to his wife, still in Baden, testify to his pleasure:

Vienna, 7-8 October, 1791
Friday, half past ten at night

Dearest, Most beloved Little Wife!
I have this moment returned from the opera, which was as full as ever. As usual the duet "Mann und Weib" and Papageno's glockenspiel in Act 1 had to be repeated and also the trio of the boys in Act 2. But what always gives me most pleasure is the

silent approval! You can see how this opera is becoming more and more esteemed. Now for an account of my own doings. Immediately after your departure I played two games of billiards with Herr von Mozart, the fellow who wrote the opera which is running at Schikaneder's theatre; then I sold my nag for fourteen ducats; then I told Joseph to get Primus to fetch me some black coffee, with which I smoked a splendid pipe of tobacco . . .

Mozart is happy again in these letters; the reception of the opera has helped him recapture a little of his former good humor. The next night, he wrote Constanze again after his return from *The Magic Flute*:

Vienna
Saturday night at half past ten

Dearest, Most beloved Little Wife,
I was exceedingly delighted and overjoyed to find your letter on my return from the opera. Although Saturday, as it is post-day, is always a bad night, the opera was performed to a full house and with the usual applause and repetition of numbers . . . The . . . [a name has been deleted] had a box this evening . . . applauded everything most heartily. But he, the know-all, showed himself to be such a thorough Bavarian that I could not remain or I should have had to call him an ass. Unfortunately, I was there just when the second act began, that is, at the solemn scene. He made fun of everything. At first I was patient enough to draw his attention to a few passages. But he laughed at everything. Well, I could stand it no longer. I called him a Papageno and cleared out. But I don't think that the idiot understood my remark. So I went into another box where Flamm and his wife happened to be. There everything was very pleasant and I stayed to the end. But during Papageno's aria with the glockenspiel I went behind the scenes, as I felt a sort of impulse today to play it myself. Well, just for fun, at the point where Schikaneder has a pause, I played an arpeggio. He was startled,

looked behind the wings and saw me. When he had his next pause, I played no arpeggio. This time he stopped and refused to go on. I guessed what he was thinking and again played a chord. He then struck the glockenspiel and said, "Shut up." Whereupon everyone laughed. I am inclined to think that this joke taught many of the audience for the first time that Papageno does not play the instrument himself.

Mozart had less than two months to live when he wrote that exuberant letter. He had traveled a fair bit during the year and had made one last trip to Prague with Constanze to present another new opera, an opera seria called *La Clemenza di Tito*, at the coronation of Leopold II in the Bohemian capital. The last performance of *Tito* coincided with the first of *The Magic Flute*. *Tito* was not a great success, and Mozart may well have fallen ill during the trip. By mid-November, he had taken to his bed.

Controversy rages to this day about Mozart's final illness. In 1791, it was diagnosed as a severe rheumatic fever; today we believe Mozart to have suffered from kidney disease. It is hard to tell for sure, but Mozart does not seem to have been ill for a long time before he died; certainly there is no hint of illness in the letters he wrote to Constanze in early October about the reception of *The Magic Flute*.

Mozart himself created some of the mystery surrounding his own death, for it seems he believed he was being poisoned. This version of events surfaced and resurfaced on a regular basis in the years following his death. Although no one can answer the obvious question as to why anyone would want to poison the poverty-stricken and forgotten composer in the fall of 1791, the story was revived in 1823 when Antonio Salieri, court composer to Joseph II and Mozart's competitor in Vienna throughout the 1780s, confessed to the crime in a lunatic asylum where he had been confined. Although there remains no evidence of any kind to implicate Salieri, the notion of the second-rate, but established, Salieri, taking revenge on the ignored genius, Mozart, has fired imaginations for 150 years, from the opera written by Nicholas Rimsky-Korsakov in the late 1800s to Peter Shaffer's *Amadeus* in the 1970s.

Another story about Mozart's last days seems to have more basis in reality. It concerns his very last composition, the *Requiem*, which lay unfinished at Mozart's death and has taken on mythic significance in the Mozart biography. In the late summer of 1791, Mozart was approached by a mysterious stranger in a gray cloak, who commissioned him to write a Requiem Mass, although he would not identify himself or explain why he had commissioned the work. The stranger reappeared at least once in the fall of 1791 to inquire after the state of the work.

Mozart seems, by several accounts, to have become obsessed with the stranger in gray, and to have believed that the stranger was some sort of emissary demanding that Mozart compose this *Requiem* for himself. Actually, the stranger was the servant of one Count Walsegg, who was in the habit of buying works from famous composers and then passing them off as his own. The Count's wife had recently died, and he wanted a service in her memory with Mozart's music. Some feel that Mozart's desperate attempts to compose the *Requiem*, late at night, when he was not well, hastened his death. Whether or not any of these stories are true, the *Requiem* has taken on a significance due as much to the stories surrounding its creation as to the music itself, although the music does present Mozart in a unique mood.

It is odd that Mozart's last composition would be a piece of sacred music. His last sacred work had been written almost ten years earlier, in 1783, and that Mass in C minor had never been completed. Of course, Mozart had written a great deal of sacred music during the years of his service to the Archbishop of Salzburg, and it was to one of the works of Michael Haydn, Joseph's brother and a fellow Salzburger, that Mozart looked for a model when he began the *Requiem*. Mozart never finished the work; at his death, the first seven of twelve sections had been completed, with sketches made for an additional two sections. A friend and pupil of Mozart, Franz Süssmayr, eventually finished the work for Constanze. Because of its incomplete nature, the total effect of the *Requiem* is somewhat muted. Süssmayr's sections, needless to say, are not in the same league as Mozart's, and there is a fair degree of uncertainty as to exactly where Mozart left off and Süssmayr took over.

Certainly there are many musical beauties in the sections which we know to be by Mozart; much of the music is influenced by the contrapuntal techniques that Mozart was using more and more frequently in his final years. The Dies Irae is a furiously energetic treatment of the text on The Day of Wrath, which follows the more peaceful Requiem Aeternam and highly contrapuntal Kyrie Eleison. A solo trombone announces the Tuba Mirum section, the Trumpet's Mighty Blast. Perhaps the most affecting section of the work is the highly chromatic, soft and painful Lacrymosa. This was the last section that Mozart composed, and a more Romantic portrait cannot be imagined: the dying artist struggling with his last breath to compose the music for the Day of Tears, for Christ and perhaps for himself. It is in fact the sheer Romanticism of the portrait that makes it suspect.

As Mozart was composing the *Requiem, The Magic Flute* was still running. It had opened at the end of September and went on at least until the beginning of November. How many performances Mozart was able to attend we will never know. He was working hard on the *Requiem* and still finding time to compose and conduct a piece to inaugurate a new temple of the "New Crowned Hope" Masonic Lodge. This was on the 18th of November. On the 20th, Mozart took to his bed, desperately ill. He was never to recover. On the afternoon of the 4th of December, a mini-rehearsal of the unfinished *Requiem* was held by Mozart's bedside, with the composer taking the alto part. That evening, Mozart's condition worsened; the doctor was called, but nothing could be done. Just after midnight on the 5th of December, he died. Constanze had to be dragged forcibly from his bedside.

The next day, Mozart was buried in an unmarked grave in the municipal cemetery. Constanze, deep in debt, had arranged the cheapest possible funeral and interment. Tradition has had the weather foul and miserable that day; it was more likely mild and misty. No mourners followed his coffin to the cemetery, although this may have been common practice in Vienna. Whatever the circumstances of the funeral, Mozart's grave was unmarked, and no mourners witnessed the interment to later identify the spot where the remains of one of the world's great geniuses were interred. To this day, his burial plot is unknown. The tragic abandonment of Mozart by the city he served for a decade had found a perfect symbol, the unmarked grave.

With no marked grave and no headstone, Mozart had no epitaph, but posterity has provided him with many to make up the loss. George Bernard Shaw, one of Mozart's great champions, has imagined for us the true story of the disputed funeral and interment:

> There is no shadow of death anywhere in Mozart's music. Even his own funeral was a failure. It was dispersed by a shower of rain; to this day nobody knows where he was buried or whether he was buried at all or not. My own belief is that he was not. Depend on it, they had no sooner put up their umbrellas and bolted for the nearest shelter than he got up, shook off his bones into the common grave of the people, and soared off into universality.

"Soaring into universality": an epitaph that many musicians and music lovers would subscribe to. Mozart's music seems to come closer to embodying a divine presence than any music in the history of the art; his formal clarity, the perfection of his phrases, the care and completeness of his musical works bear the mark of an almost otherworldly mind and spirit.

But there is another epitaph for Mozart, one that strikes at his active quality, the quality that made him a pariah in Vienna for his musical avant-gardism. This epitaph comes from Beethoven, the one musician who may be said to be Mozart's musical heir, who came to Vienna hoping to study with Mozart just a few months after Wolfgang's untimely death. Looking over Mozart's String Quartet in A major, K. 464, one of the Haydn quartets, Beethoven remarked to a pupil of his, Carl Czerny, "That's a work! That's where Mozart said to the world: Behold what I might have done for you if the time were right!"

That's an epitaph. "Behold what I might have done for you if the time were right!" Mozart's time was certainly not right. A freelance artist just before such a thing was possible, he suffered terrible financial difficulties. A composer beginning to write for himself, and for his art, he ran into an uncomprehending wall of patrons expecting light entertainment. A closet revolutionary, who abandoned his own patron and then set his revolt to music in *Figaro,* he never lived to see the full force of revolutionary France destroy the institutions of Church and state that caused him such difficulty. For many today, Beethoven's epitaph rings as true as Shaw's. While respecting Mozart's achievement and recognizing the superb quality of his music, many listeners wish that Mozart had been able to live a little longer, or to have been born in a different decade or century, where his time might have been very right.

It pains us on the one hand to see, even at two centuries' remove, the tragic course of Mozart's life, the suffering his neglected state caused him. And we can only speculate what might have happened to Mozart and to music had he lived a longer life. What would it have meant for Mozart, let us say in 1803, when he would have been forty-seven, to have walked through the streets of Vienna, now liberated by the armies of the French Revolution, and to spot Hieronymus Colloredo coming towards him, now a mere nobleman, as Salzburg had been secularized that year, and the Archbishop's court disbanded. What would he have thought had he heard that year's premiere of Beethoven's *Eroica* Symphony, a work seemingly foreign to his entire aesthetic? Could he have realized what enormous changes were to take place in his society and in music a mere ten years after his death? Would he have understood or accepted any of them?

In the end, as tantalizing as these speculations may be, they are fruitless, and if we wish to find a true epitaph for Mozart, perhaps we should look to his own statements and writings. He did provide himself with perhaps the best epitaph of all. In 1781, he wrote to his father concerning his trials in composing *The Abduction from the Seraglio.* In one of these letters, he comes as close as he ever did to defining his own musical aesthetic. He speaks of an aria he is writing for a character called Osmin, a character not unlike Monostatos in *The Magic Flute.* Osmin, a servant in the court of the Pasha Selim, is enraged that the hero of the opera, Belmonte, might be successful in his attempts to free his beloved, Constanze. Writes Mozart:

> As Osmin's rage gradually increases, there comes the allegro assai, which is in a totally different tempo and in a different key; this is bound to be very effective. For just as a man in such a towering rage oversteps all the bounds of order, moderation and propriety and completely forgets himself, so must the music too forget itself. But since passions, whether violent or not, must never be expressed to the point of exciting disgust, and as music, even in the most terrible situations, must never offend the ear, but must please the listener, or in other words must never cease to be music, so I have not chosen a key remote from F (in which the aria is written) but one related to it.

Music must never cease to please the listener, in other words never cease to be music. Although Mozart was destined to scale artistic heights far beyond those he reached in *The Abduction from the Seraglio,* he never seems to have abandoned that musical credo. Even in his most difficult music, Mozart never forgets the listeners, never forgets us. He is the most generous composer who ever lived. He showered upon us melody after melody, character upon character, beauty upon beauty. Mozart speaks to us, two hundred years after his death, as one human being to another. Born in a specific place and time, and very much a product of that time, socially and musically, Mozart is nevertheless an artist who defines universality. His enduring legacy, as ambiguous as it is, will continue to intrigue us as long as there are ears to hear and minds to ponder. In the end, we look upon Mozart as he looks upon us in the few portraits of him that remain. Cool, detached and sardonic, with a carefully hidden intelligence, his passion overcomes all else in the end.

Nonetheless, once you can understand his musical language, you may find that this enigmatic genius speaks to you as intensely as any musician who ever lived. Mozart has endured for two centuries and will endure many more, because he found a secret in music that allows us to hear his world in sound forever.

APPENDIX ONE

Mozart's
Top Fifty

IN ADDITION to the four instrumental works mentioned earlier — *Eine Kleine Nachtmusik*, the *Haffner* Serenade, the *Elvira Madigan* Piano Concerto, and the *Jupiter* Symphony — the following make up my personal selection of Mozart's Top Fifty works.

SYMPHONIES

Symphony no. 25 in G minor, K. 183

This work sprang from Mozart's imagination in October of 1773, when the composer was seventeen. It was completely unlike any other work Mozart had written up to that time. The first movement is a passionate, dark, stormy journey through tragic emotions almost impossible for a teenager to comprehend. Nonetheless, Mozart here for the first time comes to grips with musical sentiments he will revisit several times in his career — in his next G minor Symphony (K. 550), and his G minor Quintet (K. 516). The first movement is written in a type of sonata-allegro form, but with a shortened development. The second movement provides a heavenly contrast to all the storm and passion of the first. The finale is lighter than the preceding movements; it would take Mozart a decade to realize the power a finale could have. However, the "little" G minor, as this symphony is often called (to distinguish it from its powerful cousin, the 40th Symphony) remains one of Mozart's most astounding early works.

Symphony no. 35 in D major, K. 385 (The Haffner Symphony)

This is the second piece in the Mozart repertoire named after the Haffner family of Salzburg. Mozart had written the *Haffner* Serenade in the summer of 1776; this symphony was written in the summer of 1782. Originally, this piece as well was intended to be cast as a serenade, with several added movements. As it turned out, it marks a transition from Mozart's Salzburg exuberance to his mature Viennese style.

Despite the less than mature style of the *Haffner,* it contains some of Mozart's most assured and polished music. The first movement begins with a fierce unison passage which turns out to be something of a little Mozartean joke; it is quickly followed by a simple, short passage in the strings. The movement is in a form of sonata-allegro organization, but with a shortened development. The second movement, andante, harks back to the spirit of the first *Haffner* Serenade — beautiful ideas tumble after one another as fast as Mozart can imagine them. The andante is the longest movement of the work; Mozart poured into it many of his most polished musical thoughts.

The third movement minuet sounds like it was left over from an earlier Mozart work. It is stiff, formal, elegant to the point of uncomfortable artificiality. In his Salzburg days, Mozart composed many such formal minuets; here one pops up in the beginning of his Vienna years. The trio is equally formal, unlike many later Mozart compositions where the trio provides a definite respite from the cold elegance of the minuet. The final presto is Mozart at his most exuberant and boyish. It caps off a work which is hardly profound, but which does exhibit the composer at complete ease, splashing about in his musical universe, totally absorbed with the musical fun at hand.

Symphony no. 36 in C major, K. 425 (The Linz)

In the fall of 1783, Constanze and Wolfgang were making their way back from Salzburg to Vienna. The two had finally gotten to Salzburg a year after their marriage, and the dreaded meeting between Leopold and Constanze had gone better than expected. They stopped at Linz at the end of October, where Wolfgang immediately made arrangements to give a concert. Since he had no symphony with him to perform, he set about to write one — in less than a week. The *Linz* Symphony is the result.

This is the first of Mozart's mature symphonies, written after the move to Vienna had solidified his musical language. C major was always a heroic key for Mozart, and the *Linz* shares this character. The first movement has a sly opening theme after a slow introduction, but opens up into a broad, expansive, happy ten minutes of music. Mozart's abiding genius for melody finds ample opportunity for expression in the second movement of the symphony; the third movement is a boisterous minuet and trio. The finale sounds as if it came from *The Abduction from the Seraglio*; it has a definite comic opera feel to it. The good burghers of Linz got their money's worth from the four days Mozart stayed in their town in 1783. The *Linz* is one of Mozart's sunniest, most tuneful symphonies.

Symphony no. 38 in D major, K. 504 (The Prague)

Like the *Linz*, the *Prague* Symphony was written when Mozart was traveling, this time to the Bohemian capital in late 1786. Mozart was hard at work on *Don Giovanni* at the time of the visit, and the depth of emotion expressed in the opera is evident in this symphony as well.

The *Prague* shows Mozart at his most profound and moving. From the first bars of the slow introduction, you can sense that a new depth has entered Mozart's musical language. Notice how he changes back and forth from major to minor in this introduction, moving into the minor to heighten the emotion of the moment. The introduction itself lasts over three minutes, almost an overture to the symphony proper (an overture not that dissimilar to the real overture to *Don Giovanni* that Mozart was to write only a few months later). Counterpoint and polyphony abound in the first movement, which has for its main theme a seemingly innocent bit of music. The intensity of the exposition is new for Mozart; he is heading towards the simple and direct style of the *Jupiter* Symphony in this work. The development section is one long moment of the most intense counterpoint; bits and pieces of the exposition are combined in a thrilling and emotional section. The recapitulation presents a fair amount of new material, in keeping with the heightened intensity of the entire movement.

The second-movement andante continues the intensity of the first. What a pity that in Vienna Mozart chose to write so few symphonies before the three he tossed off in 1788. The perfection of expression found in this movement is virtually unrivaled anywhere in his output. The finale (there is no minuet and trio in this symphony) is a rousing romp through several themes and different combinations of instruments, but with a development section that returns to the serious tone of the first movement. It completes one of Mozart's most serious works; an instrumental counterpart to the emotional landscape of *Don Giovanni*.

Symphony no. 39 in E flat major, K. 543

The E flat major Symphony was the first of the trio of symphonies that Mozart wrote in the summer of 1788 — his last three symphonies. It has always stood somewhat in the shadow of the two other, more spectacular works in the trilogy: the 40th Symphony in G minor and the C major *Jupiter*. It is certainly a gentler, more lyrical work.

The opening theme of the first movement is almost pastoral, the kind of open-air writing that Mozart created quite rarely. The form of the first movement is quite conventional; the development especially is brief and emotionally calm, more and more a rarity in the late music of Mozart. The second movement, an andante con moto, is extremely regular in its phrase lengths: check for the uniformity of the four-bar phrases that begin the movement. The movement sounds as though Mozart was deliberately holding back some deeply felt emotions. It is clear and simple, but with a hint of darker forces lying just beneath the surface.

A charming minuet and trio is followed by a tuneful, simple finale. The 39th Symphony sees Mozart in a lighter mood, with music full of divine grace that only he could write.

Symphony no. 40 in G minor, K. 550

Mozart's 40th Symphony is one of the most famous works he ever composed. In this single work, he created perhaps the most concentrated musical language he was ever to use, a language that looks ahead to the work of Beethoven, with its constant thematic repetition. And the minor element in this music may be the most pathetic that Mozart ever employed. The G minor Symphony has been a staple of European music since the early nineteenth century. Unbelievably, it may never have been performed in Mozart's lifetime.

The first movement is based on a simple motif that first made its appearance in Mozart's music years earlier in the first movement of the *Elvira Madigan* Piano Concerto. Remember this little G minor motif in the first movement? In the concerto, it is there to provide a little harmonic spice; here it is the foundation on which an entire passionate movement is based. The 40th uses the same simplicity that Mozart employed in the *Jupiter*; the slightest of musical means are stretched to provide the greatest possible emotional content. The first movement is a model of tautness and musical efficiency.

The slow movement, an andante, continues the tragic character of the symphony, even though it is in a major key, E flat major. Mozart's genius in sustaining a mood over seven or eight minutes (a long time in musical terms) is unparalleled here. With slight shadings and contrast, a uniformity of texture and emotion is expertly crafted in this second movement.

The minuet and trio of the 40th shows Mozart at his chromatic best. The opening minuet is reminiscent of the first minuet in the *Haffner* Serenade, with its slinky chromatic descents in the strings, and wonderful counterpoint between the strings and winds. The trio is a mischievous Mozart confection, where he constantly plays around with the meter. Try to find the downbeat in this trio; Mozart keeps shifting it from beat to beat.

The finale of the 40th is light in texture but demonic in intent. Different generations have heard quite different sentiments in this music. Some have heard only "Grecian lightness and grace," to quote Robert Schumann; others have heard pain and torment in this and all the other movements of the symphony. Listen especially for one moment in this finale: the beginning of the development where Mozart writes a passage that seems astoundingly modern. Glenn Gould, who generally detested Mozart, loved this moment. It was, as he said, Mozart reaching out his hand to touch the spirit of the twentieth century.

Mozart's Mona Lisa, the 40th Symphony will always remain a mystery. In it, perhaps more than in any other work, he combines the elegant and the tragic in a mixture that is uniquely his.

STRING QUARTETS

Our main focus in this book has been on Mozart's orchestral music. But Mozart excelled in writing chamber music as well. His string quartets, string quintets and other pieces written for various combinations of instruments have been in the standard repertoire for generations.

Chamber music has to be listened to slightly differently than orchestral music. Generally there are only four or five instruments playing in a chamber work, and each instrument is extremely important. Train yourself to listen carefully for each part; all contribute to the overall impact of the music. Because of the tight balance of most chamber music, it takes a little more concentration to appreciate than orchestral music. You really have to focus on each line as well as on the overall effect the music is creating.

Chamber music is intimate music; often composers reserved for their chamber works their most heartfelt expression, preferring the small forces and deep concentration of this genre to the grand statement an orchestra can make. However, although the texture of chamber music differs from that of orchestral or vocal music, the style that Mozart uses for his chamber pieces is identical to that of his other works. In fact, it was in his string quartets that his mature instrumental style first emerged.

String Quartet in G major, K. 387

Between 1782 and 1785, Mozart wrote six string quartets, which he eventually published and dedicated to Joseph Haydn. These "Haydn Quartets," as they have come to be known, are extremely important in Mozart's development as a composer. Mozart worked hard at them, studying Haydn's quartets as he went and assimilating the new dramatic language that Haydn first used in his chamber works. In some ways, these quartets mark the beginning of Mozart's mature style, the style we talked about in Chapters 3 and 6.

The first of these was the Quartet in G major, finished on the last day of 1782. The freshness of this quartet announces the beginning of a new musical world for Mozart. The first movement is one of the first fully formed sonata-allegro movements he was to write; it adds to the two exposition themes a relatively long "third" theme before the beginning of the development. The minuet movement of this quartet appears not as the third movement, which is the most common position, but as the second. It is a wonderfully elegant, yet highly chromatic piece of music. Normally Mozart reserved his chromatic writing for moments of great emotional stress; this is one of the few instances where the chromaticism is wedded to lightness of touch. As always in chamber music, listen for the way Mozart throws this thematic material back and forth between his four instruments (two violins, a viola and a cello).

There is great interplay between instruments in all chamber music. The trio of this movement is a dramatic little interlude in a minor key before the sunniness of the opening is restored.

After an elegaic third movement, Mozart launches into what seems to be a fugue for his finale, but it quickly changes character to become the opera buffa kind of finale that Mozart most often wrote for his pieces. Nonetheless, there is a great deal of counterpoint in this short movement, including the first appearance of the four-note theme that was to serve as the basis of the last movement of the *Jupiter*, Mozart's most complex polyphonic movement.

String Quartet in D minor, K. 421

This, the second quartet in the Haydn series, was composed in June 1783. It is the first of Mozart's mature D minor works, which include the Piano Concerto in D minor, K. 466, and *Don Giovanni*. Constanze Mozart claimed that Mozart was composing this work as she went into labor with their first child, and that Wolfgang composed her labor pains into the opening theme of the first movement. Whether or not this story is true, there is an intensity to the first movement that is new to Mozart with this work.

A simple andante is followed by yet another chromatically based minuet and trio (a favorite trick of Mozart's; we first saw it in the *Haffner* Serenade). The finale begins with a beautiful, rocking figure, extremely dance-like in its rhythm. This movement is actually a theme and variations, a form Mozart used occasionally in his last movements (Beethoven used this form considerably more frequently). In a theme and variations, a simple musical idea is played and then repeated over and over again, with slight changes or variations to it with each repetition. The form imposes a great burden on the composer, who has to continually reinvent the same bit of music. By varying the rhythms or the instrumentation (the harmony always stays the same), a master like Mozart can use the same idea half a dozen times without ever repeating himself or boring us.

String Quartet in E flat major, K. 428

Although there are twelve different major and twelve different minor keys in our harmonic system, Mozart returned to the same half dozen tonalities time and time again in his career. Whole musicological theories (and a not unsubstantial number of Ph.D. theses) have been built on attempts to relate the emotional content of various Mozart works that were written in the same key. If D minor is the key Mozart seems to have reserved for his most demonic music, E flat major is his key for assertive, positive music. It is the key of most of his Masonic music, as well as the key for *The Magic Flute*.

However, this third Haydn quartet, also written in the summer of 1783, seems to break the E flat mold. The first movement is strangely disquieting and nervous, full of wild figuration and wide melodic leaps. The same emotional sense invades the second movement, which begins in an eerily chromatic way, and continues for almost ten minutes, perhaps the most harmonically rich movement Mozart was ever to write. Even the third movement is somewhat uncharacteristic of Mozart; the lightness of touch normally associated with these kinds of movements has been replaced here with a heavier hand. Mozart seems to be struggling towards a new kind of expression in this work, a new depth which doesn't quite come off. The finale is similarly nervous and jerky; Mozart is testing new waters with this work. However, even when he is testing the new, Mozart provides music of unforgettable quality, and such is the case in this somewhat strained quartet.

String Quartet in B flat major, K. 458 (The Hunt)

This enchanting work begins with a boisterous, rollicking theme, which gave the quartet its nickname: it sounds like the kind of music that would accompany a hunting expedition. Where the E flat major Quartet is testing new emotional ground, and is fascinating for that reason, Mozart here has gained a new maturity and confidence. Not a note is out of place in its dramatic first movement. Again, Mozart uses a minuet and trio for his second movement: not for the first time, he plays around with the rhythm of the minuet theme, moving the downbeat of the various bars of the phrase. The same assurance in handling the musical material makes the third-movement andante one of Mozart's most dramatic slow movements. About a third of the way through the movement, Mozart composes a moment that seems to come straight out of the Romantic era. A few chromatic changes in an accompaniment figure, and the music sounds like Schumann or Chopin.

The finale to the *Hunt* is one of Mozart's most famous and tuneful; it almost defines the Mozartean finale — high-spirited yet dramatic, engaging but never overly emotional. The last movement caps off one of Mozart's most splendid works. No surprise that it was at a concert where this quartet was played along with K. 464 and K. 465 that Haydn made his famous remark about Wolfgang to Leopold. These chamber works by Mozart show him at the height of his powers just at the time when he was about to turn his attention to the piano concerto.

String Quartet in A major, K. 464

It was of this work that Beethoven was speaking when he said to Carl Czerny, "What a work. It was here that Mozart said to the world, Behold what I might have done for you if the time were right." Beethoven was very much taken with this A major Quartet; he copied out the last movement by hand to better learn its secrets. And it is no surprise that Beethoven discovered in it many of the features that were to predominate in his own style. The A major Quartet is an intense, contrapuntal, serious exercise from beginning to end.

Its first movement is distinguished by an extremely long and complex development section, exactly the same kind of development Beethoven himself was to write. Mozart takes his theme through many harmonic and melodic regions before returning to the simple thematic idea with which he began the piece. In the second-movement menuetto, he strives for a light-heartedness that he never quite achieves; single instruments are constantly set off against the rest of the ensemble, creating a sense of unease that the movement never shakes off. The third-movement andante is a longish, intense theme and variations. The final movement, the one that so captivated Beethoven, is full of contrapuntal and chromatic figures, two giveaways that Mozart is in a serious mood in this movement. Mozart was seldom as abrupt and terse in any work as he was in this quartet.

String Quartet in C major, K. 465 (The Dissonance)

The *Dissonance* Quartet gets its name from the strange, other-worldly, almost ugly slow introduction with which the first movement begins. Whether this is a Mozartean joke, or some attempt to push back the boundaries of traditional harmony, we will never know. For a minute or so, Mozart plunges us into a completely foreign harmonic world, but one from which he emerges with the simplest of themes in that simplest of keys — C major. From this moment on, the first movement takes off into a joyous, upbeat mood. The anxiety of the introduction is long forgotten. One fine theme after another breezes our way. As in the A major Quartet, the development section of the first movement of the *Dissonance* is longer and more exciting than is usual with Mozart. And the main theme is given quite a different treatment at the beginning of the recapitulation, another uncommon twist.

The second movement is full of the interplay between instruments that lies at the heart of the texture of all the Haydn Quartets — it may be their single most striking feature. The movement is made up of a string of beautiful melodic and harmonic moments. The third movement minuet and trio is one of Mozart's wittiest; accents are misplaced all over the place, contrasts are sharply and humorously drawn. The trio is a moving, exciting two minutes or so of music, in sharpest contrast to the outward simplicity of the minuet. The bright finale shows Mozart in full control of his material; an energetic theme is transformed into an emotional roller-coaster of harmonies and thematic ideas until we are safely deposited back at the emotional point where we began the movement. The *Dissonance* Quartet ended the Haydn series; Mozart never wrote as fluid a work, combining light and dark textures so completely and effortlessly.

String Quartet in D major, K. 499 (The Hoffmeister)

Mozart was to write only four more quartets after the Haydn series: a group of three originally intended for the King of Prussia in the late 1780s, and this single quartet, written in mid-1786. Hoffmeister, after whom the quartet was named, was a publisher and one of Mozart's creditors.

In some ways, the *Hoffmeister* Quartet represents something of a retreat for Mozart, if such a thing is possible. Much of the textural complexity and emotional intensity of the Haydn Quartets is missing here. A master is at work, but a master in a more relaxed mood. All is smoothness and transparency in the graceful first movement. The second-movement menuetto sounds like something right out of the nineteenth century; it has the Romantic harmonies of the quartets of Alexander Borodin. The "typical" moving slow movement and brilliant finale close out this often-neglected quartet. By this point in his career Mozart is in such command of his musical language that we expect him to write something more than a masterpiece every time he picks up his pen. But the *Hoffmeister* Quartet is just another masterpiece that a lesser composer would have killed to have written. For Mozart, just another day at the office.

String Quartet in D major, K. 575 (The Prussian)

Mozart's last three quartets were written in 1789 and 1790, originally for the King of Prussia, to coincide with a visit Mozart made to Berlin in early 1789. K. 575, the first *Prussian*, is perhaps the least emotionally wrenching. The first movement of the work shows the same compactness of style that entered Mozart's symphonic writing at about the same time. As with his other instrumental music of this period, every note in this work counts for something. The development of the first movement carries us through many harmonic twists and turns, before the graceful first theme returns. The spirit of power through gracefulness continues through the second movement and the playful menuetto. The finale takes its opening motif from the opening of the first movement, and proceeds in a happy frame of mind. Mozart, in the depths of his Viennese poverty and isolation, breaks through that despair with this uniformly upbeat and outgoing chamber work, one of his most positive statements in any medium.

String Quartet in B flat major, K. 589 (The Second Prussian)

Mozart's last two quartets date from the summer of 1790, when the composer's circumstances were at their worst. Both these quartets show a greater depth than the first *Prussian*, composed a year earlier. There is more contrapuntal play in this work, and greater harmonic intensity. Mozart also travels through more key changes at a greater rate in this work than in K. 575. Although more intense, the musical statements are briefer in this work as well. The opening movement is about two-thirds the length of many other first movements. The second-movement larghetto and third-movement allegretto share this same characteristic: concentrated, to the point, but extremely powerful nonetheless. Mozart has packed into the twenty minutes of this quartet a great deal of musical meaning. The finale is a typical Mozartean gallop: lots of fun and excitement, but plenty of musical sophistication as well. Listen especially for that quick descending line in the first violins as the movement gets under way. Mozart was to return to this idea at the beginning of his last quartet, written only a month later.

String Quartet in F major, K. 590 (The Third Prussian)

Mozart's last string quartet opens with one of his most surprising musical ideas: a unison figure which balances a slow three-note rise with a violent eight-note decline. This is where the elegant Mozart of the early 1780s had come: to an expressiveness more character-istic of Beethoven at his most overwhelming. Though it bears all the marks of Mozart's style, this movement is charged with electric excitement from the first note to the last. The development starts out slyly, almost as a parody of elegant quartet writing, before it takes off into more complex musical directions. The second-move-ment allegretto is also Beethoven-ish in style. It begins with a simple chordal figure, which is developed to a more and more intense pitch within the six minutes of this movement. Beethoven may well have admired the A major Quartet of the Haydn series, but it is this work (which he may or may not have known) that actually anticipated many of his own chamber works.

All claim to elegance leaves the piece during what is often the most elegant movement in any work, its minuet and trio. Listen for the incredible roughness of the cello line in this short movement, its simple, repeated notes. Here Mozart is straining to break the conventional bounds that circumscribed almost all his previous chamber music. This is an extraordinary movement, full of passion and depth. Without any doubt, it is the most expressionistic movement Mozart ever wrote. A lively, contrapuntal finale finishes off this masterpiece among masterpieces in Mozart's quartet output.

Since chamber music is performed less frequently in our modern era of large concert halls and world-famous orchestras, Mozart's chamber output is somewhat neglected. However, the third *Prussian* Quartet is one of Mozart's most significant works in any medium. Never again in any form did he achieve such power, such "Romantic" expression while still remaining true to the style of elegance and balance he cultivated throughout his career.

PIANO CONCERTOS

Mozart was not an innovator in the use of form; by and large, he was content to use the formal plans other composers had created. The one exception to this rule was in his mature piano concertos, perhaps because the available forms were not as well developed as those that could be used in symphonic or chamber works. Joseph Haydn created sophisticated models for other composers in the realm of the symphony or the string quartet, but possibly because he was not a pianist himself, he did not do the same for composers of piano concertos. Mozart was left more or less on his own in adapting the new musical language of well-defined phrases and dramatic formal structures to the piano concerto. The results are perhaps Mozart's greatest orchestral compositions — almost a dozen works, written over several years, that sparkle with charm, wit and musical good humor as well as depth and emotional daring. For many, the Mozart of the piano concertos is the greatest Mozart of all.

Piano Concerto no. 9 in E flat major, K. 371 (The Jeunehomme)

All the Mozart concertos worth including in a list of greatest hits were written in Vienna — apart from this youthful work, composed in Salzburg in 1777, when the composer was twenty-one. The *Jeunehomme* Concerto is like the "Little" G minor Symphony. Out of nowhere, seemingly, comes this extraordinary work, mature beyond its years, that takes the composer from apprenticeship to maturity in a single compositional bound. The *Jeunehomme* is full of unique compositional effects.

Each movement of K. 371 includes some exceptional musical techniques, as though Mozart were experimenting with the whole notion of what a concerto could be. Amazingly, some of these techniques were never used by him again, representing some fascinating roads not taken. In the first movement, soloist and orchestra are combined in as intimate a relationship as Mozart was ever to create. The very opening theme is shared by soloist and orchestra: two bars of orchestra followed by two bars of piano, then repeated. Never in twenty-seven concertos did Mozart again attempt so audacious an opening, having the piano interrupt the orchestra almost before it starts. And this is only one of many innovations in the work. Throughout the first movement, Mozart crafts one of his most careful thematic sets: ideas return in constantly changing patterns throughout the development and recapitulation, with a complexity he used infrequently later in his career.

The second movement opens with a dirge-like theme that sounds as if it could only have been composed by Mozart at the end of his career, but here it appears in the Salzburg of the late 1770s. It is a powerful, pulsating theme that instantly creates a despondent mood. But perhaps the most striking innovation in the *Jeunehomme* Concerto comes in the third movement. Right in the middle of a normal allegro, Mozart stops the music entirely and writes an exquisitely charming minuet, in a different key, in a different emotional space, almost as a different piece. Never again did he try such a wonderful trick, of combining two movements in one, as it were. And listen for the chordal passage that ends this section; Mozart has leaped into the nineteenth century with these few bars. Chopin would have been proud to have written this moment.

The *Jeunehomme* is a fascinating work, as much for the paths it sketches out but does not follow as for its many musical charms. It would be several years before Mozart wrote another concerto that had the power and originality of this work.

Piano Concerto no. 17 in G major, K. 453

This concerto was written in the spring of 1784, not for Mozart himself, but for a talented pupil, Barbara Ployer. Mozart never wrote another work that combined more successfully deeply felt emotion with the most iridescent charm and lightness. The first movement opens with deceptive simplicity: a series of brightly colored phrases that do not amount to much individually, are woven together to create a wonderful melodic texture. Mozart loved the alternation of orchestra and soloist; the combination of the two sets of forces called forth some of his greatest writing, especially in this work. The second movement, the andante, is long, and reminiscent of an aria, with the piano taking the role of the prima donna pouring forth emotion as on an operatic stage. There is no end to Mozart's melodic extravagance in this movement, or to his play with orchestral colors. The final movement, one of Mozart's most joyous, is a theme and variations that begins simply and never betrays its light-hearted origins. More than a romp, the final movement of K. 453 is Mozart at contented play, creating wonderful music and high-spirited fun at the same time. Mozart wrote many works more profound than K. 453, but none where the joy of music making is more apparent.

Piano Concerto no. 19 in F major, K. 459

In most of his mature concertos, Mozart balanced charm and musical depth. But the F major concerto, written in the fall of 1784, is in some ways an exception to this rule. In fact, it has been somewhat overlooked because it seems to place too much emphasis on the charm and too little on the depth. A tinkly little dotted-note motif opens the first movement, promising nothing but a "*style galant*" kind of charm, but before long, the musical universe darkens a bit, and Mozart adds musical pungency to his compositional mix. The entire movement is a tuneful gem, with that dotted-note opening motif never very far from the surface.

The second movement is an allegretto, rather than an andante — that is, a movement that goes a bit faster than usual. And Mozart keeps up that pace throughout the movement. There is almost always some accompaniment figure in the strings keeping the pulse going. This second movement is more a conversation about issues of depth than an extended meditation upon them, as is more often the case in Mozartean slow movements. The final allegro vivace takes its lead from its first strange, syncopated motif, an opening relatively uncommon for Mozart, and then enters into a lively dialogue between piano and orchestra and within various orchestral groups. The F major is not the greatest concerto Mozart ever wrote, but it is infected with a celestial good humor that carries it forward from the first note to the last.

Piano Concerto no. 20 in D minor, K. 466

In the spring of 1785, Mozart wrote two monumental concertos: the *Elvira Madigan*, which we discussed in Chapter 6, and this Piano Concerto in D minor. We know the significance of D minor as a key for Mozart; he reserved for it his darkest and strongest statements. The D minor Concerto, no. 20, the first Mozart ever wrote in a minor key, is probably also the most famous large work that Mozart ever composed. During the nineteenth century, it was virtually the only Mozart piece that was performed regularly and often, so audiences of that period based their opinions of Mozart almost entirely on their reactions to this work. Beethoven performed the D minor on several occasions, though it was rare for him to perform the work of another composer. His cadenzas for the concerto have been preserved, and are often used in contemporary performances. As in the case of *Don Giovanni*, also in D minor, the nineteenth century was transfixed by the brooding, dark quality of this concerto.

The tone is set right from the beginning. The orchestra outlines a fascinating theme, almost a mood rather than a melody, that creates a sense of deep anxiety, though the tones are hushed. The exposition continues by piling up phrases, each one more tragic and fearful than the last. By the time the piano enters, a mood of deep foreboding has been created. The soloist enters, not with a repetition of the first theme, but with a brand new bit of music; the alternation of soloist and orchestra is very pronounced in this work. The development constantly returns to the opening motif, as often now in the major as in the minor, giving the same music a slightly different interpretation each time it recurs. Finally, the forces of the development gather strength and the recapitulation plunges us back into D minor for the rest of the movement.

If you are going to listen to a performance of this work, try to get one that uses the Beethoven cadenza in the first movement. There is no greater lesson on the difference between these two composers than this cadenza. Beethoven takes the drama of Mozart's movement and strips it of its overlay of elegance and charm. The music of the cadenza becomes pure drama — powerful, fearful, intensely exciting. As the music returns to Mozart for the final coda, we feel that we have been given a glimpse of the future, and can never quite return to the relative calm of Mozart.

A simple movement in a major key labeled "Romance" balances off the fervor of the first movement. Piano and orchestra engage in an ongoing conversation, throwing musical phrases back and forth. The final movement gives us D minor at its most demonic. A rushing figure that seems to miss its first beat time and time again begins the movement, the devil enjoying a jest at our expense. The rest of the movement is an uncanny combination of the fearful and the fun. From one moment to the next, Mozart changes the emotional coloration, like some musical chameleon. The movement is a fitting conclusion to a concerto with such a wide range. In the twentieth century, we have developed a greater appreciation of every aspect of Mozart's art than the single-minded Romantics of the nineteenth century; we know that Mozart can be just as profound and rich in the C major of the *Elvira Madigan* Concerto or the *Jupiter* Symphony as in the D minor of this work. However, the nineteenth century was not wrong about K. 466; it is one of Mozart's greatest and most profound works.

Piano Concerto no. 22 in E flat major, K. 482

As is often the case, Mozart returned to a simpler style after writing the two monumental concertos of 1785. This E flat Concerto sounds a bit like some of the Salzburg concertos he wrote in his late teens and early twenties, although it shares in all the musical sophistication of the Vienna years. The first movement is a lively mix of wind tone coloration and sweet piano phrases. The second-movement andante is one of Mozart's more heartfelt slow movements; the genial style of the first movement has been replaced by something akin to real tragic feeling here. The final movement is a dance-like jig that returns to the emotional landscape of the first movement. Mozart is in a relaxed mood in this concerto, despite the intensity of the second movement. His public may have needed a break after the rigors of the previous concertos. Mozart gave them just that, without sacrificing his musical integrity or inventiveness.

Piano Concerto no. 23 in A major, K. 488

The A major Concerto was written in the spring of 1786 while Mozart was writing *The Marriage of Figaro*. The key of A major was the key of seduction for Mozart (Don Giovanni woos Zerlina in A major) and this concerto is one of the most seductive pieces Mozart ever wrote. What a smooth, unassuming opening he created for this work! It almost sounds as though we had missed the first few "real" bars of the piece and were coming in at the second or third phrase. Mozart never wrote a more gentle, smooth, lyrical movement than the first movement of this work. Everything is calm and ordered, the major key prevails in virtually every phrase. The piano enters with a repetition of the opening and engages in only the slightest deviation from the mood of the movement. The deep tones of the lower register of the piano give the second theme a rosy, dark-edged hue. However, in all this musical geniality, originality and expressiveness are not sacrificed for an instant. Indeed, this is one of Mozart's most original works. A completely new theme enters just before the exposition's coda, giving rise to an extended original section in the development. Piano and orchestra collaborate in an extremely balanced way to recap the material from the exposition, and the first movement draws to a close.

The adagio of the A major Concerto is in F sharp minor, the only movement Mozart ever wrote in this key. It is one profound meditation on the deepest subjects, blending the song-like character of the piano with a simple orchestral accompaniment. The simplicity of the first movement, seductive in its charms, is here matched by another form of simplicity, the simplicity of the direct emotional appeal — never overstated, but never unwavering. In some ways, Mozart had never before composed a movement as unaffectedly serious as this, or as simply beautiful. The movement is short, but breathes the spirit of perfection; not another note could be added without destroying the effect. A simple, straightforward motif opens the outgoing third movement. The movement continues by combining the seductive innocence of the first movement with the overwhelming simplicity of the second. A minor flavoring reminds us of the second movement as well. As much as on anything else, the greatness of Mozart's concertos rests on the supremely individual character of each work. In its blend of sweetness and bitterness, the A major Concerto has a unique place in Mozart's output.

Piano Concerto no. 24 in C minor, K. 491

The second concerto that Mozart composed in a minor key (after the D minor, K. 466) was written in March of 1786, the same month as the A major Concerto. It begins with one of Mozart's most unusual musical statements, an extended theme that for once puts aside the principle of phrase balance that Mozart used most of his career. If the minor mood is not maintained as scrupulously in this work as it is in the D minor, the form of this concerto is more interesting. A wealth of material is presented in the orchestral exposition; the piano then enters with a brand new theme, and goes on to take over the main orchestral theme, moving it in new musical directions. The C minor is more varied emotionally than the D minor; though it is certainly less harrowing, it is more kaleidoscopic in its moods. The development picks up on the brief piano figure that introduced the solo instrument and uses this figure as often as the main C minor theme. The proportions of the first movement are very broad; musically the movement is complex.

Mozart rewrote the original opening of the second movement of this concerto. He scratched out the first draft after a dozen or so bars, preferring this cool, sublime, simple opening, to provide contrast with the wild, complicated structure of the first movement. The piano has the first word in the second movement, and with its entry, the phrase balance that was missing in the first movement returns. In fact, balance, both musical and emotional, is the essence of this movement. Mozart gives us a number of contrasting moods, some happier, others more tragic, but all presented in perfect balance. The last movement, a theme and variations, opens with a friendly C minor theme (minor themes can be friendly, as major ones can sometimes be somber). As in all parts of this work, Mozart here puts aside some of the obvious expressive possibilities of his minor key to concentrate on structural innovations. Perhaps no other concerto is as full of new formal ideas as this one. Mozart was at his most thoughtful and theoretical when writing this powerful and subtle work.

Piano Concerto no. 25 in C major, K. 503

K. 503 was composed in the winter of 1786, between *Figaro* and *Don Giovanni*. Although it is not one of Mozart's best-known concertos, it is one of his most significant. In this work, Mozart returns to the exploration of large-scale formal principles that we saw in the *Elvira Madigan* Concerto and to some extent in the C minor Concerto, K. 491. Listen for the broad, martial opening; it doesn't sound like a real theme at all, more like a series of chords. But a theme it is, and Mozart develops it again and again in his spacious first movement. The entire movement is operatic; it all sounds like one of those wonderful finales that Mozart composed for *Figaro* or *Don Giovanni*, with one idea tripping over the next. The concentration of ideas, the manner in which Mozart combines themes and motifs is very rare for him. It is almost a cut and paste job, as ideas are continually juxtaposed with new sounds and combinations. Nowhere in his output, not even in the similar first movement to the other C major concerto, the *Elvira Madigan*, is the feeling of majesty and spaciousness so complete. The first movement of this concerto is one of the longest Mozart was ever to write.

The feeling of space and solidity is carried through to the second-movement andante, which continues the technique of adding idea to idea, like a sort of collage. In its avoidance of the easy melodic turns that characterized his earlier concertos, even those of only a few years earlier, Mozart has created here his own "late style," like that of Beethoven. He is trying to wrest from his musical materials all the meaning and passion they contain, worried less about their pleasing effect and more about their significance. The final rondo is also a serious movement, showing the first signs of a tendency Mozart developed in his later works — that of investing the final movement with as much meaning as the first. K. 503 is one of Mozart's most powerful statements, a dense, challenging work that bears repeated listening to fathom all its secrets and connections.

Piano Concerto no. 26 in D major, K. 537 (The Coronation)

Musicologists often like to get angry at the public for enjoying works that they're not supposed to enjoy, and snubbing works they are supposed to find "worthy." This concerto falls into the first category, a category, by the way, that Mozart would have found mystifying. He wrote his music to be enjoyed, even his more challenging pieces. He cannot be blamed because his musical mind raced ahead of his contemporaries' near the end of his life. The *Coronation* Concerto was written for Mozart's visit to Frankfurt for the coronation of the new Austrian emperor, Leopold II. It certainly contains none of the deep musical thoughts of either the C major Concerto, K. 503, or the C minor Concerto, K. 491. However, as in *Eine Kleine Nachtmusik*, Mozart, in his maturity, invested this lighter music with skill he simply did not possess earlier in his life when he wrote light music for a living, in Salzburg.

After the passion and drama of his later concertos, the first movement of the *Coronation* seems like a miniature, tuneful and graceful. Although it was clearly a piece written to make a royal impression, all it does is charm thoroughly and convincingly. The slow movement is similarly tuneful and charming; Mozart calling forth with no effort the kind of elegant phrases that he had spent a lifetime discovering. The finale carries this spirit into the third movement as well. Mozart was so skilful in crafting tuneful melodies that a little bauble like this concerto is still immensely satisfying. It was not only in his grander works that Mozart could make a lasting impression.

Piano Concerto no. 27 in B flat major, K. 595

Mozart's final piano concerto was written in January of 1791. It breathes a spirit of resignation and nostalgia in all three movements. The first movement is full of wonderful interchanges between soloist and orchestra, some of them untried since the *Jeunehomme* Concerto written fifteen years earlier. The passion and angry drama of the earlier concertos is absent here; Mozart is in a mood to reflect and consider, with a combination of sadness and rueful laughter. The peaceful second movement continues the emotional theme; nowhere else is Mozart so untroubled musically. An allegro which is the essence of charm closes off this autumnal work, in which Mozart, at the end of two miserable years, and facing a third, seems to be summing up some of the things that music and life have meant to him.

PIANO SONATAS

Mozart was the greatest piano virtuoso of his generation, and most of his sonatas were written to show off his extraordinary skill. However, unlike the concerto, Mozart did not always fill his sonatas with his most exalted musical thoughts. It is interesting to observe the various uses composers made of certain forms. Because Haydn wrote few concertos, Mozart concentrated a great deal of attention on this form. Similarly, because Mozart wrote relatively few piano sonatas, Beethoven, desperate to make a significant reputation for himself in the same Vienna in which Mozart had lived for a decade, invested this form with his greatest musical utterances. Because Beethoven exhausted the possibilities of the sonata, few composers after him dared write many works in the form. Mozart's sonatas, in comparison with Beethoven's, may appear insubstantial, but he wrote them for a different purpose, and they still show the composer at his most felicitous and engaging. Some of his most famous melodies first appeared in the sonatas. By and large, Mozart's sonatas belong to his pre-Vienna period; in Vienna, he preferred to write concertos for himself.

Sonata in G major, K. 283

Mozart was in Munich for the premiere of his opera *La finta giardiniera* in 1775 when he wrote this, one of his best-known sonatas, part of a group of six. He was only nineteen at the time, and had already composed his first great symphonies, including the little G minor a few months before.

Like all the sonatas, this is a good one to use when you are first learning to listen to Mozart because it is usually easier to hear the structure in a sonata than in the larger orchestral pieces. The movements are often short, and the development of the first and second themes and the recaps in the first movements are generally quite clear. Such is certainly the case in this G major Sonata. From the graceful opening, the piece moves quite quickly to the second theme, using a figure that pops up again in the *Elvira Madigan* Concerto (a lot of the ideas from the sonatas make their way into the later concertos). Mozart has often been criticized for the slightness of his writing in his piano sonatas, but, as usual, this criticism is misplaced. Mozart used each medium as he needed it; sonatas for him were a way of impressing a smaller, noble audience with intimate fare. The concert hall received his more far-reaching musical thoughts. The textbook sonata-allegro form of the first movement of this sonata is followed by a famous and graceful second movement; you can almost hear the missing orchestral parts in this lovely aria-like movement. A finale worthy of any of the later concertos finishes off this polished work, an extraordinary creation for a nineteen-year-old, even a nineteen-year-old Mozart.

Sonata in D major, K. 311

Although it has a higher Köchel number than the A minor Sonata, K. 310, this sonata was written first, during the abortive trip Mozart made to Mannheim and Paris in 1777 and 1778. The work was written in Mannheim, the city where Mozart made his fateful acquaintance with the Weber family. The D major Sonata is full of brilliance, with quick alternation between darkness and light. Again, the opening movement is short, but not without a wealth of musical ideas. We can just imagine Mozart playing this sonata for a gathering of nobility in Mannheim or Paris. (Often the sonatas began life as improvisations, unbelievably, and were only written down later.) The first movement is a wonderfully compact set of musical ideas and themes. The style of these early sonatas, as we have noted, is not as fully developed as Mozart's later Viennese works, but they are perfect expressions of his musical taste and skill at that time of his life. Like K. 283, the slow movement of this work resembles an operatic aria, a beautiful, drawn-out, song-like moment frozen in time and space. A rocking, "hunt-like" theme begins the final movement and is then juxtaposed with a wide variety of musical ideas. The whole movement is a crazy quilt of musical themes, tied together by a joyous, youthful spirit.

Sonata in A minor, K. 310

The A minor Sonata was written during the summer of 1778, in Paris, the summer in which Mozart watched his mother die, his fortunes dwindle and his attempts to liberate himself from Salzburg fade. Perhaps — and only perhaps — the events of that summer account for the aggressive, almost angry opening of this tough, insistent work. Mozart is working on a different emotional plane with this sonata than he was only a few months earlier with K. 311. The first movement is twice the length of the D major, indeed the entire work is 25 percent longer. And it is not just longer, but more assured and musically more varied and dramatic. Listen for the repeated bass notes in the development; this is music of a tragic character that Mozart had written only rarely up to this point in his life.

The second-movement andante cantabile seems to have the emotional depth of the work of an extremely mature and assured artist. But even in Mozart's most deeply felt emotional moments, his way with tuneful melodies never deserts him; and this movement is full of singable, memorable little phrases. A beautiful minor tune opens the third movement, recovering the mood of the first movement; for three dense minutes, this final presto carries through to its dark-hued conclusion. The A minor Sonata was never equaled in Mozart's solo piano output; as an outpouring of the darker side that Mozart revealed when the mood welled up in him, it stands with his other famous minor creations in the concerto, quartet and quintet families.

Sonata in C major, K. 330

This is one of Mozart's clearest, most open works. Responding to the key of C major, he composed a cheery, good-spirited first movement without a hint of darkness to ruin the fun. A free-flowing andante and an allegretto written in the *style galant* close out this charming sonata. This is Mozart at his untroubled best — full of sophistication, both musical and emotional, but graceful and aristocratic from first to last.

Sonata in A major, K. 331

This may be Mozart's most famous sonata; it's the one that begins, unconventionally, with a theme and variations and ends with the well-known Rondo à la turque. The opening theme is one of the most graceful melodies that Mozart ever composed. Rocking back and forth on an A major triad, it conveys a striking sense of peace. Before the first movement is over, Mozart will have subjected this idea to a number of musical tricks and transformations, but in all its changes, it never loses that tranquil character. The minuet and trio that make up the second movement play around with time a little bit; it sounds as though the opening theme is a beat short somewhere. The movement itself is simple compared to the originality of the first and the familiarity of the third. The Rondo à la turque is, of course, something of a joke. Turkish themes were all the rage in Vienna, which had something of a love-hate relationship with all things Turkish. Mozart has a lot of fun in this short movement creating a musical portrait of sultans and their servants running to and fro in their desert camps. If it is a bit stereotypical, it has nevertheless remained popular for two centuries.

Sonata in B flat major, K. 333

This sonata was composed during Mozart's early days in Vienna and may have been written for a visit he made to Linz in 1783, the same visit that saw the composition of the *Linz* Symphony. Many have called this sonata the most "Mozartean" piano composition of all. It exudes a freshness and warmth that make it extremely appealing. The first movement seems simple, and might lack the emotional depth of some earlier sonatas, but it carries the listener forward on a wave of luxurious music making. The andante is controlled and somewhat restrained; it is nonetheless moving for this fact. Indeed, some of the academic style of this movement lends it a certain expressiveness. "Allegretto grazioso" is the marking for the third movement, which lives up to its billing. It is gracious from first note to last, the kind of light, yet sensitive music making that for many decades was seen to represent all that Mozart had to offer as a composer. There is more to Mozart, of course, than these jeweled finales, but they are precious nonetheless.

Fantasia in C minor, K. 475, and Sonata in C minor, K .457

The C minor Sonata is one of the few piano sonatas that Mozart wrote in his full maturity as a composer. He wrote the work in October of 1784, only a few months before his D minor Concerto. This is a work full of the power and explosive expressiveness of Mozart at the height of his powers. The entire first movement is suffused with a sense of overwhelming drama; moments appear suddenly, strongly defined, then disappear just as quickly. Mozart uses alternation of louds and softs to make up for the absence of the orchestral colors that he could have written into a concerto or even a chamber piece featuring the piano. In K. 457, we do not feel the absence of the other colors as we sometimes do in other sonatas, so cleverly has Mozart mixed his musical ideas and textures. For the first time in his solo piano writing, we begin to sense the depth of writing possible for the instrument: a depth that Beethoven was to exploit in almost unbelievable ways during the decade following the composition of this sonata.

The second movement provides a brief respite from the *sturm und drang* of the first movement (with a middle section that prefigures the slow movement of Beethoven's *Pathétique* Sonata) before we are plunged back into the C minor of the third movement. A syncopated figure opens this movement, then Mozart takes us on a wild, demonic ride through musical open country. The entire sonata, not just this movement, almost breaks open the restraints commonly associated with the form; the power in the writing is almost too much for the poor piano sonata to bear. Perhaps for that reason, Mozart wrote something of an introduction to the work a few months later, the Fantasia in C minor, and published the two works together, as a unit.

The Fantasia is an extraordinary work, and gives us the truest idea of what it must have been like to hear Mozart improvise at the piano. Imagine yourself in a drawing room, or someone's living room, listening to Mozart in front of you, making up this kind of music as he went along, now inspired, now tragic, now moving from one idea to the next, now returning to an earlier idea. The Fantasia may be Mozart's most evocative piece for the piano, precisely because it follows no prearranged form, allowing us to follow the musical thoughts of the composer as they came to him, apparently on the spot.

Sonata in C major, K. 545

This "easy" sonata in C major is the piano equivalent of *Eine Kleine Nachtmusik*, an extremely sophisticated work, written purposely as a miniature. It begins with what is perhaps Mozart's most famous first theme: a triadic theme featuring the C major chord, which every beginning piano student has either learned or heard. The first movement itself is tiny, but nearly perfect. The sonata was truly written as a beginner's piece, so technical difficulties are kept to a minimum; formally it is also quite clear and simple. The middle movement carries this beginner's notion through to the slow movement, without sacrificing musical taste or interest. A rondo that lasts a minute and a half closes out this charming work, justly famous despite its self-imposed limitations.

OTHER ORCHESTRAL WORKS

Serenade in B flat major, K. 361

Mozart wrote a number of serenades (open-air wind or string pieces) during his youth in Salzburg, but composed relatively few of these kinds of compositions once he got to Vienna, as there were few opportunities to perform them. This "Gran Partita," as it is called, was an exception. It was probably written in 1782 or 1783, for a unique combination of twelve wind instruments and a double bass. Mozart experimented with different combinations of instruments all his life; he loved the variety of textures he could create with different groupings. In the Serenade in B flat major, Mozart added maturity of formal expression to this lifelong interest in texture. There are seven moments altogether in the Serenade; the first may be the most perfect sonata-allegro movement Mozart ever composed. The opening theme is Mozart at his most balanced and witty. You can't get a theme simpler or more direct than the little four-note grouping Mozart uses here. Between the various combinations of sounds that Mozart creates with his ensemble and his various compositional tricks, this is a wonderful movement.

Of the remaining six movements (two minuets, a romance, an adagio, a theme and variations and the finale), the third-movement andante takes full advantage of the wind sonority to create a rolling accompaniment to a melody based on the sound of the oboe and clarinet. Mozart's wind music exists in a world of its own; nothing so celestial ever again escaped his pen. The fourth-movement minuet charms with its rustic opening; a trio in the minor, then one in a major key balance off the remainder of this movement. Each movement in this work has its own special charms; the K. 361 Serenade may be Mozart's most relaxed work, combining the skill of a mature composer with the love of sound that characterized the youth.

Sinfonia Concertante, K. 364

The Sinfonia Concertante is in reality a double concerto, that is, a concerto for two different instruments, in this case, a violin and a viola. It was composed in Salzburg in 1779, eighteen months before Mozart was to leave that city for his new life in Vienna. As much as Mozart detested his servitude in Salzburg, some of his most interesting compositions were composed in his home town, rather than on the road. It was as though he absorbed influence after influence in foreign cities, then waited until he got home to try them out. So the G minor Symphony (the little one), the *Jeunehomme* Concerto and this double concerto were all composed in the provincial Austrian town in which Mozart was born.

In effect, the Sinfonia Concertante is one of Mozart's first mature concertos, but it still borrows heavily from Baroque forms. The first movement has the same superabundance of thematic material that we saw in the first movement of the *Haffner* Serenade in Chapter 4. One idea follows another in quick succession; there is less concern with developing or even linking the ideas. But the music itself is, as always, melodic, graceful and appealing. The two solo instruments give Mozart the opportunity to write a dialogue between soloists that was normally impossible. The slow movement presents its minor thematic material in something of an old-fashioned, stylized setting. Compared to later minor movements, where Mozart seems to strip away all compositional artifice and speak right from the heart, this movement seems unnecessarily theatrical. The finale sounds like a scene from an opera buffa, with lots of frenetic activity, all in the name of a good theatrical time. The movement is charming, as is the entire concerto, an indication of where Mozart was in his development as he stood on the threshold of his Viennese adventure.

Violin Concerto no. 4 in D major, K. 218

Mozart wrote only five violin concertos in his life, all, it was thought until recently, between the months of April and December of 1775 (though musicologists now think that the first two were written earlier). The first two concertos belong very much to the stylistic past; they are more Baroque than Classical. The last three are more Mozartean. Of these, the fourth, in D major, is the best known. All three movements of this concerto are full of the thematic material Mozart made familiar in many of his earlier compositions — balanced phrases, abrupt changes of register in his solo instrument, play back and forth between soloist and orchestra.

Mozart does not seem to have enjoyed either playing or writing for the violin, although he was constantly exhorted by his father to do so. And when Mozart did not like writing for an instrument, he simply did not do it. Countless generations of violinists must have gnashed their teeth at the slim pickings Mozart left them, compared to the one-hundred-plus compositions that feature the piano in one way or another. This concerto represents the best that Mozart could make of the violin; it is by turns vigorous, masculine, whimsical, and in the second movement, nostalgic and sentimental.

Horn Concerto no. 4 in E flat major, K. 495

All of Mozart's four horn concertos were inspired by his friendship with one Ignaz Leutgeb, a horn player and cheese merchant. Mozart became friendly with Leutgeb in Vienna and filled the manuscripts of these concertos with a series of uncomplimentary and slightly obscene marginal remarks about Leutgeb and his horn. Of the four concertos, only two truly deserve the name. The first has only two movements, the third having been lost. The second is really a compilation of three separate movements for horn that have been turned into a finished work. Only the last two works are fully developed Mozart concertos, and of these, no. 4 is the more accomplished and significant. All of the works contain wonderful melodies for horn, but the E flat, which was composed in the heyday of Mozart's success in Vienna, during the period of the great piano concertos, also has a first movement that is well-constructed musically and formally. The second-movement romanza is a beautiful song for horn and orchestra. The final rondo has been immortalized by the British musical comedians Flanders and Swann, who set lyrics to this movement and performed it, allegro vivace, as a perennial favorite for their many fans. For one generation of British music-hall audiences, Flanders and Swann made this Mozart's most famous piece, though they may not have known who wrote it.

Clarinet Concerto in A major, K. 622

Unlike his concertos for violin and horn, which were written partly as novelties and partly to pay the bills, Mozart's Clarinet Concerto is one of the most significant pieces in his output. Its high K. number gives its significance away; it was Mozart's last concerto, and one of his very last compositions. What an extraordinary work it is. From the silky beauty of the opening movement, with its many musical ideas and changing moods, all concentrated on the sonority — rich and languid, by turns — of the clarinet, the piece emanates an air of resigned sadness. Interestingly, Brahms, too, turned to the sound of the clarinet to express his autumnal mood at the end of his life.

The concerto's second movement represents Mozart at his most introspective; slow and stately, the clarinet sounds as if it is pondering aloud the steady progression of life from birth to death. Listen especially for the dramatic harmonic interchange between soloist and orchestra just after the movement's opening. Mozart never wrote more poignant music. As an antidote to this almost painful movement, Mozart closes out the concerto with a finale from his earlier days — full of the naïve simplicity and charm that generations have come to associate with his name. Except in this case, Mozart was not writing this kind of a finale because he was incapable of conceiving of a last movement in more dramatic terms. He chose to leave us, as with *The Magic Flute*, in a mood of optimism and joy.

OTHER CHAMBER MUSIC

Clarinet Quintet in A major, K. 581

The Clarinet Quintet, like the Clarinet Concerto, was inspired by Anton Stadler, one of two famous clarinetist brothers in the Vienna of the late 1780s. Mozart had performed with and become friendly with Anton in the mid-1780s. This work was composed in 1789, around the time of *Così fan tutte*. In a way, it is a quieter, more reflective version of the Clarinet Concerto. The sound of the clarinet obviously inspired a whole set of musical emotions in Mozart that the violin, piano or horn could not evoke. The first movement of the Quintet is a lovely, hushed poem set to music.

The sense of fireside warmth established in the first movement is sustained in the second-movement larghetto, a movement that combines the sonorities of the clarinet and the string quartet with an unerring instinct for expressing emotion through sound. The third-movement minuet has two trios, the first for strings, the second featuring the clarinet. A rustic, peasant-like dance finishes off this smooth, romantic work, shot through, as it is, with the seductive sound of the clarinet, an instrument capable of conveying the widest range of emotion in the hands of a composer like Mozart.

Piano Trio in E major, K. 542

The piano trio was one of the most common forms of chamber music in Europe for over a century, from the mid-1600s to the end of the eighteenth century. The combination of a violin, cello and keyboard instrument was one that could easily be found in most musical households, so the piano trio became one of the chief methods of domestic entertainment in the noble Europe of the seventeenth and eighteenth centuries. Not that this work was necessarily intended for musical amateurs; Mozart composed it just before beginning work on his last three symphonies in the summer of 1788.

The masterful way in which Mozart combines the violin, cello and piano is the first thing to notice in this work. Somehow the power of the piano is never allowed to overwhelm the two stringed instruments, and the three enter into a friendly partnership. The opening allegro is a straightforward, lively first movement, with piano and strings collaborating at every turn to expose the thematic material of the movement. The andante is open and pastoral, evoking the rustic charms of a country home. The closing allegro harkens back to an easier time in Mozart's life and musical career, where pure joyousness could find unfettered release. Mozart re-entered that world just before he plunged himself into the most intensely creative period of his life — the month and a half that saw the creation of the E flat major, G minor and *Jupiter* symphonies.

Piano Quartet no. 1 in G minor, K. 478

The piano quartet differs from the piano trio in that a viola joins the violin and cello to balance off the sonority of the piano. This form was something of a novelty in Mozart's Vienna. Haydn never composed for this arrangement, nor had many other previous composers. Add to this the fact that this G minor work, like so many others in that key, is a dense, serious, passionate piece, and you will understand why it was unpopular in Mozart's day.

When the piece was published in late 1785 or 1786, it was intended to be the first of three such works, but it sold so poorly

that Mozart withdrew it from the public. It was universally con-
demned for being too difficult, and hard to understand, completely
divorced as it was from the sensibilities of the young cultured ladies
and gentlemen who were the intended audience for such a chamber
work. From this point on, common wisdom had it that Mozart
wrote music too complex to be enjoyed. He was never able to escape
that charge, and his popularity began the nosedive which ended in
the desperate poverty of the last years of his life.

Today, it is hard to understand why this work, of all others,
should have precipitated such a crisis in Mozart's fortunes. Yes, it
is a serious work, but it is also a glorious one, with a first movement
which cleverly integrates the piano with the three stringed instruments in a collaboration of grace as well as depth. In the development, especially, listen for the way in which Mozart combines the
sounds of the four instruments to create a moment of true musical
explosiveness. The second movement provides a restful contrast to
the bustle and seriousness of the first, and the third begins with a
magical theme which sets off a little bundle of charm and happiness
to end this exceptional, if rarely heard, work.

STRING QUINTETS

Mozart's string quartets are among the greatest ever written, but,
by general agreement, Mozart outdid his achievements in the
quartet genre with his string quintets. A quintet is made up of two
violins, two violas (instead of the single viola in the quartet) and a
cello. It may not seem that significant a change from the quartet,
but the addition of the second viola allows a composer a much
warmer and potentially more expressive texture to work with.
Again, as in the concerto, Mozart could look to few models while
writing his quartets. Haydn, for one, had written only a couple of
them. Mozart's great quintets all come from the last years of his life,
when his growing musical maturity demanded a richer combination of instruments and a broader conception of form for its
expression. Some of the most significant musical statements he left
us are in these works.

Quintet in C major, K. 515

Mozart wrote this quintet and its relative, K. 516, in the spring of 1787 in the hopes of receiving a position in the Prussian court. He never received the position, but did get a commission for the Prussian quartets which he completed within the next couple of years. Something about the quintet form must have held a mysterious appeal for Mozart. Right from the opening bars of this massive work, a strong sensibility is at work. There are no wasted notes in the highly expressive first movement; full of melodic and contrapuntal charm and interest, it holds our breathless interest from first note to last. A different Mozart lurks behind this movement — a powerful personality staring from behind the mask of the perpetual musical youth he had worn all his life.

Mozart becomes playful again in the blissful andante, matching sonorities brilliantly to provide constant textural interest. Listen to how many different combinations of instruments Mozart manages to create during the eight minutes of this section. As became increasingly common in Mozart's later works, the minuet movement does not provide the light-hearted contrast of so many early Mozart minuets; this is a serious movement, in keeping with the heightened expressiveness of the entire work. The finale begins with a lively theme which, coming at the end of a different work, might be heard as elegant and graceful, but here is heard as the lightness that comes with great understanding and wisdom. It is the lightness of wisdom that informs this whole movement, just as a sense of overwhelming musical maturity and understanding permeates this entire, extraordinary composition.

Quintet in G minor, K. 516

If it is possible for a work to have a deeper musical expression than that of the C major Quartet, it is this work in G minor that does so. Mozart wrote it a few weeks after finishing the C major. Only a few months later, in 1788, he would write two major works within weeks, also in G minor and C major — the G minor Symphony, and the *Jupiter*. A startlingly chromatic theme introduces this work and plunges us right into the world of emotional turbulence from which we will not escape for the next thirty-five minutes. For many, this is Mozart's deepest, most telling work. Throughout the first movement, the deeper sonorities of the violas and cello are set off against the brighter sounds of the violins. Listen also for the various treatments that Mozart creates for that original idea; it is constantly transformed throughout this movement. The development section is a masterful elongation of that idea, turned into counterpoint and performed against itself time and again. As in the C major Quintet, Mozart seems completely liberated and free in his treatment of his material in this piece, as though he had finally discovered the means to translate every nuance of his inner feelings directly and immediately into musical expression.

The minuet precedes the slow movement in this quintet. If anything, it is more intense than the movement which preceded it. Rough syncopation defines the minuet theme, before the introduction of calmer phrases, which then prevail. A lighter trio balances off the sadness of the minuet theme, which nevertheless returns to fill out the movement. The adagio is a lonely plea for help and guidance in the midst of an apparently darkened world; Mozart never wrote as personal a statement. With this movement, we enter a new and unfamiliar musical world. Without ever deserting the conventions within which he worked his entire life, Mozart has nonetheless led us into a brand new musical world here. Nothing looks backwards to the Baroque; nothing really looks forward to the Romantic era, either. This is pure music, speaking to us in its own place and time.

The final movement, not unsurprisingly, begins with a slow introduction. Mozart could not possibly have followed that adagio with anything lively or upbeat. The slow introduction, with its pizzicato cello line, helps move us slowly out of the rarified regions in which we wandered in the third movement. Finally, a wonderfully frisky theme erupts into the finale proper, but even this tune contains its own seeds of discontent and darkness. The most powerful piece Mozart ever composed, the G minor Quintet represents the Everest of his musical achievement: it remains proud in

its isolation, able to be scaled, but not without effort and preparation on the part of anyone willing to take the test.

Quintet in D major, K. 593

Mozart's last two quintets were composed about two years after the
massive duo of K. 515 and 516. The ferocious intensity of those
two works is muted here and Mozart's mood is more reflective, but
the expressiveness of the music is not dimmed. K. 593 begins with
a slow introduction, with the cello apparently thinking out loud
about the piece to follow. A brisk allegro theme is then introduced.
It avoids the drama of the earlier quintets, but still involves all five
instruments in dialogue with each other. The development section
is a witty examination of the first theme, with its share of contrapuntal writing, but where humor and fun overcome depth of
expression. As a final surprise in the movement, the slow introduction returns just before the closing coda — yet another example of
the freedom with which Mozart treated his formal patterns in his
late works.

A gently moving adagio follows the classic first movement,
keeping up the spirit of resignation and late-evening warmth that
the first movement introduced. In just the same spirit, the minuet
movement follows. The finale sounds as if it came right out of the
Hunt Quartet — it is a jumpy little hunting theme shot full of
humor, as well as a certain pathos. The first violin takes the lead in
a quintet often dominated by the darker sounds of the cello and
violas. The movement is full of the contrapuntal filigree so common
in Mozart's later works, but it never loses the spirit of impishness
with which it begins. K. 593 does not take us to the expressive
heights of either K. 515 or 516, but it is the work of an accomplished
artist nonetheless. If it puts aside the dramatic gestures of the earlier
works, it is no less meaningful for that reason.

Quintet in E flat major, K. 614

This last chamber work was completed in April of 1791, eight months or so before Mozart's death. More than perhaps any of his chamber works, even the set of quartets dedicated to him, this work shows the influence of Joseph Haydn. The opening theme has the rustic, almost peasant-like charm so often associated with Haydn's music. The mood here is considerably less anguished than in Mozart's previous quintets, but the music is still captivating. The middle movements — an adagio and a minuet and trio — carry this spirit forward. Haydn is present in both movements, in both the manner in which the themes are written and the way they are developed. The minuet especially is a model of terse writing; its ideas are developed tightly and quickly. The finale is a warm-hearted romp, running through its thematic material in the manner of a French farce. Mozart's final chamber work may lack the breadth of composition of the other mature quintets, but it serves as a fitting valedictory to this chamber-music form, which Mozart single-handedly raised to the heights of musical expression.

The Elvira Madigan Piano Concerto

Chromatic ascending theme

Four-note theme
(First theme)

This book was typeset by Tony Gordon
Limited in Berkeley Oldstyle, a typeface cut
by Monotype in 1958 as a reissue of
University of California Old Style. Frederic
W. Goudy designed it in 1938 as a private
type for the University of California Press.

Cover and text design by Tania Craan
Cover illustration by David E. Smith
Music engraving by Maestro Laser